*Convergences—Rhetoric and Poetic
in Seventeenth-Century France*

Convergences

RHETORIC AND POETIC
IN SEVENTEENTH-CENTURY FRANCE

ESSAYS FOR HUGH M. DAVIDSON

EDITED BY

David Lee Rubin
and Mary B. McKinley

OHIO STATE UNIVERSITY PRESS
Columbus

Library of Congress Cataloging-in-Publication Data

Convergences—rhetoric and poetic in seventeenth-century France:
essays for Hugh M. Davidson / edited by David Lee Rubin and Mary B.
McKinley.
p. cm.
Includes index.
ISBN 0–8142–0468–6 (alk. paper)
1. French literature—17th century—History and criticism.
2. Davidson, Hugh McCullough, 1918– . I. Davidson, Hugh
McCullough, 1918– . II. Rubin, David Lee. III. McKinley, Mary B.
PQ243.C66   1989
840'.9'004—dc19   89–30177
                                                                          CIP

The paper in this book meets the guidelines for permanence and
durability of the Committee on Production Guidelines for Book
Longevity of the Council on Library Resources.

Printed in the U.S.A.

9 8 7 6 5 4 3 2 1

Contents

Acknowledgments

ix

Publications of Hugh M. Davidson

x

Introduction

xv

I.   LITERARY THEORY

Jean Mesnard
Vraie et fausse beauté dans l'esthétique au dix-septième siècle

3

Robert Garapon
Sur le sens du mot "raison" au dix-septième siècle

34

H. Gaston Hall
Desmarets's "L'Art de la poésie": Poetics or Politics?

45

II.   THEATER

Odette de Mourgues
Poetry and the Comic—A Subtle Partnership

65

Terence Cave
Corneille, Oedipus, Racine

82

Judd D. Hubert
A Theatrical Reading of *Cinna*
101

Marie-Odile Sweetser
"Docere et delectare": Richesses de l'*Avare*
110

III.   FICTION

Charles G. S. Williams
Doubling and Omission in the Text of Anne Ferrand/Bélise
123

IV.   THE LYRIC

Jules Brody
La Fontaine, *Les Vautours et les pigeons* (VII, 8):
An Intertextual Reading
143

Robert T. Corum, Jr.
Generic Modulation in Consolations by Malherbe,
Tristan l'Hermite, and Théophile de Viau
161

V.   THE MORALISTS

John D. Lyons
Camera Obscura: Image and Imagination in Descartes's *Méditations*
179

Peter Bayley
A Reading of the First *Liasse*
196

Roland A. Champagne
Toward a Semiotics of Blaise Pascal's *Pensées*: A Model for
Geometrical and Rhetorical Persuasions
208

Bruce H. Davis
Resisting the Pull: Pierre Nicole on the Inclination to Sin
217

Contributors
235

Index
237

Acknowledgments

The editors gratefully record their indebtedness to Robert T. Denommé, chairman of the Department of French Language and Literature, University of Virginia, for his encouragement at every stage of this project; to Loretta Davidson, for sound, well-timed support and advice; to Peter John Givler, director, Charles G. S. Williams, member of the editorial board, and Alex Holzman, acquisitions editor, of the Ohio State University Press, as well as their advisors, who welcomed our proposal and assumed the risk of judging this book strictly on its merits; and, finally, to Cécile Danehy, Bruce Davis, Mary Herndon, Jane McGuire, Jeffery Persels, for their invaluable assistance.

Publications of Hugh M. Davidson

BOOKS

The Idea and Practice of General Education (Editor). (Chicago: University of Chicago Press, 1948).

Audience, Words, and Art. (Columbus: The Ohio State University Press, 1965).

A Concordance to the *Pensées* of Pascal (with P. H. Dubé). (Ithaca: Cornell University Press, 1975).

The Origins of Certainty: Means and Meanings in Pascal's *Pensées*. (Chicago: University of Chicago Press, 1979).

A Concordance to Pascal's *Les Provinciales* (with P. H. Dubé). (New York: Garland Publishing, Inc., 1980).

Blaise Pascal. (Boston: G. K. Hall, 1983).

In preparation: Pascal and the Arts of the Mind.

BOOK CHAPTERS

"The Literary Arts of Boileau and Longinus." In *Studies in Seventeenth-Century French Literature,* presented to Professor Morris Bishop, ed. by Jean-Jacques Demorest. (Ithaca: Cornell University Press, 1962).

"Recent Histories of Eighteenth-Century French Literature." In the *Cabeen Critical Bibliography of French Literature,* vol. 4 (Syracuse: Syracuse University Press, 1968).

"The Critical Position of Roland Barthes." In *Criticism: Speculative and Analytical Essays,* ed. by L. S. Dembo (Madison: University of Wisconsin Press, 1968).

"The Problem of Scientific Order vs. Alphabetical Order in the *Encyclopédie.*" In *Studies in Eighteenth-Century Culture,* vol. 2, ed. by H. E. Pagliaro (Cleveland: Case Western Reserve University Press, 1972).

"Sign, Sense, and Roland Barthes." In *Approaches to Poetics,* ed. by Seymour Chatman (New York: Columbia University Press, 1973).

"Meaning and Method in Pascal's *Pensées.*" In *Expression, Communication and Experience in Literature and Language,* ed. by Ronald G. Popperwell (London: Modern Humanities Research Association, 1973).

"Fontenelle, Perrault and the Realignment of the Arts." In *Literature and History in the Age of Ideas, Essays on the French Enlightenment Presented to George R. Havens,* ed. by Charles G. S. Williams (Columbus: Ohio State University Press, 1974).

"Rhétorique et pratique du théâtre: étude sur le vocabulaire et la méthode de d'Aubignac." In *Critique et création littéraires en France au XVIIe siècle,* ed. by M. Fumaroli (Paris: Centre national de la recherche scientifique, 1977).

"French Literary Criticism in the Seventeenth Century: Its Nature and Status." In *French Literature Studies,* ed. by Phillip Crant (Columbia, S.C.: French Literature Conference, 1977).

"Pluralisme méthodologique chez Pascal." In *Méthodes chez Pascal,* Actes du colloque tenu à Clermont-Ferrand, 10–13 juin 1976 (Paris: Presses universitaires de France, 1979).

"Remarques sur la concordance des *Pensées.*" In *Méthodes chez Pascal* (see preceding item).

"Dialectical Order and Movement in *La Nouvelle Héloïse.*" In *Enlightenment Studies in Honour of Lester G. Crocker,* ed. by Alfred J. Bingham and Virgil W. Topazio (Oxford: The Voltaire Foundation, 1979).

"Pascal's Arts of Persuasion," In *Renaissance Eloquence: Studies in the Theory and Practice of Renaissance Rhetoric,* ed. by James J. Murphy (Berkeley: University of California Press, 1983).

"Voltaire Explains Newton." In *The Dialectic of Discovery: Essays Presented to Lawrence E. Harvey,* ed. by J. D. Lyons and Nancy J. Vickers (Lexington: French Forum, 1984).

"Pascal." In *The Age of Reason and the Enlightenment,* vol. 4 of the *European Writers Series,* ed. by George Stade (New York: Charles Scribner's Sons, 1984).

"Pascal's Concept of the Infinite." In the proceedings of the International Conference on the *Pensées* of Pascal, held at London, Ontario, Canada, April 26–28, 1984 (1988).

"Options disciplinaires et littérature au XVIIe siècle." In *Destins et enjeux du XVIIe siècle,* ed. by Philippe Sellier et al. (Paris: Presses universitaires de France, 1985).

"Corneille interprète d'Aristote dans les trois *Discours.*" In *Pierre Corneille,* ed. A. Niderst (Paris: Presses universitaires de France, 1985).

ARTICLES

"The *Essais de psychologie contemporaine* and the Character of Adrien Sixte." *Modern Philology* 46, 1 (August, 1948).

"Language and Languages in the Liberal Curriculum." *Journal of General Education* 6, 4 (July, 1952).

"On the Future of College French." *French Review* 48, 4 (February, 1955).

"The Argument of Pascal's 'Pari.'" *Romanic Review* 47, 2 (April, 1956).

"Conflict and Resolution in Pascal's *Pensées*." *Romanic Review* 49, 1 (February, 1956).

"Descartes on the Utility of the Passions." *Romanic Review* 51, 1 (February, 1960).

"The Idea of Literary History in Boileau's *Art poétique*." *Symposium* (Summer, 1964).

"Yet Another View of French Classicism." *Bucknell Review* 3, 1 (March, 1965).

"French Literature and Undergraduates: Texts and Contexts." *French Review* 39, 4 (February, 1966).

Review article, based on *Critics of Consciousness*, by Sarah Lawall, in *Contemporary Literature* 10, 3 (Summer, 1969).

"Myth, Mathematics, and Rhetoric: The Example of Pascal." *Iowa State Journal of Research* 51, 2 (1976).

Review article on *Of Grammatology*, by J. Derrida, trans. by Gayatri Chakravorty Spivak, in *Comparative Literature* 31, 2 (Spring, 1979).

"Disciplinary Options and the Discussion of Literature in Seventeenth-Century France." In *New Literary History* 17 (1985–86).

REVIEWS

Review of *Paul Bourget and the* nouvelle, by Walter Todd Secor, *Modern Philology* 46, 4 (May, 1949).

Review of *The Continental Model*, by Scott Elledge and Donald Schier, *Modern Philology* 59, 2 (November, 1961).

Review of *Men and Masks*, by Lionel Gossman, *Modern Language Notes* 80, 3 (May, 1965).

Review of Arthur H. Beattie, *Selections from Pascal's Thoughts, Modern Language Journal* 50, 5 (May, 1966).

Review of *An Anthology of French 17th Century Lyric Poetry*, ed. by Odette de Mourgues, *Modern Language Review* 62, 2 (1967).

Review of *The Sixth Sense: Individualism in French Poetry, 1686–1760*, by Robert Finch, *Comparative Literature* 19, 3 (Winter, 1968).

Review of Pascal's *Lettres provinciales*, ed. by L. Cognet, *Modern Language Notes* 83, 4 (May, 1968).

Review of *The Rhetoric of Pascal*, by Patricia Topliss, *Modern Philology* 66, 3 (February, 1969).

Review of *L'Enseignement de la littérature française aux étrangers*, by G. Raillard et al., *French Review* 45, 2 (December, 1971).

Review of *French Individualist Poetry 1686–1760: An Anthology*, by Robert Finch and Eugène Joliat, *University of Toronto Quarterly* 41, 4 (Summer, 1972).

Review of *Rousseau and His Reader: The Rhetorical Situation of the Major Works,* by Robert Ellrich, *Modern Philology* 70, 1 (August, 1972).

Review of *Truth and Rhetoric in France: From Descartes to Diderot,* by Peter France, *French Review* 48, 1 (October, 1974).

Review of *Bookmaking in Diderot's* Encyclopédie, by C. G. Barber, *Eighteenth-Century Studies* 8, 4 (Summer, 1975).

Review of *L'Ecriture et le reste: The* Pensées *of Pascal in the Exegetical Tradition of Port-Royal,* by David Wetsel, *Romanic Review* 63, 4 (November, 1982).

Review of Jules Brody, *Du style à la pensée: trois études sur Les Caractères de La Bruyère,* in *Esprit créateur* 22 (1982).

Introduction

Speaking several years ago of Nathan Edelman, Jules Brody remarked that some writers are superior to their books, and others inferior, while a few—by some miracle of inner harmony—are equal. To the third category belongs Hugh M. Davidson, whose qualities as a colleague, teacher, and friend as well as a scholar and critic have inspired this garland of essays, presented to him with affection and esteem on his seventy-second birthday.

THE MAN
BY MARY B. McKINLEY

A skillful balance of the art of listening and the art of questioning contributes to Hugh Davidson's esteemed success as a teacher and colleague. During his years at Chicago, Dartmouth, Ohio State, Yale, and, since 1973, Virginia he has developed an educational philosophy as distinctive as his signature. In the classroom he helps his students to discover knowledge by an ongoing process of dialogue, a process constantly nourished by the unfailing respect that characterizes his attitude toward them. Whether in his French composition classes, in his advanced undergraduate literature courses or in his doctoral seminars, Hugh tries to discern the individual strengths of each person in the group and encourages them to value and to question their ideas while learning to articulate them. His course on the moralists has become a cherished tradition among French majors. Students who approached the reading of Descartes, La Bruyère, La Rochefoucauld, and Pascal with trepidation find that those writers offer fascinating perspectives on the human mind and soul. They seem to engage each other in dialogue under Hugh's direction and gradually to entice the students into their discussions. A recurring topic in those colloquia is the continuity prevailing behind the appearances of change, a concern that reappears regularly in Hugh's teaching and scholarly writing. In 1975 he gave a post-doctoral seminar sponsored by the National

Endowment for the Humanities on "Underlying Constants in the Changing Methods of Literary Study." The title, like the attitude toward criticism that it implies, characterizes his approach to literature in his graduate courses. Unfazed by the latest critical fad but willing to consider its possible merits, he likewise eschews imposing rigid methodologies on his students while welcoming their cogent proposals for any critical approach. That open attitude represents an enduring conviction about critical discourse. In an article published in the *Bucknell Review* in 1965, "Yet Another View of French Classicism," Hugh argued that the survival of humanistic studies today depends upon the willing acceptance of a variety of critical approaches to literature. He emphasizes the need for continuing dialectical confrontation between various methods and schools if criticism is to thrive as a vital tool of scholarship. The perfect setting for such dialogue is Hugh's doctoral seminar on Pascal, a true *locus amoenus* for graduate students at Virginia. Discussions generated in it continue outside the seminar itself and flow naturally into courses on other writers and other centuries. It has helped to convert many students to the seventeenth century and has planted the seeds for several excellent dissertations. Hugh's calm, quietly expressed confidence in his doctoral candidates acts as a catalyst, urging them to pursue intellectual challenges because that is their common endeavor. As one such student put it: "Monsieur Davidson voit dans chaque étudiant un potentiel intellectuel à développer, et il s'occupe à le développer étape par étape jusqu'à ce que l'étudiant puisse voler de ses propres ailes." Recognition of Hugh's teaching has taken him far beyond the university community of Charlottesville. In 1980 and 1989 the Folger Institute invited him to give postdoctoral seminars on Pascal at the Folger Library in Washington, and in 1984 he was invited to give a course on "Les Anciens dans la littérature du XVIIe siècle" at the Sorbonne.

The arts of listening and questioning are not left behind when Hugh Davidson leaves the classroom. An artist attempting his caricature would do well to portray a man at lunch intently sketching with pen on paper napkin while an interested student or colleague looks on. Those familiar diagrams speak of his talent for gently taking another's awkward disorder of expression and deftly recasting it into an eloquent statement of compelling intellectual clarity—while giving the other full credit for both the idea and its eloquence. That generosity is particularly appreciated by junior colleagues, whose books and articles owe much to those lunches.

In departmental and university affairs Hugh draws upon his characteristic equilibrium and clear thinking to suggest innovative programs, to argue for the highest intellectual standards and to recall the voice of reason whenever necessary. As graduate student advisor from 1977 to 1985 he led the graduate program through a crucial period in its growth, chairing the committee that revised and restructured the M.A. and Ph.D. programs in 1985. As a highly respected consultant to deans and other administrators, he frequently serves in roles that have a significant impact on the future direction of the university. His birthday provides a welcome opportunity for his students and colleagues to celebrate his career. Modestly and unobtrusively Hugh Davidson has come to embody the highest ideals of intellectual inquiry and its promulgation.

His Work
by David Lee Rubin

Tel arbre, tel fruit: if Hugh Davidson himself is a model of magnanimity, lucidity, and elegance, his contributions to the study of seventeenth-century French literature possess corresponding qualities: broad learning and instinctive pluralism; incisiveness and rigor of thought; as well as a style whose polish is matched only by its naturalness. Ideally, of course, these remarks would do justice to his entire achievement. Space limitations, however, preclude such exhaustiveness, and, as a result, we shall confine ourselves to an overview of the work that has exercised the widest and deepest influence.

Audience, Words, Art (1965)

The six exquisitely written essays that compose this volume recount, step by step, the official French effort to reinstate the discipline of rhetoric. After tracing rhetoric's Latin origins and its naturalization by Vaugelas and Rapin, Hugh discusses four other facets of the problem: cartesianism and its impact (especially on Port Royal, whose *Logique* sought to redefine rhetoric in terms of logic); Pascal's shift from polemic to apology; and finally, the absorption of rhetorical theory into the widely diverging critical and programmatic statements of Corneille, Racine, and Molière.

Methodologically, *Audience, Words, Art* achieves for its subject what Bernard Weinberg's history did for Italian Renaissance criticism: it clarifies the subtly shifting assumptions and the diverse modes of argument marshaled in a debate which compels our attention not only for its own sake and as a chapter in the history of ideas, but above all for its impact on the creative enterprise itself.

One of the particular strengths of *Audience, Words, Art* is Hugh's treatment of the *Provinciales* and the *Pensées*. His analysis of these works in the light of the fragments, *De l'esprit de géométrie* and *L'art de persuader,* still stands, by common consent, as the best we possess. It is fitting, then, that from the general question of rhetoric, Hugh passed, in his next four books, to the work of Blaise Pascal.

Two Concordances

Hugh recognized early that the daunting vastness and complexity of Pascal's work had tempted more than one critic to launch incandescent, if tenuous theories. From the experience of writing *Audience, Words, Art*—in which he applied and extended the semantics of thought modes proposed by Richard McKeon and Ronald Crane—Hugh also understood why such purely intuitive flights so frequently fall short: the author's key terms, in all their resonance and polyvalence, are imperfectly known. To preserve intuition, yet impose needed controls, in both his own work and that of his fellow *pascalisants,* Hugh concluded that a concordance would be necessary—an instrument that would exhaustively, precisely, and accurately identify the verbal building blocks of Pascal's system as they appear in (and are modified by) their immediate contexts. A manually produced reference, however, was immediately ruled out: to achieve the desired degree of adequacy, its compilation would have left neither time nor energy for the more important work that the concordance was to support. Computerization and the assistance of programmer Pierre Budé overcame these obstacles, with spectacular results, in *A Concordance to Pascal's* Pensées (1975) and *A Concordance to Pascal's* Provinciales (1980). With these tools, the analysis of Pascal's most important texts could, and did, proceed with greater confidence.

The Origins of Certainty (1979)

If proof were needed of the uses to which a sound concordance might be put, this bold yet graceful volume would more than suffice. As Charles G. S. Williams wrote, "Davidson approach[es] and promot[es] the intelligibility [of the *Pensées*] by the study of complexes of words, terms, and designations surrounding them, which establish, as they interact and converge in the text . . . a matrix that will . . . fix any important [element] in Pascal's thought and . . . [reveal] some of its overarching principles, including the relationship of faith to scientific certainty." What results is a diagrammatic treatment of the *moyens de croire* (reason, custom, and inspiration), by which Hugh transcends ancient and inconclusive debates concerning the completeness of sequential order of the *Pensées* to discover something far more essential: what Robert J. Nelson has called their "*intra*-relatedness" or "symbiotic" connection. Through his reconstructive readings, Hugh created a new, richly promising critical framework—indeed a new hermeneutic genre—for exploration and elaboration by future students of the *Pensées,* to say nothing of other works which have come down to us in fragmentary form.

Pascal (1983)

Creation of new genres goes hand in hand with a revitalizing of the old. Thus in this volume—a contribution to the Twayne World Authors' Series—Hugh works within the limits of the "l'homme et l'oeuvre" format, but infuses it with extraordinary coherence, vigor, and depth. Conceding the doubleness of Pascal's formative experiences and the intensity of his commitment to scientific inquiry as well as religious faith and reflection, Hugh nevertheless insists on the unity of the author's spirit and method. This he then traces through a series of condensed, crystalline analyses of the major works and résumés of the *opuscules*. Particularly stimulating is a supplementary account of Pascal's changing image and presence in literature and scholarship not only during his own century but those to follow.

* * *

That, at this writing, Hugh is in the midst of other book-length projects on Pascal and nonrhetorical aspects of seventeenth-century French esthetics makes this introduction incomplete in more senses than the one already mentioned: the authors and the editors honor Hugh Davidson not at the conclusion of a long and distinguished career, but at the very height of his powers and productivity. To paraphrase Mallarmé, "nous les voulons perpétuer."

I
Literary Theory

Vraie et fausse beauté dans l'esthétique au dix-septième siècle

Jean Mesnard

Au long du XVIIe siècle, si le terme de "beauté" est aussi couramment employé qu'à toute autre époque, la catégorie qui lui correspond n'a guère sollicité la réflexion des philosophes et des artistes. Le siècle s'est intéressé aux règles de l'art plutôt qu'à la théorie du beau. A s'en tenir au domaine des lettres, il a essentiellement constitué une rhétorique, prolongée par une poétique dont Hugh Davidson se plaît justement à souligner qu'elle est elle-même pénétrée de rhétorique. L'esthétique demeure assez étrangère à l'époque.[1] Le terme n'apparaîtra d'ailleurs qu'en 1750, avec le premier volume des *Aesthetica* de l'allemand Baumgarten. C'est au XVIIIe siècle, en France et en Allemagne, qu'on verra s'élaborer la discipline. Au milieu du XIXe siècle, Victor Cousin pouvait composer "la philosophie tout entière" avec les "trois problèmes du vrai, du beau et du bien."[2] Il est clair que le XVIIe siècle, passionné de science rigoureuse et d'analyse morale, n'a pas mis le second terme sur le même pied que les deux autres.

Peut-être lui a-t-il pourtant prêté plus d'attention qu'il ne le semble. C'est sans doute l'importance qu'il accorde à l'étude des rapports entre le beau et le vrai qui constitue son originalité principale sur ce sujet. Mais ces rapports peuvent être envisagés de diverses manières. La formule un peu tranchante de Boileau, "Rien n'est beau que le vrai,"[3] n'est peut-être pas celle qui répond le mieux à l'esprit de l'époque. Il y a plus de finesse dans les réflexions inspirées de divers côtés par le souci de distinguer une vraie et une fausse beauté. Notre propos est d'analyser le sens de cette distinction, en nous arrêtant aux divers auteurs qui l'ont pratiquée—du moins ceux que des sondages assez étendus nous ont permis de repérer— et en essayant de dégager, des uns aux autres, les tendances communes et les positions originales.

C'est un écrivain de premier ordre, à propos d'une oeuvre majeure, qui, dans l'état actuel des recherches, fournit notre plus ancien exemple, d'une

3

netteté remarquable. Dédiant à Mme de Combalet, future duchesse d'Aiguillon, nièce de Richelieu, sa tragi-comédie du *Cid,* dont l'édition originale porte un achevé d'imprimer du 23 mars 1637, Corneille se félicite que la pièce ait eu le bonheur de plaire à la grande dame, et il ajoute: "le jugement que vous en faites est une marque assurée de son prix; et comme vous donnez toujours libéralement aux véritables beautés l'estime qu'elles méritent, les fausses n'ont jamais le pouvoir de vous éblouir." [4]

Comme il est naturel, la distinction entre vraie et fausse beauté acquiert sa pertinence lorsque l'attention se porte, non sur les lois qui président à la création de l'oeuvre, mais sur le jugement qu'appelle l'oeuvre constituée. Elle s'adresse essentiellement au critique et, par-delà, à tout homme. C'est indirectement qu'elle peut toucher le créateur, dans la mesure où il est obligé lui-même de se critiquer.

Mais la même idée n'aurait-elle pu s'exprimer sans recours aux catégories du vrai et du faux? Corneille lui-même pourrait nous inviter à répondre par l'affirmative. En 1632, pour la première de ses pièces qu'il ait fait imprimer, la tragi-comédie de *Clitandre,* il avait adressé au duc de Longueville, destinataire de l'épître dédicatoire, une flatterie semblable à celle dont il gratifia plus tard Mme de Combalet, mais en termes différents: "Vous avez un tel dégoût des mauvaises choses, et les savez si nettement démêler d'avec les bonnes, qu'on fait paraître plus de manque de jugement à vous les présenter qu'à les concevoir." [5] Ce sont donc simplement de bonnes et de mauvaises choses auxquelles se substitueront plus tard de vraies et de fausses beautés. Il est évident que la seconde formule est incomparablement plus originale, qu'elle seule engage certains principes esthétiques.

Par quel cheminement Corneille est-il passé de la première à la seconde? Il serait tentant d'invoquer l'influence de Descartes et de rappeler, dès les premières lignes du *Discours de la Méthode,* le prix exceptionnel reconnu à "la puissance de bien juger et distinguer le vrai d'avec le faux, qui est proprement ce qu'on nomme le bon sens ou la raison," puissance "naturellement égale en tous les hommes," mais plus ou moins bien exercée selon les individus.[6] Cette "puissance" n'a-t-elle pas à jouer son rôle en matière de beauté comme en tout autre domaine? Corneille nous autorise à le conclure. Mais il ne doit rien à Descartes. Le *Discours de la Méthode,* premier ouvrage publié par le philosophe, porte un achevé d'imprimer du 8 juin 1637: un peu plus de deux mois après *Le Cid.* Est-ce à dire que Corneille a devancé Descartes sur ce point, comme il le fera dans la conception du "généreux," mis en scène dans les grandes tragédies de 1637 à 1643, avant d'être aussi l'objet d'une définition en 1649 dans le *Traité des Passions?* Il est plus naturel de considérer que Corneille et Descartes procèdent d'un même courant.

Le *Discours de la Méthode* n'est d'ailleurs pas le seul ouvrage du temps qui mette à haut prix la capacité de "discerner le vrai d'avec le faux." La formule se trouve dès 1630 dans un livre promis à une large diffusion et à un long succès, *L'Honnête homme ou l'Art de plaire à la Cour* de Nicolas Faret.[7] L'auteur s'indigne du poids que peut avoir l'"opinion"—ce que Descartes appellera la "prévention"—sur l'esprit des hommes, et il fait du recours à la "raison" l'une des caractéristiques de l'"honnête homme." Ce n'est pas à dire que l'homme idéal, l'homme capable de plaire, soit un raisonneur, mais qu'il doit avoir l'esprit juste. Sa faculté principale est le "jugement," moins éclatant que les dons de l'imagination ou de la mémoire, mais permettant seul une communication intime entre les hommes fondée sur ce qui leur est commun.[8] La raison est une faculté souple et vivante. Elle sert de rempart contre le pédantisme et contre le prestige de l'autorité. Il est plus profitable "d'étudier dans le grand livre du monde que dans Aristote."[9] Descartes en dira autant, un Descartes à qui l'ouvrage de Faret n'était sans doute pas inconnu. Si *L'Honnête homme* rend, à plusieurs endroits, un son précartésien, on peut dire non moins justement que le début du *Discours de la Méthode* est un plaidoyer en faveur de l'"honnêteté": la nouvelle philosophie que Descartes entend fonder repose sur des principes que chacun peut trouver en soi et qui peuvent assurer une communication authentique. Faret et Descartes sont les témoins d'une même modernité.

Dans les milieux modernes du début de XVIIᵉ siècle, les catégories du vrai et du faux semblent avoir été appliquées d'abord aux valeurs morales et spirituelles. On en découvre l'emploi chez le rénovateur audacieux de la *devotio moderna* qu'a été saint François de Sales. En 1608, l'*Introduction à la Vie dévote* s'ouvre par un chapitre intitulé *Description de la vraie dévotion.*[10] Dans ce titre, "vrai" n'est pas un banal synonyme d'"excellente." Son emploi repose sur une distinction formelle entre la dévotion vraie, qui est unique, et les "fausses et vaines," qui sont en "grande quantité." Ces "statues et fantômes de dévotion" ne sont évidemment pas à confondre avec l'hypocrisie d'un Tartuffe; ce sont de fausses idées d'une dévotion qui, par manque de jugement, demeure "impertinente et superstitieuse." Les actes extérieurs y sont préférés à l'attitude intérieure. Son contraire est "la vraie et vivante dévotion."

Le même distinction reparaît dans un chapitre *Des vraies amitiés,* suivi d'un autre intitulé *Des vraies et des vaines amitiés*.[11] Le sens de toutes ces distinctions peut être condensé dans le précepte: "Ne recevez pas la fausse monnaie avec la bonne," et leur principe est bien exprimé par un autre titre de chapitre, *Qu'il faut avoir l'esprit juste et raisonnable*.[12]

De saint François de Sales et de Faret à la fois procède un autre écrivain, Jacques Du Bose, dont le gros ouvrage sur *L'Honnête femme*—encore un grand succès de librairie du siècle—paru en trois parties de 1632 à 1636, est contemporain des premiers succès de Corneille. La distinction du vrai et du faux en matière de vertus morales y est opérée fréquemment. Aux vraies et aux fausses amitiés répondent vraie et fausse simplicité, vraie et fausse probité, vraie et fausse civilité.[13] Le chapitre *De la vraie science d'une honnête femme* traite, plus de trente ans avant Molière et en termes comparables, de la question des femmes savantes.[14] La distinction se fonde sur celle très générale, qui oppose la vérité à l'apparence, la conscience à l'opinion, ou, plus précisément, la mesure, la discrétion, au "faste," à la "parade."[15] L'idée s'applique indirectement à la beauté, même si les termes de vrai et de faux ne sont pas employés à son sujet. Observant que Caton estimait fort la beauté, Du Bose commente: "Il parlait de la naturelle, et non pas de celle qui est pleine d'étude et d'afféterie."[16] La faculté qui, dans tous les cas, permet d'opérer cette distinction, c'est la raison, le jugement ou, pour retenir encore une expression précartésienne, la "lumière naturelle."[17]

Une origine plus lointaine, plus imprécise, de cette manière de penser, peut être relevée, en termes explicites ou implicites, dans un texte spirituel prestigieux, *L'Imitation de Jésus-Christ*. Lorsque Corneille le traduisit, il se plut à faire ressortir le procédé plus nettement que son original. Un chapitre est ainsi intitulé *De la véritable patience*, un autre *En quoi consiste la véritable paix*.[18] Entre les fragments de *L'Imitation* joints en 1670 à *L'Office de la Vierge*, figurent les belles stances intitulées *De la vraie liberté*.[19] La distinction établie dans la dédicace du *Cid* ne constitue donc pas un simple accident.

Mais, dans ce cas particulier, quelle signification précise faut-il lui prêter? Le contexte n'est pas d'un grand secours. Il n'y a pas non plus beaucoup à attendre des préfaces, examens et discours où Corneille entend surtout s'expliquer auprès des doctes et se place sur le terrain de la rhétorique et de la poétique. Pour définir ce qu'il appelle beauté, d'autres textes sont à prendre en considération.

Dans les scènes qui, à la fin du premier acte de *La Galerie du Palais*, publiée, comme *Le Cid*, en 1637, ont pour décor le lieu qui a donné son titre à la comédie, les conversations qui se déroulent devant la boutique de la lingère et devant celle du libraire donnent lieu à des propos d'"honnêtes gens" qui touchent de près à ce sujet.

A la lingère montrant des collets de dentelle, Hippolyte, qui représente assez bien le type de l'"honnête femme," déclare:

Ceci n'est guère bon qu'à des gens de campagne.

La suivante Florice critique un

. . . ouvrage . . . confus
Bien que l'invention de près soit assez belle,

et constate qu'en un autre modèle,

. . . la dentelle
Est fort mal assortie avec le passement.

Puis encore:

Cet autre n'a de beau que le couronnement.²⁰

Propos moins superficiels qu'il ne pourrait sembler et dont se dégage, en tout cas, l'idée d'une beauté fondée sur l'harmonie de divers éléments et dont seuls les gens de goût savent juger d'une manière correcte.

Aux deux jeunes premiers fort "honnêtes" que sont Lysandre et Dorimant, les livres exposés dans l'autre boutique suggèrent des réflexions beaucoup plus intéressantes, révélatrices de l'esthétique cornélienne. Dorimant, qui ne s'encombre guère de nuances, prononce par exemple:

Quantité d'ignorants ne songent qu'à la rime.

La rime est opposée implicitement, comme chez Boileau, à la raison, le brillant du son à la netteté du sens. Au libraire qui lui vante un recueil de vers:

Considérez ce trait, on le trouve divin,

le même Dorimant répond sans hésiter:

Il n'est que mal traduit du Cavalier Marin.²¹

Dénonciation significative d'une fausse beauté. Sur la poésie en général, Lysandre observe:

Beaucoup, dont l'entreprise excède le pouvoir,
Veulent parler d'amour sans aucune pratique.

Sur quoi Dorimant précise:

On n'y sait guère alors que la vieille rubrique.
Faute de le connaître, on l'habille en fureur,
Et loin d'en faire envie, on nous en fait horreur.
Lui seul de ses effets a droit de nous instruire;
Notre plume à lui seul doit se laisser conduire.
Pour en bien discourir, il faut l'avoir bien fait;
Un bon poète ne vient que d'un amant parfait.

Tous les "secrets" de l'amour, poursuit-il,

Quoi que tous nos rimeurs en mettent par écrit,
Ne se savent jamais par un effort d'esprit;
Et je n'ai jamais vu de cervelles bien faites
Qui traitassent l'amour à la façon des poètes.
C'est un tout autre jeu. . . .[22]

La vraie poésie se moque de la poésie, pourrait-on dire. Ou bien: un vrai poète est d'abord "honnête homme." Corneille revendique en faveur de la vie contre un art tout d'invention, contre une beauté empruntant des traits forcés à la "vieille rubrique," c'est-à-dire à la tradition antique, se guindant en des "efforts d'esprit" qui produisent des inventions artificielles, et oubliant le seul vrai modèle qui est la nature.

On ne saurait trouver meilleur commentaire à ces réflexions qu'en se reportant de nouveau à la première partie du *Discours de la Méthode* et en relevant ce passage dont la portée esthétique n'a peut-être pas été suffisamment perçue:

J'estimais fort l'éloquence et j'étais amoureux de la poésie. Mais je pensais que l'une et l'autre étaient des dons de l'esprit plutôt que des fruits de l'étude. Ceux qui ont le raisonnement le plus fort et qui digèrent le mieux leurs pensées afin de les rendre claires et intelligibles peuvent toujours mieux persuader ce qu'ils proposent, encore qu'ils ne parlassent que bas-breton, et qu'ils n'eussent jamais appris de rhétorique. Et ceux qui ont les inventions les plus agréables, et qui les savent exprimer avec le plus d'ornement et de douceur, ne laisseraient pas d'être les meilleurs poètes, encore que l'art poétique leur fût inconnu.[23]

Déclaration typique d'"honnête homme" et qui, même si les mots ne sont pas prononcés, aboutit à distinguer une vraie et une fausse beauté, opposées comme l'enseignement de la nature à celui de l'école. Il va de soi que, chez Descartes, la continuité est parfaite entre cette conception d'une beauté moderne, directement ouverte sur l'homme, et celle d'une nouvelle mathématique et d'une nouvelle métaphysique reposant sur des principes communs à tous les hommes.

"Vraie et vivante," disait saint François de Sales de la dévotion. Vraie et vivante, telle est aussi, pour Corneille et Descartes, la beauté. L'invocation du bon sens et de la raison ne signifie pas autre chose, et pas davantage. La vraie beauté se situe dans une voie moyenne entre le mauvais goût rustique et les lourdeurs du pédantisme ou les faux brillants d'une imagination déchaînée.

Tels sont les enseignements qui se dégagent de textes malheureusement fort brefs, touchant à notre sujet d'une manière seulement incidente, mais que leur conjonction rend fort suggestifs. Nous nous établirons sur un terrain plus solide en abordant l'écrit qui fournit naturellement son centre à notre étude.

En 1659—exactement le 20 août—l'un des plus fidèles imprimeurs de Port-Royal, Charles Savreux, faisait paraître, sans nom d'auteur, un *Epigrammatum delectus,* choix d'épigrammes empruntées au maître du genre, Martial, et à d'autres poètes latins et néo-latins. En tête, des pièces préliminaires aussi en latin, toujours anonymes: une *Praefatio,* puis une *Dissertatio de vera pulchritudine et adumbrata,* d'une quarantaine de pages. Consacrée expressément, comme l'indique le titre, au problème de la vraie et de la fausse beauté, cette dissertation, comme aussi la préface et le choix des épigrammes, est indubitablement de Nicole, qui fut d'abord maître aux *petites écoles* de Port-Royal, et dont le talent de latiniste se reconnaît au choix ingénieux de l'adjectif *adumbrata* pour exprimer l'idée de *falsa* ou de *ficta,* le premier de ces adjectifs étant d'ailleurs employé le plus souvent dans le corps de l'ouvrage. *L'Epigrammatum delectus* remporta un grand succès. Il fournissait des modèles d'expression brève et dense qui allaient s'imposer dans la prose avec les *Maximes* de La Rochefoucauld et les *Pensées* de Pascal. Mais c'est surtout la dissertation qui fut remarquée. En 1669, un jésuite fort versé dans les belles-lettres, le P. Vavasseur, publia un *De Epigrammate liber* dans lequel il crut devoir consacrer une centaine de pages à la critique de son devancier. Trait significatif, il ne reprend nulle part, fût-ce pour en contester le bien fondé, la distinction de la vraie et de la fausse beauté: silence compréhensible, car le principe de cette distinction s'accordait mal avec l'idée, chère aux jésuites, d'un art tendant à rivaliser avec la nature. La dissertation fit aussi l'objet de deux traductions, accompagnant de nouveaux recueils d'épigrammes: l'une du Toulousain Germain de La Faille, en 1689, l'autre de l'avocat auvergnat Brugière de Barante, en 1698, rééditée en 1700 et 1720. Traductions peu satisfaisantes et que nous négligerons au profit de l'original latin, mais qui signalent un succès durable. Aucun ouvrage d'esthétique du XVIIe siècle ne connut pareille diffusion.[24]

Sous la plume de Nicole comme sous celle de Corneille, la distinction entre vraie et fausse beauté suppose qu'est adoptée sur l'oeuvre d'art une perspective critique. C'est même en vue du choix des épigrammes à faire entrer dans le recueil que l'auteur aurait élaboré ses principes.[25] En fait, son dessein a pris une tout autre ampleur. Il entend traiter de la beauté comme Descartes a traité de la vérité.

La démarche initiale de Nicole est calquée sur celle du *Discours de la Méthode*. Prenant acte de la diversité des opinions, Descartes dénonce les tendances humaines qui empêchent l'esprit de bien juger, notamment la précipitation et la prévention. Contre la tentation du scepticisme, il a recours, non à la leçon des Anciens, mais à l'usage du bon sens commun à tous les hommes et qu'il s'agit seulement de bien employer. Il construit donc une méthode permettant de "bien conduire sa raison et chercher la vérité dans les sciences." Nicole commence aussi par remarquer la diversité des opinions, fût-ce entre hommes cultivés, touchant la beauté de ce qu'il nomme "scripta," de ce qu'on appellerait aujourd'hui les oeuvres littéraires. C'est que la prévention et la précipitation gâtent le jugement esthétique: "*Ommes temere conceptam opinionem ac impressum sibi sine animaduersione et judicio sensum in judicando sequuntur.*"[26] Il n'en faut pas pour autant tomber dans le scepticisme, qui réduit le jugement esthétique au jeu des fantaisies individuelles. Il n'est que de s'en rapporter à la raison, qui fournira une idée de la vraie beauté propre à servir de pierre de touche et à la distinguer de la fausse. N'allons pas nous méprendre sur le sens du mot "raison," qui demeure très souple. Il conduit essentiellement à la nature, une nature dans laquelle seront mis en valeur les traits universels. Il n'exclut pas que l'oeuvre d'art soit d'abord faite pour plaire et que toute beauté vise le plaisir, mais ce plaisir doit être, non mobile et changeant, mais ferme et stable.[27] Nous demeurons dans l'univers de l'"honnête homme."

Nicole élabore donc à son tour une méthode, aussi différente des règles édictées par les doctes que la méthode cartésienne de la logique d'Aristote. Mais, par la force des choses, le parallélisme avec le *Discours de la Méthode* se fait moins rigoureux. La beauté ne peut pas se composer, comme la vérité, à partir de l'évidence et en allant du simple au complexe. Elle ne peut être reconnue par une déduction conduite selon le modèle géométrique. Elle ne peut être saisie que globalement. Même s'il existe des beautés de détail, ce n'est pas leur simple somme qui constitue la beauté d'un ensemble. Aussi les règles de la méthode de Nicole sont-elles en même temps des principes caractérisant la structure de la beauté, un peu comme chez Descartes, au-delà de la méthode, est posé, comme fondement de la physique, le principe que tout, dans la naturel corporelle, se fait par figure et mouvement.

Nicole pose donc deux principes, qui sont en même temps deux règles: Pour être belle, une chose doit avoir convenance avec sa propre nature et avoir convenance avec la nature de l'homme, entendons de l'homme en général.[28] La perception de la beauté est donc celle d'un double rapport, l'un interne à l'objet, l'autre unissant l'objet à l'homme. La difficulté du système de Nicole réside, non pas dans ces principes, première expression cohérente et profonde d'une esthétique moderne, mais dans leur application. Le souci de rationalisation dont ils témoignent ne va pas, comme on peut l'observer aussi dans la physique cartésienne, sans porter atteinte à la complexité des choses. La conciliation nécessaire de l'un et du divers forme le grand écueil de toute théorie esthétique: Nicole s'y est heurté. Il est permis de douter que sa vraie beauté soit une beauté universelle.

La puissance de sa synthèse n'en est pas moins remarquable. Les deux règles posées s'appliquent d'abord au beau dans la nature. Une chose convient à sa propre nature lorsqu'elle ne comporte ni excès ni défaut, en somme lorsqu'elle est *"recte constituta."* Elle convient à la nature de l'homme lorsqu'elle plaît—à la fois aux sens et à l'esprit—mais d'un plaisir tel que peut l'éprouver une nature *"emendata et bene composita."*[29] La norme est assez vague. La véritable beauté se situe dans une sorte de juste milieu.

Mais c'est surtout aux oeuvres d'art, et principalement aux oeuvres littéraires, que Nicole entend appliquer ses principes. L'art littéraire use comme instrument du discours, sous les deux formes traditionnelles que sont l'éloquence et la poésie. Trois composantes s'y reconnaissent: les sons, qui s'adressent à l'oreille, les mots, qui signifient les choses, les idées, *"sententiae,"* qui viennent de l'auteur. En ces trois domaines, la vraie beauté résulte de la convenance établie avec la nature des choses et avec la nature de l'homme.

A propos des choses, la situation change lorsqu'on passe de la beauté naturelle à la beauté artistique et littéraire. La nature est à elle-même son propre référent: la convenance à reconnaître réside, comme on l'a vu, à l'intérieur de l'objet. Dans l'oeuvre littéraire, deux catégories d'objets sont à considérer, ceux de la nature et ceux du discours, les seconds se référant aux premiers. La convenance doit s'établir entre les uns et les autres.

Il ne fait pas l'ombre d'un doute, pour Nicole, que l'art est imitation. Les sons, les mots et les idées sont à prendre comme le moyen d'une imitation fidèle. L'idée de vivacité, par exemple, sera suggérée par un son rapide. La convenance des mots avec les choses sera respectée lorsque les grands mots seront employés pour désigner les grandes choses et les mots simples pour désigner les choses simples. Les figures et les ornements ont leurs emplois appropriés, en rapport avec les choses auxquelles ils s'appliquent. Pour les idées, qui expriment la personnalité de l'auteur, reflétée aussi bien par ses opinions que par sa manière, par le fond comme par la forme, elles ne s'accorderont avec les choses que si elles se réfèrent au seul vrai. Même la fiction ne peut être belle que si son mensonge dit la vérité. Les auteurs ne se réfugient dans le faux que par impuissance: car la vérité est enfermée en d'étroites limites, alors que le champ de l'erreur est infini. Qu'est-ce donc que la vérité dans les idées? On admettra sans peine que les passions doivent être conformes à la nature des personnages auxquelles elles sont prêtées. Mais la sévérité de Nicole va parfois très loin: il blâme les allusions mythologiques, les pointes reposant sur des équivoques, les hyperboles et toutes les formes d'exagération, ce qui condamne l'oeuvre d'un Rabelais, le manque de clarté dans les intentions, les descriptions négatives, en somme tout ce qui, dans l'art, est jeu sur la matière même de l'art, c'est-à-dire sur le langage, tout ce qui manifeste indiscrètement la présence de l'auteur.[30]

Lorsqu'il s'agit de définir la vraie beauté par sa convenance à la nature de l'homme, la considération successive du son, des mots et des pensées s'impose de nouveau. Mais désormais il n'est plus nécessaire d'aller jusqu'à l'objet; l'analyse porte entièrement sur le discours. Le plaisir de l'homme raisonnable devient le critère de la vraie beauté.

En quoi consiste l'agrément du son? Nicole tire de Cicéron l'idée que, dans l'éloquence, ce qui charme l'oreille est un juste équilibre entre le long et le bref, qu'il s'agisse des syllabes, des phrases ou du discours dans son ensemble. En matière de poésie, l'exigence de produire des sons agréables est encore plus contraignante, d'autant que la poésie est un discours harmonieux, *oratio modulata*. Mais le charme des vers suppose encore réalisé un équilibre difficile entre deux extrêmes. L'harmonie est insuffisante lorsque le poète se contente de suivre les règles de la prosodie sans tenir compte de la valeur et du rapport des sons. Elle est excessive, ou plutôt vaine et vide, lorsqu'elle est recherchée pour elle-même, sans que le son soit soutenu par le sens. La vérité de la nature humaine, comme celle de l'art, réside dans le juste milieu.[31]

Dans l'emploi des mots, Nicole estime que ce qui plaît est la conformité à l'usage: en quoi il se révèle disciple de Vaugelas et fidèle à l'idéal de l'"honnête homme." Dans la ligne de ses principes, il conçoit l'usage comme un juste milieu entre l'archaïsme et la néologisme. Il n'est pas toutefois sans percevoir une contradiction entre ce respect de l'usage et la quête d'une beauté éternelle. Aussi, pour instaurer une liaison plus fondamentale entre la nature humaine et l'usage des mots, est-il conduit à avancer une des idées les plus originales, sinon les plus convaincantes, de son étude. Dans la nature humaine, selon un schéma que l'on trouve aussi exploité, à d'autres fins, dans le *Traité des Passions* de Descartes,[32] il voit un mélange de force et de faiblesse. La tension constante est insupportable, de même que le relâchement continuel. De là vient qu'en musique, la tension des consonances appelle le relâchement des dissonances. Dans le discours, la grandeur continue fatigue, de même qu'une trop longue simplicité. La variété est nécessaire. Conséquence principale: l'expression directe de la vérité, par un discours sans figures, manifestation de force, doit parfois céder le pas à l'expression métaphorique, qui, introduisant un écart avec la pure vérité, contente la nature humaine avide de changement, manifestation de faiblesse. Reste qu'il faut user sobrement de cette nécessité; la poésie, par exemple, ne doit pas devenir mascarade. Le juste milieu demeure la règle.[33]

Dans l'expression des idées, obtenir la convenance avec la nature humaine n'est encore autre chose que de rechercher ce qui plaît et de fuir ce qui déplaît. C'est, en définitive, respecter strictement les bienséances. Est condamné comme fausse beauté tout ce qui choque la pudeur, toute peinture d'un objet repoussant: une vieille édentée, un poète crotté, toute bouffonnerie et toute bassesse, toute manifestation gratuite de malignité qui fait rire de malheurs dont les victimes ne sont pas responsables. S'il faut fuir certains sujets, il ne faut pas moins éviter, dans l'expression, ce qui détruit l'équilibre entre le langage et la pensée: surabondance des paroles, banalité des idées, jeux de mots artificiels. Comme il lui arrive souvent, Nicole insiste plus ici sur ce qui déplaît que sur ce qui plaît.[34]

En définitive, si, dans l'application des principes, son système offre quelque rigidité, ce n'est pas par fidélité aux lois de la rhétorique antique, qu'il s'agit au contraire de dépasser: ce système est moderne. Ce n'est pas non plus pour se réclamer de la raison et de la vérité, notions souples qui renvoient à l'art de plaire. C'est pour s'appuyer sur une conception trop étroite du plaisir de l'art et de l'esprit de l'"honnête homme" pris pour référence. Le désir d'élaborer un modèle d'humanité générale et constante aboutit à plaider pour un juste milieu, au fond aristotélicien, qui risque fort de déboucher sur la convention et l'académisme.

Pour aller plus au fond de cette pensée et en faire apercevoir malgré tout la profondeur, il est bon de faire ressortir que Nicole se représente constamment l'art littéraire sur le modèle, moins de la peinture, comme dans la tradition rhétorique, que de la musique. Les comparaisons musicales sont fréquentes sous sa plume et l'idée d'harmonie y revient constamment. La théorie même de la vraie beauté lui emprunte ses fondements. La convenance interne de l'oeuvre se constitue comme une sorte d'unité musicale, comparable à celle d'un accord. Le rapport des sons, des mots et des idées avec les choses apparaît moins comme un reflet que comme une harmonie. Quant à la convenance externe entre l'oeuvre et la nature de l'homme, elle rappelle les théories fort en vogue au XVIIᵉ siècle sur le rapport de la musique avec les moeurs. On ne sera donc pas surpris de relever d'étroites affinités entre l'esthétique de Nicole et celle qui s'exprime dans le *Compendium musicae,* écrit de jeunesse de Descartes, composé en 1618, inconnu du public avant la traduction qu'en donna le P. Poisson en 1668, mais dont les cartésiens de Port-Royal pouvaient avoir quelque idée. Raisonnant en "honnête homme," Descartes affirme fortement que la fin de la musique est de plaire. Sans méconnaître les caractères internes de l'harmonie musicale, il insiste sur l'idée que la beauté, en musique, est liée à la structure de l'homme. Le plaisir éprouvé à l'audition du son dépend de la disposition de l'oreille: "Ce qui fait que la voix de l'homme nous agrée plus que les autres, c'est seulement parce qu'elle est plus conforme à la nature de nos espirts."[35] La musique doit être perçue avec clarté mais l'excès de facilité est aussi blâmable que l'excès de difficulté. La variété est aussi une exigence de notre nature: elle veut que les dissonances viennent briser la continuité des consonances. En somme, la musique établit un rapport constant entre les sons et les passions. Chez Nicole comme chez Descartes, la référence à la musique dénote un certain climat platonicien, qui n'exclut pas les éléments aristotéliciens déjà mentionnés.[36]

Sans nous écarter beaucoup de Nicole, nous découvrirons une nouvelle mise en oeuvre de la distinction entre vraie et fausse beauté dans les *Pensées* de Pascal. A vrai dire, la distinction n'y est pas opérée d'une manière aussi formelle que dans la *Dissertation*. Mais, si les termes "vrai" et "faux" n'y sont jamais opposés symétriquement, c'est sans doute pour éviter toute lourdeur pédante. En fait, la distinction existe d'une manière sous-jacente dans la plupart des fragments des *Pensées* qui touchent à l'esthétique.

Dès lors, une question se pose. Comment expliquer les nombreuses affinités décelables entre ces pensées, dont la rédaction a pu s'échelonner entre 1656 et 1662, et la *Dissertation* publiée en 1659, mais peut-être sur le chantier, ou déjà composée, vers 1655–1656?[37] Les *Pensées* sont-elles inspirées de la *Dissertation*? Ou bien Pascal a-t-il été l'initiateur et Nicole a-t-il tiré un parti décisif de sa conversation?[38] Ou bien les deux écrits demeurent-ils indépendants?

L'examen des textes autorise une seule certitude. Une pensée, intitulée *Epigrammes de Martial*,[39] se réfère incontestablement au recueil publié en 1659 et lui est postérieure. On observera que Pascal y émet, à propos d'une épigramme, des réserves sur le choix effectué dans le recueil, et qu'il nuance la théorie qui, dans la *Dissertation,* donnait la malignité pour toujours déplaisante. Par rapport à l'*Epigrammatum delectus* dans son ensemble, Pascal se situe donc comme devant un ouvrage étranger. Il n'a pas participé à son élaboration.

Est-ce à dire que Nicole n'ait pas reçu certaines suggestions de Pascal? A la fin de la préface, l'auteur déclare n'avoir pas seulement puisé ses principes dans son propre esprit et dans les livres des Anciens, mais dans la conversation des "honnêtes gens": "*ex virorum omni eruditione praestantium, et multo vitae elegantioris usu verae urbanitatis intelligentium sermonibus.*"[40] Ses principales sources sont donc modernes et orales. De tous ceux dont les réflexions ont pu l'enrichir, Pascal est sans aucun doute celui que, depuis 1655, il rencontrait le plus fréquemment.

Ce n'est pas à dire que Pascal n'ait aussi profité de la fréquentation de Nicole et que chacun d'eux n'ait pu faire sur l'autre l'essai de ses idées. Mais il y a tout lieu de croire que les deux systèmes sont indépendants.

Aux idées exprimées dans la *Dissertation* beaucoup de pensées font exactement écho, un écho toujours plus dense et plus brillant: "Je hais également le bouffon et l'enflé. . . . On ne consulte que l'oreille parce qu'on manque de coeur"; "L'éloquence continue ennuie"; "Changer de figure à cause de notre faiblesse." [41] Ailleurs la pensée est encore la même, mais elle est exprimée avec une précision et une virulence étrangères à la *Dissertation:* "Toutes les fausses beautés que nous blâmons en Cicéron ont des admirateurs et en grand nombre." [42] Ou bien elle s'enrichit et se nuance: "Il faut de l'agréable et du réel, mais il faut que cet agréable soit lui-même pris du vrai." [43] Ou bien encore, à partir d'un même principe, elle fournit une vue tout à fait originale: "Symétrie: en ce qu'on voit d'une vue . . . et fondée aussi sur la figure de l'homme: d'où il arrive qu'on ne veut la symétrie qu'en largeur, non en hauteur ni profondeur." [44] Enfin le modèle musical est brillamment exploité: "On croit toucher des orgues ordinaires en touchant l'homme. . . ." [45] Mais Pascal est beaucoup plus sensible que Nicole à la difficulté de trouver la convenance entre l'homme et les choses qui constitue la vraie beauté. Adopte-t-il les mêmes principes qu'il est beaucoup plus prudent dans leur application.

Si l'on aborde les deux séries de pensées où sont opposées, de la manière la plus précise, la vraie et la fausse beauté, on découvre de grandes différences de perspective entre Nicole et Pascal.

La première série est formée de trois fragments, qui figurent ensemble sur le même papier, celui qui est au centre portant seul un titre, *Beauté poétique.*[46] Pris sous la dictée, ils sont de la main d'un des secrétaires de Pascal et figurent dans l'unité XXIII de la seconde partie de la *Copie* des *Pensées,* intitulée *Miscellanea.* Leur date exacte est actuellement impossible à déterminer, mais ils ont de fortes chances d'être antérieurs à la publication de l'*Epigrammatum delectus.*

Le premier offre le caractère le plus général. L'idée fondamentale est exprimée dès le début:

> Il y a un certain modèle d'agrément et de beauté qui consiste en un certain rapport entre notre nature, faible ou forte, telle qu'elle est, et la chose qui nous plaît.

Des rapprochements avec la *Dissertation* s'imposent: la considération de la force et de la faiblesse de la nature humaine, l'idée d'une beauté définie par le rapport que l'objet reconnu beau entretient avec l'homme.

Mais les différences sautent aux yeux. Dans la définition de la vraie beauté par Nicole, Pascal néglige tout l'élément objectif, ou interne, tout ce qui tient à la structure de l'objet ou à la relation entre l'oeuvre d'art et le réel. Pour lui, semble-t-il, la connaissance de l'objet étant déjà relative à l'homme, l'objectivité véritable n'existe pas; seule compte la relation de l'homme à l'objet: la pensée déjà citée sur la symétrie montre dans l'harmonie interne de l'objet le reflet de la structure de l'homme. De plus, Pascal complète l'idée de beauté par celle d'agrément, source d'un plaisir esthétique plus simple, plus familier: Pascal a, plus profondément que Nicole, reçu l'empreinte de la société mondaine. Mais surtout son effort de systématisation est plus pénétrant. Il introduit la notion capitale de modèle.[47] Au lieu d'énumérer, comme le fait Nicole, les exigences de la nature humaine dont la satisfaction détermine la reconnaissance de la beauté, il s'attache à saisir globalement, synthétiquement, le rapport de l'homme à l'objet qui définit le modèle de la beauté. Une beauté qui n'est pas située dans l'objet même, mais se présente comme une qualité autonome, un mode de la relation que l'objet entretient avec l'homme.

Posant un principe plus profond que Nicole, Pascal en déduit aussi des conséquences plus générales. Le modèle est indépendant de l'objet qui a servi à le définir. Il peut convenir à d'autres objets: "Tout ce qui est formé sur ce modèle nous agrée, soit maison, chanson, discours, vers, prose, femme, oiseaux, rivières, arbres, chambres, habits, etc." Autre trait de généralisation: la beauté ainsi définie n'est pas seulement celle des oeuvres d'art, mais aussi celle des objets de la nature. Entre toutes les beautés particulières s'établissent des correspondances, au sens baudelairien du terme.

Le modèle est-il uniqeu? On pourrait assurément distinguer plusieurs types de beautés, et l'analyse de Pascal n'exclut pas ce prolongement de sa thèse. Mais ce n'est pas dans cette voie qu'il s'engage. Il n'y a pour lui qu'un seule modèle de ce que Nicole appelait la vraie beauté: "Tout ce qui n'est point fait sur ce modèle déplaît à ceux qui ont le goût bon."

Ce n'est pas la raison, comme chez Nicole, mais le goût[48] qui fait distinguer la vraie et la fausse beauté. La différence est moins sensible que le vocabulaire, entendu selon ses connotations actuelles, pourrait le laisser croire. Mais chez Pascal, Descartes semble bien loin et la référence à l'idéal de l'"honnête homme" est plus accusée. De plus, au lieu de définir, comme l'aurait fait Nicole, les caractéristiques du bon goût, Pascal en fait le privilège de certaines personnes. Le goût peut sans doute s'apprendre, mais il peut difficilement se raisonner.

Unique est donc le "bon modèle." Il y a aussi de "mauvais modèles": il y en a même "une infinité." Pour chaque mauvais modèle, le même jeu de correspondances s'établit qu'à propos de l'unique vrai: "Chaque mauvais sonnet, sur quelque faux modèle qu'il soit fait, ressemble parfaitement à une femme vêtue sur ce modèle."

On voit que Pascal change progressivement d'adjectif, "mauvais" lais-

sant la place à "faux." Il parle ensuite d'un "faux sonnet," c'est-à-dire
non pas d'un sonnet infidèle aux lois du genre, mais chargé d'une fausse
beauté. On reconnaît le mouvement de langage déjà signalé à propos de
Corneille.

Comment se construit le "faux modèle"? Sans doute sur une discordance entre la nature humaine et l'objet jugé beau. Toutefois, le goût se
révèle plus juste, plus universel, pour certains objets que pour d'autres:
la beauté d'une femme—il s'agit plutôt de sa parure—est plus aisée à
juger que celle d'un sonnet. Pour apprécier un sonnet, il faut en dégager
le modèle et imaginer une femme qui lui corresponde. C'est le jeu des
ressemblances qui fonde la rationalité du système pascalien.

Cette méthode de correspondance est plus amplement développée dans
le fragment intitulé *Beauté poétique*. Mais elle est introduite par une
autre voie:

> Comme on dit beauté poétique on devrait aussi dire beauté géométrique
> et beauté médicinale; mais on ne le dit pas, et la raison en est qu'on sait
> bien quel est l'objet de la géométrie et qu'il consiste en preuve, et quel est
> l'objet de la médecine et qu'il consiste en la guérison. Mais on ne sait pas
> en quoi consiste l'agrément, qui est l'objet de la poésie. On ne sait ce que
> c'est que ce modèle naturel qu'il faut imiter et, à faute de cette connais-
> sance, on a inventé de certains termes bizarres, *siècle d'or, merveille de
> nos jours, fatal*, etc., et on appelle ce jargon beauté poétique.

Pourquoi cette comparaison entre poésie, géométrie et médecine? Cha-
cune de ces disciplines entretient un certain rapport avec l'homme et vise
à son sujet un certain but: la preuve, pour la géométrie; la guérison, pour
la médecine; l'agrément, pour la poésie. Preuve et guérison s'imposent à
l'esprit et aux sens: on ne peut s'y méprendre. La catégorie du vrai suffit
à en rendre compte; il n'y a pas lieu de faire appel au beau. C'est
lorsqu'une preuve est douteuse, peut-être aussi lorsqu'un traitement mé-
dical est jugé indépendamment de son effet, qu'on peut parler, comme le
fait Pascal ironisant sur les théories du P. Noël à propos du vide, de "belle
pensée." [49] Or l'objet de la poésie est insaisissable et sujet à discussion.
Dès lors s'applique la loi définie dans une autre pensée: "L'esprit croit
naturellement et la volonté aime naturellement, de sorte qu'à faute de
vrais objets il faut qu'ils s'attachent aux faux." [50] Faute de connaître la
beauté naturelle, l'esprit invente une beauté artificielle, qu'il nomme
"beauté poétique." Pascal, comme le montrent les variantes, avait

d'abord pensé dire "langage poétique." La fausse beauté est en effet rapportée à l'emploi d'un certain "jargon."

Un tel raisonnement devrait aboutir au scepticisme esthétique. En fait, la dénonciation d'une fausse beauté implique l'existence d'une vraie beauté, si difficile qu'elle soit à percevoir. La règle du modèle permet de saisir la beauté des vers par comparaison avec la beauté d'une femme. Elle invite à exclure la surcharge et l'abus des ornements, qui dénotent le mauvais goût populaire ou pédant:

> Mais qui s'imaginera une femme sur ce modèle-là, qui consiste à dire de petites choses avec de grands mots, verra une jolie demoiselle toute pleine de miroirs et de chaînes, dont il rira, parce qu'il sait mieux en quoi consiste l'agrément d'une femme que l'agrément des vers. Mais ceux qui ne s'y connaîtraient pas l'admireraient en cet équipage, et il y a bien des villages où on la prendrait pour la reine; et c'est pourquoi nous appelons les sonnets faits sur ce modèle-là les reines de village.

Au fond, le domaine de la beauté est celui de l'apparence. La vraie beauté se distingue de la vérité en ce qu'elle est vérité d'une apparence, dont les caractéristiques tiennent à celles de la nature humaine. Elle n'a pas le même statut que la preuve ou la guérison, qui appartiennent au réel. Le troisième fragment montre bien sur quel terrain se situe Pascal: celui de l'"honnête homme," conçu par lui comme l'homme universel, porteur au suprême degré de la nature humaine et s'exprimant en son nom: "Les gens universels ne sont appelés ni poètes, ni géomètres, etc. Mais ils sont tout cela et juges de tous ceux-là. . . . C'est donc une fausse louange qu'on donne à un homme quand on dit de lui lorsqu'il entre qu'il est fort habile en poésie; et c'est une mauvaise marque quand on n'a pas recours à un homme quand il s'agit de juger de quelques vers." "Poète et non honnête homme," dit ailleurs Pascal.[51] Et, en même temps: "La règle est l'honnêteté." Le poète n'est pas celui qui fait métier de poésie. Il n'a pas une spécialité, il n'use pas d'un langage qui lui serait propre. La vraie poésie exprime l'humanité même. On a vu que l'auteur de *Discours de la Méthode* ne pensait guère autrement.

Le seconde série de pensées s'applique particulièrement à l'autre volet de l'art littéraire: l'éloquence, "La vraie éloquence se moque de l'éloquence; la vraie morale se moque de la morale. C'est-à-dire que la morale du jugement se moque de la morale de l'esprit, qui est sans règles. Car le jugement est celui à qui appartient le sentiment, comme les sciences appartiennent à l'esprit. La finesse est la part du jugement; la géométrie est celle de l'esprit." [52] Comme la prétendue "beauté poétique" était une fausse beauté, l'éloquence pure et simple est ici une fausse éloquence. C'est celle qui relève de la rhétorique et non de la vie: nous retrouvons l'idée de Descartes.

Mais la pensée de Pascal, par rapport à celle de Descartes comme à celle de Nicole, comporte d'importants éléments nouveaux. Elle introduit d'abord une comparaison très éclairante entre l'éloquence et la morale. L'éloquence a pour fin de persuader. La vraie éloquence entend s'adapter aux lois de la nature humaine, qu'il s'agit de toucher. La fausse éloquence se veut essentiellement fidèle aux lois de la rhétorique. De même, la vraie morale conduit l'homme vers le bien par l'éducation de sa conscience. La fausse morale substitue à la considération du vécu celle de préceptes artificiels qui, à la limite, dispensent de la conscience: c'est l'une des leçons des *Provinciales*.

On voit comment s'établit l'opposition fondamentale entre le jugement et l'esprit. Le premier s'applique à la vraie éloquence et à la vraie morale; le second à la fausse éloquence et à la fausse morale. Les deux termes se précisent par deux autres: la finesse, qui ressortit au jugement; la géométrie, qui ressortit à l'esprit. A quoi s'ajoute un autre terme, qui se rapporte au jugement, le sentiment, sorte d'intuition, proche du goût esthétique et de la conscience morale.

L'esprit s'exerce normalement dans le domaine de la géométrie, où "les principes sont palpables, mais éloignés de l'usage commun." [53] La géométrie est une construction intellectuelle, dont le rapport à la réalité est sans importance. Le jugement est un autre nom de l'esprit de finesse, qui est aussi un esprit, mais pour lequel "les principes sont dans l'usage commun et devant les yeux de tout le monde." C'est en effet à l'homme et à la vie qu'il s'applique: où les principes sont faciles à voir, mais tellement nombreux qu'il est presque impossible d'en oublier, c'est-à-dire d'éviter l'erreur. Pour reprendre l'idée de *Beauté poétique,* il n'y a pas de beauté en géométrie parce que la vérité y est atteinte d'une manière rigoureuse. Il y a beauté en éloquence parce qu'il est presque impossible de persuader en vérité. Selon les analyses de l'écrit intitulé *De l'Art de persuader,* l'orateur doit à la fois toucher l'esprit et le coeur, convaincre et agréer, s'adapter aux opinions et aux désirs de son auditoire: tâche d'une complexité extrême, surtout dans sa seconde partie. Toutefois, par cette distinction de la géométrie et de la finesse, Pascal se dégage du scepticisme sans tomber dans le rationalisme très sec de Nicole.

Reste la difficulté majeure du texte. Qu'est-ce qui est sans règles, le jugement ou l'esprit? Grammaticalement, c'est l'esprit. Faut-il, avec plusieurs éditeurs, rapporter le relatif à l'antécédent la plus éloigné? Rien ne permet de croire que pour Pascal le jugement n'obéisse à aucune règle. Ainsi déclare-t-il qu'il y a "des règles aussi sûres pour plaire que pour démontrer," [54] encore qu'il soit presque "impossible d'y arriver." Ces règles sont en effet beaucoup plus souples que celles qui regardent l'esprit. On peut en définir l'orientation générale par la pensée déjà citée: "La règle est l'honnêteté." Nous proposerons donc de prêter au texte son sens le plus naturel, mais en interprétant "sans règles véritables" ou "adéquates."

Fait curieux, un autre fragment des *Pensées* traitant des règles comporte une difficulté analogue: "Ceux qui jugent d'un ouvrage sans règle sont à l'égard des autres comme ceux qui ont une montre à l'égard des autres. L'un dit: il y a deux heures; l'autre dit: il n'y a que trois quarts d'heure. Je regarde ma montre et je dis à l'un: vous vous ennuyez; et à l'autre: le temps ne vous dure guère, car il y a une heure et demie. Et je me moque de ceux qui disent que le temps me dure à moi et que j'en juge par fantaisie. Ils ne savent pas que j'en juge par ma montre." [55]

Incontestablement, la nécessité d'une règle est ici affirmée. Faut-il corriger en substituant, soit, au début, avec l'édition de Port-Royal, "par règle," soit, dans la suite, avec Brunschvicg, "n'ont pas de montre"? Il suffit de reconnaître qu'involontairement, Pascal a pratiqué une inversion, une sorte de chiasme, qui rend erronée la lettre du texte, mais sans obscurcir son sens. Il va de soi que cette règle est la nature humaine essentielle, idéale, à laquelle s'opposent les fantaisies des individus. La vraie mesure du temps est perçue par l'homme équilibré.

Si Pascal n'utilise pas le mot de "beauté" à propos de l'éloquence, la notion est impliquée dans ses analyses d'une manière analogue à celle qui s'exprime à propos de la poésie.

Pascal introduit une complexité, une souplesse et une profondeur toutes nouvelles dans des réflexions qu'il est impossible de réduire à celles de Nicole. Les deux auteurs se distinguent encore d'une façon remarquable par la portée qu'ils assignent à leur théorie de la beauté. Nicole se situe étroitement sur le terrain du jugement esthétique, négligeant tout prolongement philosophique et surtout religieux. Au contraire, chez Pascal, la conception de la vraie et de la fausse beauté entre dans une vision du monde plus vaste. Les deux esthétiques sont de caractère strictement anthropologique. Si elles débordent le scepticisme, elles n'aboutissent ni l'une ni l'autre à une conception ontologique du beau, à la manière de Platon, auquel saint Augustin fait écho, notamment dans le *De vera religione*. Mais, si la *Dissertation* laisse de côté christianisme et augustinisme, les *Pensées* s'attachent à saisir le rapport entre la partie et le tout.

L'esthétique de Pascal se rapporte clairement au domaine de l'homme sans Dieu. La beauté, on l'a vu, n'est que d'apparences; elle ne touche à rien d'essentiel. Lorsque la vérité est accessible, fût-ce la vérité humaine de la géométrie, la beauté n'a plus sa place. De même, les vérités divines ne sont pas sujettes à l'art de persuader.[56] La preuve de l'existence de Dieu par l'harmonie de la nature, "le ciel et les oiseaux,"[57] est inefficace et ridicule. L'homme avec Dieu s'élève au-delà de la beauté.

Peut-être vaudrait-il mieux dire que le beau change alors de nature et qu'il se confond avec le bien. En tout cas, le passage de la nature à Dieu s'opère selon un schéma qui comporte aussi les deux termes de "vrai" et de "faux," appliqués désormais au Bien. "L'homme sans la foi" s'attache à une multitude d'objets, ombres, fantômes du "vrai bien" qui est seul l'objet réel de sa quête. Comme "l'homme universel" était juge de la vraie beauté terrestre, le vrai bien, qui se confond avec Dieu, présente aussi ce caractère d'universalité.[58] La théorie janséniste de la "délectation" peut rendre compte de ces affinités entre l'art de plaire et le jeu de la grâce.

C'est encore un passage du faux au vrai, plus précisément de l'apparence à la réalité, que l'on saisit par l'interprétation des figures de la Bible, capitale dans l'argumentation apologétique de Pascal. "Vrai jeûne, vrai sacrifice, vrai temple," vraie liberté, "vrai pain du ciel":[59] les figures de la Bible sont comme les figures de rhétorique telles que les analyse Nicole. Elles s'écartent du vrai, mais leur seule justification est de signifier le vrai. En s'exprimant par figures et en vérité, Dieu s'adapte à la nature humaine, faible et forte à la fois. "L'unique objet de l'Ecriture est la charité." Mais cet "unique but" n'est pas toujours désigné au sens propre, il l'est parfois au sens figuré. "Dieu diversifie ainsi cet unique précepte de charité pour satisfaire notre curiosité qui recherche la diversité par cette diversité qui nous mène toujours à notre unique nécessaire."[60] Les lois qui président à l'expression de la beauté humaine président aussi à celle de la vérité divine.

Le propre de Dieu parlant aux hommes est donc d'employer le langage de la vraie beauté. La "modestie"—la mesure—est le caractère du style évangélique:[61] nulle outrance, nulle "affectation." Jésus-Christ "dit les choses grandes . . . simplement" et "nettement."[62] Clarté et "naïveté"—

naturel—qui caractérisent le sublime. Dieu n'a pas besoin du beau pour lui-même, mais il se sert du beau par convenance à la nature humaine. Ainsi, dans le système de Pascal, la plus grande ampleur se concilie avec la plus rigoureuse cohérence.

Entre Pascal et le chevalier de Méré, comme entre Nicole et Pascal, la question d'une influence réciproque est à la fois inévitable et insoluble avec précision. De seize ans l'aîné, s'étant acquis quelque réputation dans les cercles parisiens dès les alentours de 1640, le gentilhomme poitevin se trouvait en position d'autorité vis-à-vis de celui dont il fit la connaissance au plus tard en 1653, et qu'il ne cessa de revoir à l'époque des *Pensées,* lors de ses séjours à Paris.[63] Mais pas une seule ligne de lui ne fut publiée avant la mort de Pascal. C'est en 1668 que parut son premier et plus important ouvrage, ses *Conversations* avec le maréchal de Clérambault, suivies du *Discours de la Justesse.* Des publications ultérieures, il faut surtout retenir les trois discours de 1677, *Des Agréments, De l'Esprit, De la Conversation.* Les *Lettres,* mises au jour en 1682, ne portent pas de dates, et, même si leur destinataire ou leur sujet invite à les tenir pour anciennes—c'est le cas pour une longue lettre à Pascal—rien ne prouve qu'elles n'aient pas été remaniées, peut-être même fabriquées, pour le recueil imprimé qui seul les fait connaître. A sa mort, en 1684, le chevalier laissait encore quelques "discours," publiés comme *Oeuvres posthumes* par l'abbé Nadal en 1700.[64] Entre ces divers écrits et les *Pensées,* des rapprochements nombreux s'imposent. On ne peut les expliquer d'une manière plausible que par le fait des rapports directs entre les deux hommes, qui ont permis une fécondation mutuelle des deux esprits, impossible à analyser dans le détail. Mais l'originalité de chacun d'eux est indubitable. Il suffit, sur le sujet qui nous occupe, de définir leurs positions respectives pour faire éclater, à côté des ressemblances, des divergences considérables.

Nul auteur au XVIIᵉ siècle n'a usé plus que Méré de la distinction entre le vrai et le faux, dans le domaine de la morale comme dans celui de l'esthétique. Avec lui, d'ailleurs, tous les sujets s'interpénètrent. Plus complètement que les auteurs précédents, il ne sépare pas la conception du beau de celle des rapports humains. L'"honnête homme" en quête de ce qui plaît est comme le modèle de l'artiste. Il fournit en même temps le modèle de l'oeuvre d'art, puisque plaire, c'est éveiller chez les autres un plaisir de nature presque esthétique. Dans le "commerce du monde," les mêmes lois s'exercent que dans le domaine des arts. Partout le vrai et le faux s'opposent semblablement.

Dans cette perspective, le regard de Méré explore trois domaines principaux. Le plus amplement étudié est celui de l'"honnêteté" comme art de vivre. Un traité entier est intitulé *De la vraie honnêteté.*[65] Elle se définit essentiellement par le naturel. Une "douceur étudiée," affectée, se fait haïr et dénonce un "faux honnête homme."[66] La recherche du brillant, l'abus des "bons mots" a quelque chose de contraint qui déplaît. "Je ne sais quoi de libre et d'aisé fait de bien meilleurs effets."[67] La vraie honnêteté se distingue aussi d'avec la fausse en ce qu'"elle est universelle," "juste et raisonnable en tous les endroits du monde."[68]

L'attention de Méré se porte ensuite sur un domaine où s'exerce encore l'"honnêteté" vécue, mais par des moyens qui, mettant en oeuvre le langage, font songer au travail de l'artiste. Oeuvre d'art que la conversation, que la lettre, que la poésie amoureuse. En tous ces genres, la principale vertu à cultiver est la "justesse," terme directement opposé à "fausseté."[69] Dans son *Discours de la Justesse,* Méré s'en prend aux lettres de Voiture, en dépit de la réputation d'homme habile à plaire qu'elles avaient value à leur auteur. Est manque de justesse, non seulement toute impropriété de langage, mais toute discordance entre la pensée et l'expression, toute pointe et, principalement, l'équivoque:[70] on rejoint très précisément la leçon de Nicole. La sincérité est la condition du beau langage. On le constate avec Voiture. "Lorsqu'il est question de toucher le coeur, il s'amuse à subtiliser et à dire des gentillesses."[71] Au fond, il n'avait jamais bien su aimer. Jugement sévère, injuste peut-être, mais la revendication de la vérité dans l'art exige que l'on préfère les choses aux mots.

Aux arts majeurs, Méré s'attarde moins longuement. De la conversation il s'élève toutefois naturellement à l'éloquence. Sa critique de la "fausse éloquence"—l'expression est d'autant plus significative que la pensée de Pascal sur ce sujet était encore inédite—apporte l'essentiel: "Je remarque souvent, dit-il, que ceux qui parlent trop bien, à ce qu'on dit, ne parlent toujours que trop mal; que leurs discours n'ont point de rapport au sujet; que l'on sent de l'affectation dans leur manière et dans le ton de leur voix, et qu'enfin ce n'est qu'une fausse éloquence."[72] "Rien ne réussit mieux que d'être éloquent sans le paraître, comme il sied aussi fort mal d'en avoir l'apparence et de ne l'être pas."[73] Leur souci d'atteindre l'homme en vérité a fait des Grecs les maîtres de tous les arts. "On ne peut regarder sans larmes" le tableau du sacrifice d'Iphigénie par Timante. Par leur musique, "en ajustant et diversifiant de certains tons, ils savaient toucher le coeur comme ils voulaient." De même de leur sculpture, de leur éloquence et de leur poésie.[74] Aristote est donc infidèle à leur génie profond pour n'avoir pas "un peu plus naturalisé l'art et les règles"[75]—on reconnaît un mot de Montaigne. Nouvelle critique adressée à la rhétorique.

Pour mieux saisir l'originalité de Méré, il convient de s'élever au-dessus de ces domaines particuliers et de dégager sa conception générale de la beauté.

A vrai dire, ce terme est moins employé chez lui que celui d'agrément, au singulier ou au pluriel, avec encore la distinction du vrai et du faux. Le terme "agrément" est d'une application plus large que celui de "beauté"; il convient à tout ce qui plaît, de l' "honnête homme" aux divers objets de la nature et de l'art. L'unité des vues de Méré s'y reflète parfaitement. Mais il désigne aussi, comme on l'a vu, une qualité plus familière, plus accessible, que la beauté. Comment se distinguent donc vrais et faux agréments? Il n'est que de généraliser les remarques déjà présentées. Est suspect de fausseté "tout ce qui brille et qui donne dans les yeux," tout ce qui vise "le spectacle et la décoration." Si les enfants, le peuple et même les princes penchent volontiers en ce sens, parce qu'ils manquent de formation, en revanche, "les gens faits et qui jugent bien n'aiment pas les choses de montre et qui parent beaucoup, quand elles ne sont que de peu de valeur. Celles qui n'ont guère d'éclat et qui sont de grand prix leur plaisent."[76] Les "vrais et profonds agréments"—les deux adjectifs sont plusieurs fois associés—ne peuvent résider en des "grâces superficielles."[77]

Qu'est-ce à dire? Le propre des "vrais agréments" est de ne pas éblouir. Ils se révèlent peu à peu et, par suite, se renouvellent sans cesse. L'artiste doit laisser à deviner: "Rien ne témoigne tant que la manière de s'expliquer est noble et parfaite que de laisser comprendre certaines choses sans les dire."[78] "Les excellents peintres ne peignent pas tout: ils donnent de l'exercice à l'imagination et en laissent à penser plus qu'ils n'en découvrent." C'est l'une des grandes vertus de l'art grec. Homère "ne s'amuse pas à décrire Hélène. Il ne dit presque rien de son visage ni de sa taille. Cependant il a persuadé à toute la terre que c'était la plus belle femme qu'on ait jamais vue."[79] Il faut se garder de lasser: "à force de se faire admirer, on deviendrait insupportable."[80] Les "vrais agréments" résistent au temps.

On peut encore les caractériser d'une autre façon, qui fait songer à Nicole. Ils consistent dans la modération, la mesure, "dans un bon tempérament," dans une sorte de juste milieu. "Les vrais agréments ne veulent rien qui ne soit modéré: tout ce qui passe de certaines bornes les diminue, ou même les détruit."[81] Il y faut aussi une exacte proportion. Ce n'est pas le détail qui séduit, c'est l'ensemble. "Plus les parties dont une chose est composée sont comme il faut, plus elle est agréable." Elles valent "par un juste rapport qui montre qu'elles sont faites les unes pour les autres."[82] Enfin l'agréable exclut "la manière contrainte, où l'on sent beaucoup de travail." "Les agréments aiment la justesse, mais d'une façon si naïve qu'elle donne à penser que c'est un présent de la nature."[83]

Cette exaltation des agréments ne va-t-elle pas sans un certain discrédit de la beauté? Il est certain que, comme La Fontaine, Méré est tenté de trouver la grâce "plus belle encore que la beauté."[84] Il lui arrive même d'associer la beauté au faux et le vrai à l'agrément. Ainsi distingue-t-il deux sortes de "bon air," manière générale de désigner ce qui plaît: "Le premier et le plus commun est celui qui cherche la pompe et l'éclat; l'autre est plus modeste et plus caché. Le premier a beaucoup de rapport avec la beauté, et je trouve qu'il lasse aisément, mais cet autre qui se montre moins à découvert, plus on le considère et plus on l'aime. Il y a toujours dans le premier je ne sais quoi de faux et quelque espèce d'illusion; le dernier est plus réel quoique plus imperceptible, et je vois qu'il approche de l'agrément. L'un donne plus dans la vue aux jeunes gens qui d'ordinaire sont bien aises d'être éblouis, et l'autre plaît davantage à ceux qui ont le goût fait."[85]

Cette critique de la beauté n'est pas sans appel. Pour en sauvegarder le prix, il faut fuir ce qui n'en a que l'apparence.[86] Le monde est plein de choses qui passent pour belles et qui "ne sont point belles."[87] C'est ce qui se produit lorsqu'on y cherche seulement l'éclat. Mais "les bonnes choses sont ou jolies ou belles. Les jolies donnent plus de joie et les belles plus d'admiration, mais il faut qu'elles soient belles d'une véritable beauté." Le faux existe aussi bien dans les jolies choses que dans les belles; mais dans les premières il se dénonce aisément; dans les secondes, il y a souvent du "fard" qui "éblouit." Toutefois, "quand elles sont belles d'une véritable beauté, elles tiennent le premier rang."[88] La beauté possède une grandeur qui en fait le prix, mais qui rend plus difficile à satisfaire l'exigence de naturel, le refus d'une tension qui sent la contrainte et l'étude, la nécessité toujours impérieuse "d'avoir encore plus de soin de la naïveté que de la perfection des choses."[89]

Nul mieux que Méré ne permet de comprendre comment la distinction du vrai et du faux en matière de beauté risquait d'atteindre la beauté elle-même. C'est en définitive une esthétique de la grâce qu'il propose. D'autres s'engageront dans la voie du sublime, qui sauve la beauté par la simplicité. Si le terme est inconnu de Méré, l'idée ne lui est pas étrangère. Entre ce vrai et ce faux qui envahissent tous les domaines, comment l'homme peut-il s'orienter? A quelles facultés doit-il recourir pour les distinguer? Il arrive à Méré de distinguer deux sortes d'esprits, les "inventeurs" et "ceux qui n'inventent pas";[90] en d'autres termes, les génies originaux et les intelligences compréhensives. Nous sommes fort loin de Pascal et notre sujet n'en est pas éclairé.

Précieuse, en revanche, une autre distinction. "Il y a deux sortes d'étude; l'une qui ne cherche que l'art et les règles; l'autre qui n'y songe point du tout, et qui n'a d'autre but que de rencontrer par instinct et par réflexions ce qui doit plaire en tous les sujets particuliers."[91] Sans exclure tout à fait la première, qui forme les doctes et porte sur la rhétorique et la poétique, Méré affirme sa préférence pour la seconde, qui consiste au fond dans une mise en oeuvre des ressources de la nature. C'est la voie moderne, opposée à celle des Anciens.

Les termes "instinct" et "réflexions" suggèrent la possibilité d'une division à l'intérieur de cette seconde catégorie. C'est à quoi procède Méré lorsque, à plusieurs reprises, il relève deux formes de "justesse," celle de l'"esprit" et celle du "sentiment,"[92] qui contribuent toutes les deux à la distinction du vrai et du faux. La justesse de l'esprit "s'exerce sur la vérité simple et nue"; elle établit "le vrai rapport que doit avoir une chose avec une autre";[93] elle se garde de "prendre une circonstance pour le noeud de l'affaire," en somme d'"extravaguer," par exemple en critiquant la beauté d'une dame à cause de la légèreté de sa conduite.[94] La justesse du sentiment consiste à trouver "le bon tempérament . . . entre l'excès et le défaut"; elle "ne souffre pas que l'on fasse trop grand ou trop petit ce qui veut être grand ou petit."[95] Du sentiment on peut rapprocher le goût, qui s'en distingue peu: il est "le sentiment de ce qui sied bien"; il s'acquiert par une sorte d'habitude.[96] Esprit et sentiment peuvent tous les deux procéder soit par raisonnement—"réflexion," dit plus souplement Méré—soit par intuition, ou "tout d'un coup," encore que la réflexion convienne mieux à l'esprit. Pour Méré, la raison ne se confond pas avec l'esprit: elle est "une puissance de l'âme commune à l'esprit et au sentiment."[97] Le goût, d'ailleurs, "se fonde toujours sur des raisons très solides, mais sans raisonner."[98] Il reste que la justesse du sentiment est beaucoup plus subtile que celle de l'esprit.

Les affinités de cette distinction avec celle que propose Pascal entre l'esprit de géométrie et l'esprit de finesse, ou entre l'esprit et le jugement, sont assez lointaines. Si soucieux de raison que soit Méré—il critique même la "prévention" en termes quasi-cartésiens[99]—il n'en fait pas moins large place à des intuitions qui, pour être soigneusement distinguées de la fantaisie individuelle, n'en traduisent pas moins la spontanéité d'une bonne nature, cultivée par un bon maître, plutôt qu'une forme supérieure de la raison, comme l'esprit de finesse pascalien.

Que l'exigence de rationalité soit moindre chez Méré que chez Pascal, à plus forte raison que chez Nicole, on peut en donner deux preuves. Méré refuse de distinguer l'esprit et le jugement, qui sont pour lui "une même chose." [100] C'est-à-dire que les deux "esprits" pascaliens se regroupent dans la première de ses deux "justesses," la plus rationnelle. La seconde n'est cependant pas sans offrir quelques points communs avec l'esprit de finesse, mais on est loin de la netteté pascalienne. De plus, si Méré s'en prend à Aristote, dont la rhétorique et la poétique lui paraissent introduire l'artifice dans l'art, il ne s'en prend pas moins aux géomètres modernes, dont la méthode est pourtant directement opposée à la logique aristotélicienne. Nous avons établi une continuité entre la réflexion de Descartes sur la rhétorique et la poétique et la méthode qu'il élabore pour "chercher la vérité dans les sciences." Avec Méré, le géomètre, dont il trouve le modèle en Pascal, avec ses "longs raisonnements tirés de ligne en ligne," [101] est presque aussi éloigné qu'Aristote de la vraie connaissance de l'homme. Pascal n'ignore pas que la géométrie s'écarte de la vie par son objet. Mais il voit dans le raisonnement qu'elle met en oeuvre le modèle de tout bon raisonnement, indispensable même à l' "honnête homme" pour faire "l'essai," sinon "l'emploi" de ses forces.[102]

Autre différence considérable: Pascal attache la fausse éloquence—ou, du moins l'éloquence artificielle, apparente—à l'esprit et la vraie éloquence au jugement. Pour Méré, les deux justesses collaborent dans l'élimination du faux et la reconnaissance du vrai.

Pour rendre compte de ces différences et achever de caractériser la pensée de Méré sur notre sujet, on remarquera qu'il est moins un théoricien qu'un pédagogue. La relation de maître à élève est fréquemment évoquée par lui. S'il parle souvent de modèles, ce n'est pas de modèles abstraits comme ceux qu'élabore Pascal, mais de modèles humains dont il invite à recueillir l'exemple et les leçons pour acquérir un parfait "discernement." [103] C'est l'habitude du monde qui fait acquérir un goût si raffiné qu'il semble tout naturel. Pour lui plus que pour ses prédécesseurs, la

distinction de la vraie et de la fausse beauté dépend des qualités personnelles de l'homme plutôt que de l'application d'un méthode.

C'est, jusqu'à plus ample informé, en un milieu très restreint qu'on a pris
au XVIIᵉ siècle l'habitude de distinguer vraie et fausse beauté. Pascal est
tout proche de Méré, tout proche de Nicole, et il a bien connu Corneille.
Les relations personnelles ont pu jouer, mais surtout l'existence d'un courant où s'expriment à la fois une certaine culture et une certaine pensée.

Fait de culture que l'influence grandissante de la société mondaine au
détriment des cercles érudits où se regroupent les doctes; influence qui se
manifeste même à Port-Royal. L'idéal de l'"honnête homme" a contribué
à fonder sur de nouvelles bases une réflexion sur le beau distincte de la
considération des règles de l'art, à susciter l'élaboration d'une esthétique,
à côté de la rhétorique et de la poétique. L'esprit moderne s'est détourné
d'Aristote pour reconstruire totalement la philosophie; il a trouvé son
expression la plus forte chez Descartes, maître plus ou moins direct, et,
dans une large mesure, involontaire, de nos théoriciens du beau.

C'est à une pensée de type cartésien qu'ils participent. Au départ, le
refus du scepticisme, qui se plaît à dénoncer la diversité des goûts, la
conviction que la nature humaine comporte des éléments universels, raison, bon sens, qui permettent la distinction fondamentale du vrai et du
faux, attitude à la fois critique et constructive. Au centre de cette pensée,
l'homme, juge du vrai et du faux en tous domaines, et par rapport auquel
s'ordonne toute connaissance, celle de Dieu et de l'Etre étant, sinon né-
gligée, du moins rapportée à des lumières surnaturelles. Le Beau consi-
déré est le Beau pour l'homme, non le Beau absolu de Platon.

Si nos auteurs se ressemblent par ces traits communs, ils n'en offrent
pas moins des individualités différentes. Chacun d'eux se caractérise par
le dosage qu'il établit, dans le jugement esthétique, entre le jeu de la raison proprement dite et celui de diverses formes d'intuition. L'évolution
s'accomplit dans le sens d'une moindre affirmation du rôle de la raison,
ce qui risquait de faire prévaloir de nouveau le goût individuel. L'équilibre qui conditionnait leur pensée risquait alors de disparaître. Peut-être
est-ce la raison pour laquelle le courant qu'ils représentent ne se prolonge
pas au-delà de la fin du XVIIᵉ siècle.

Même quand la distinction de la vraie et de la fausse beauté n'est pas
prononcée, des idées analogues à celles qu'ils ont développées ne s'en
expriment pas moins de divers côtés. Un La Rochefoucauld, un Molière,

un Saint-Evremond et même certains aspects de Boileau seraient intéressants à considérer dans cette perspective. A plus forte raison pourrait-on s'attarder sur un traité *De la vraie et de la fausse éloquence* de Jean Le Clerc, publié à Amsterdam en 1699.[104] Dernière expression, à notre connaissance, de la distinction. En 1715, le *Traité du Beau* de Crousaz l'ignore. Mais l'esthétique naissante n'oubliera pas totalement la leçon de ses précurseurs du XVIIᵉ siècle.

NOTES

1. L'ouvrage fondamental de René Bray, *La formation de la doctrine classique* (Paris, 1927), touche peu à l'esthétique proprement dite. Il en va de même, en dépit du titre choisi, pour une série d'articles du même auteur, "L'esthétique classique," *Revue des Cours et Conférences,* XXX/2, 1929, pp. 97–111, 211–26, 363–78, 434–49, 673–84. On se reportera principalement à l'étude très contestable et, pour le moins, insuffisante, mais très stimulante, d'Emile Krantz, *Essai sur l'esthétique de Descartes, étudiée dans les rapports de la doctrine cartésienne avec la littérature classique française au XVIIᵉ siècle,* (Paris, 1882), (pour la critique, Nigel Abercrombie, "Cartesianism and Classicism," *Modern Language Review* 31 [1936]: 358–76); et à l'ouvrage trop peu connu d'Arsène Soreil, *Introduction à l'histoire de l'esthétique française, Contribution à l'étude des théories littéraires et plastiques en France de la Pléiade au XVIIIᵉ siècle* (Bruxelles-Liège, 1930; nlle éd. revue, Bruxelles, 1955). Voir aussi Ladislas Tatarkiewicz, "L'esthétique du Grand Siècle," *XVIIᵉ siècle,* no. 78 (1968): 21–35; Bernard Tocanne, *L'idée de nature en France dans la seconde moitié du XVIIᵉ siècle* (Paris, 1978), 3ᵉ partie, *La Nature et l'Art.*

2. Nous citons d'après la 20ᵉ éd. (Paris, 1878), p. 1.

3. *Epître IX,* v. 43. Dans toutes nos citations, nous rétablissons l'orthographe moderne.

4. Corneille, *Oeuvres complètes,* éd. G. Couton, I (Paris, 1980), 691.

5. Ibid., 93.

6. Descartes, *Oeuvres philosophiques,* éd. F. Alquié, I (Paris, 1963), 568.

7. Ed. M. Magendie (Paris, 1925), p. 60. Voir aussi p. 59.

8. Ibid., pp. 72–73.

9. Ibid., p. 26; et Descartes, éd. citée, I: 577.

10. Éd. A. Ravier (Paris, 1969), p. 31. Voir aussi p. 32.

11. Ibid., pp. 184–94; pour la citation, p. 192.

12. Ibid., IIIᵉ Partie, ch. 36.

13. Première partie, 2ᵉ éd. (plus complète que la première) (Paris, 1633), pp. 413, 181; Seconde partie, 1634, pp. 324 sqq.; Troisième partie, 1636, p. 82.

14. Troisième partie, pp. 1 sqq.

15. Première partie, pp. 131–33.

16. Ibid., p. 301.

17. Seconde partie, p. 338.

18. Corneille, éd. citée, II (1984): 987, 1010.

19. Corneille, éd. citée, III (1987): 898 et. *Oeuvres,* éd. Ch. Marty-Laveaux, IX (Paris, 1862): 385–86.

20. Corneille, *Oeuvres complètes,* I: 310–11.

21. Ibid., 309.

22. Ibid., 312–13.

23. Ed. citée, I: 574.

24. Sur l'*Epigrammatum delectus,* consulter principalement Sainte-Beuve, *Port-Royal,* 3ᵉ éd., III (Paris, 1867): pp. 529–31; A. Soreil, *L'Histoire de l'esthétique française,* 1930, pp. 55–59; 1955, pp. 41–45; Z. Tourneur, "*Beauté poétique,*" *Histoire critique d'une "pensée" de Pascal et de ses annexes* (Melun, 1933); J. Lafond, "Un débat d'esthétique à l'époque classique, la Théorie du Beau dans l'*Epigrammatum delectus* et sa critique par le P. Vavasseur," *Acta Conventus Neo-Latini Turonensis* (Paris, 1980), pp. 1269–77. Sur l'histoire du recueil, nous renvoyons à notre article, "L'*Epigrammatum Delectus* de Port-Royal et ses annexes (1659): Problèmes d'attribution," *Ouverture et Dialogue, Mélanges offerts à Wolfgang Leiner* (Tübingen, 1988): 305–18.

25. *Praefatio,* VI, à la fin.

26. La *Dissertation* n'étant pas paginée et ne comportant pas de divisions chiffrées dans l'éd. originale, nous renvoyons au texte, malheureusement gâté par de nombreuses coupures, qu'en a publié Tourneur, en l'accompagnant de la traduction de La Faille et en adoptant les divisions de celle-ci. Pour la présente citation, Tourneur, *Histoire critique,* p. 133.

27. Ibid., 134 et 135.

28. Ibid, 134.

29. Ibid., 134 et 135.

30. Ibid., 136–37, 138–40, 144–48.

31. Ibid., 137–38.

32. Descartes, éd. citée, III (1973): 492–93.

33. Tourneur, *Histoire critique,* pp. 140–44.

34. Ibid., 148–52.

35. Descartes, éd. citée, I: 30–31; à commenter par Geneviève Rodis-Lewis, *L'Oeuvre de Descartes,* I (Paris, 1971): 31–37; II: 440–43. Des vues générales sur le rapport entre la nature humaine et la nature extérieure sont présentées dans le *Traité des Passions,* Descartes, éd. citée, III: 1018–19.

36. Nicole est revenu plus sommairement sur les questions d'esthétique, mais sans reprendre la distinction entre vraie et fausse beauté, en participant avec Arnauld à la rédaction de *La Logique ou l'art de persuader (Logique de Port-Royal),* Paris, 1662, voir l'éd. Clair et Girbal, Paris, 1965; et en composant la préface du *Recueil de poésies chrétiennes et diverses,* procuré par Brienne et La Fontaine. Avec le temps, Nicole a beaucoup atténué le rigueur de son système. Voir J. Brody, "Pierre Nicole auteur de la préface du *Recueil de poésies chrétiennes et diverses,*" XVIIᵉ siècle, no. 64, 1964, pp. 31–54. Contrairement à ce qu'on pourrait croire,

il se rapprochait ainsi de Descartes, beaucoup moins rationaliste sur la question du beau que la *Dissertatio.*

37. Sur ces questions, nous renvoyons à notre article cité à la n. 24.

38. C'est le point de vue de Tourneur, *Histoire critique,* qui tend à identifier les positions respectives de Nicole et de Pascal.

39. *Pensées,* 798/41 (le premier numéro est celui de l'éd. Lafuma, Paris, 1951; le second, celui de l'éd. Brunschvicg).

40. *Praefatio,* VI, à la fin.

41. *Pensées,* 610/30; 771/355; 582/669. On pourrait citer aussi 637/59; 559/27; 509/49.

42. Ibid., 728/31.

43. Ibid., 667/25.

44. Ibid., 580/28.

45. Ibid., 55/111.

46. Ibid., 585–586–587/32–33–34.

47. Louis Marin, "Réflexions sur la notion de modèle chez Pascal," *Revue de Métaphysique et de Morale,* 72, 1967, pp. 89–108.

48. J.-B. Barrère, *L'idée de goût de Pascal à Valéry* (Paris, 1972), pp. 28–33.

49. Voir la lettre au P. Noël du 29 octobre 1647, dans notre éd. de Pascal, *Oeuvres complètes,* II (Paris, 1970), p. 519.

50. *Pensées,* 661/81.

51. Ibid., 611/30; cf. 732/38.

52. Ibid., 513/4.

53. Ibid., 512/1.

54. "De l'art de persuader," dans Pascal, *Oeuvres complètes,* éd. Lafuma (Paris, 1963), p. 356.

55. *Pensées,* 534/5.

56. Pascal, *Oeuvres complètes,* éd. Lafuma, p. 355.

57. *Pensées,* 3/244.

58. Ibid., 148/425.

59. Ibid., 268/683; cf. 249/681; 253/679; 835/564.

60. Ibid., 270/670.

61. Ibid., 812/798.

62. Ibid., 309/797.

63. Sur la personne du chevalier de Méré, voir notre *Pascal et les Roannez,* I (Paris, 1965), pp. 368–76 et *passim.*

64. Les *Oeuvres complètes* de Méré ont été éditées par Ch.-H. Boudhors, Paris, 1930, 3 vol. Manquent toutefois les *Lettres,* pour lesquelles il faut recourir aux éditions anciennes.

65. Méré, *Oeuvres complètes,* éd. citée, III: 69–102.

66. Ibid., II: 126.

67. Ibid., I: 9–10.

68. Ibid., III: 93.

69. Ibid., I: 108.

70. Ibid., p. 102; II: 72, 116–17.

71. Ibid., I: 57.

72. Ibid., III: 124–25.

73. Ibid., p. 125.

74. Ibid., I: 27–28.

75. Ibid., p. 29. Pour le texte de Montaigne, *Essais*, éd. Villey-Saulnier (Paris, 1965), p. 874.

76. Méré, éd. citée, I: 56; voir aussi p. 55.

77. Ibid., II: 31; cf. p. 38; et I: 75.

78. Ibid., I: 62.

79. Ibid., p. 63; cf. III: 83.

80. Ibid., II: 108.

81. Ibid., p. 15.

82. Ibid., p. 37.

83. Ibid., p. 121.

84. *Adonis*, v. 78.

85. Méré, éd. citée, II: 23; cf. 39; et I: 72.

86. Ibid., I: 56.

87. Ibid., II: 52; cf. I: 56; II: 40, 107.

88. Ibid., II: 52.

89. Ibid., p. 106.

90. Ibid., p. 79.

91. Ibid., p. 109.

92. Ibid., I: 14–96; II: 69–70, 126–27; III: 72.

93. Ibid., I: 96.

94. Ibid., II: 126.

95. Ibid., I: 96.

96. Ibid., II: 128. Sur le goût chez Méré, J.-B. Barrère, *L'Idée de goût,* pp. 34–38.

97. Méré, éd. citée, II: 69–70.

98. Ibid., p. 129.

99. Ibid., p. 35.

100. Ibid., p. 61.

101. *Lettre à Pascal,* dans Pascal, *Oeuvres,* éd. Brunschvicg, IX (Paris, 1914), p. 215.

102. *Lettre de Pascal à Fermat,* ibid., X: 5.

103. Méré, éd. citée, II: 129–30.

104. *Parrhasiana ou Pensées diverses sur des matières de critique, d'histoire, de morale et de politique,* dans la 2e éd., I, 1701: 73–131. Voir aussi, dans le même volume, les *Réflexions sur les poètes et sur la poésie,* pp. 1–73.

Sur le sens du mot "raison" au
dix-septième siècle

Robert Garapon

Il est des mots, dans notre vocabulaire critique, dont tout le monde sait qu'ils ne signifient plus la même chose qu'au XVIIᵉ siècle: ainsi le mot de *nature,* qui renvoyait alors à la nature humaine, et non à la nature extérieure. Mais il est d'autres termes, tout aussi importants, dont nous mesurons mal combien ils ont changé de sens en trois cents ans: en particulier le mot de *raison,* à propos duquel nous ne cessons de commettre quantité d'erreurs implicites, tant et si bien que nous finissons par fausser et déformer des pans entiers de l'esthétique classique. Lorsque nous rencontrons *raison* chez Boileau ou chez La Bruyère, et plus généralement dans une page de critique ou de morale du XVIIᵉ siècle, nous pensons à la capacité discursive de l'esprit qui a permis la science moderne, alors que l'auteur de l'*Art poétique* ou celui des *Caractères* pensaient à ce pouvoir quasi intuitif que nous appelons aujourd'hui discernement, goût ou tact.

Pour fixer la signification essentielle qu'a prise de nos jours le terme de raison, je me permets de donner ci-dessous la définition qu'en fournit le dictionnaire de Paul Robert, en son tome V:

> I. Pouvoir par lequel l'homme est capable d'organiser, de systématiser sa connaissance et sa conduite, d'établir des rapports vrais avec le monde. *Dans certaines théories,* système de principes qui dirigent l'activité de l'esprit et forment une règle, un modèle idéal de connaissance et d'action. . . .
> 1° La faculté pensante et son fonctionnement chez l'homme: ce qui permet à l'homme de connaître, juger et agir conformément à ses principes (considérés comme plus ou moins stables) . . . *Spécialement* La pensée discursive.

On le voit, la raison, pour nous, en cette fin du XXᵉ siècle, c'est avant tout le pouvoir qu'a l'esprit de raisonner, c'est-à-dire de joindre en une chaîne significative des propositions dépendant les unes des autres et aboutissant à une conclusion. Dès lors, la difficulté est grande, pour le

Français de 1987, de comprendre les endroits où Boileau, dans l'*Art poétique* et ailleurs, fait référence à la raison. Lorsqu'il écrit, par exemple:

> Aimez donc la raison: que toujours vos écrits
> Empruntent d'elle seule et leur lustre et leur prix[1]

nous comprenons qu'il est adversaire de tout épanchement de la sensibilité—et nous nous méprenons gravement sur l'attitude des classiques à l'égard de la sensibilité, car ce n'est pas d'elle, mais de l'imagination qu'ils se méfient, comme l'a très bien montré Jean Mesnard.[2]

Mais il y a pis: dans certains cas, en effet, le faux-sens tourne au burlesque et risque d'entraîner une incompréhension complète. Ainsi, lorsque nous lisons, toujours dans l'*Art poétique:*

> Mais la scène demande une exacte raison,
> L'étroite bienséance y veut être gardée[3]

ou encore:

> J'aime sur le théâtre un agréable auteur
> Qui, sans se diffamer aux yeux du spectateur,
> Plaît par la raison seule et jamais ne la choque[4]

nous risquons de nous méprendre du tout au tout: car comment imaginer un dramaturge qui aime raisonner et qui ne soit pas mortellement ennuyeux? Pour un peu, nous irions croire que Boileau appelle ici de ses voeux *Le Fils naturel* ou *Le Père de famille* de Diderot et l'indiscrète prédication dont ces ouvrages sont pleins.

Mais, me dira-t-on, cette acception du mot *raison* qui se présente d'abord à notre esprit aujourd'hui ne vient-elle pas de Pascal lui-même? N'est-ce pas dans les *Pensées* que l'on trouve—et dès la première édition de 1670—la fameuse distinction entre le *coeur* et la *raison*? On se souvient du passage:

> Nous connaissons la vérité non seulement par la raison mais encore par le coeur. C'est de cette dernière sorte que nous connaissons les premiers principes et c'est en vain que le raisonnement, qui n'y a point de part, essaie de les combattre. . . . Les connaissances des premiers principes: espace, temps, mouvement, nombres, sont aussi fermes qu'aucune de celles que nos raisonnements nous donnent et c'est sur ces connaissances du coeur et de l'instinct qu'il faut que la raison s'appuie et qu'elle y fonde tout son discours. Le coeur sent qu'il y a trois dimensions dans l'espace et

que les nombres sont infinis et la raison démontre ensuite qu'il n'y a point deux nombres carrés dont l'un soit double de l'autre. Les principes se sentent, les propositions se concluent, et le tout avec certitude quoique par différentes voies . . .[5]

On ne saurait mieux opposer le caractère successif et logique des opérations de la *raison* et l'immédiateté contraignante de l'évidence que définit le *coeur* au sens pascalien!

Oui, certainement, le XVIIᵉ siècle connaissait le sens du terme *raison* qui nous paraît actuellement essentiel. Seulement, cette acception était-elle la première qui vînt à l'esprit des Français d'alors? Là encore, la réponse s'impose, et elle est négative. Le sens dominant du mot est très différent vers 1680 de ce qu'il est devenu trois siècles plus tard; *raison,* à l'époque, équivaut très souvent à "discernement," et l'on peut déjà s'en convaincre en se reportant à la définition que Furetière donne du mot dans son *Dictionnaire:*

RAISON. Entendement; faculté, puissance de l'âme qui discerne le bien du mal, le vrai d'avec le faux. . . .
RAISON dans la même idée signifie le jugement, le bon sens, la faculté de concevoir, de réfléchir; la compréhension; l'étendue et la pénétration de l'entendement . . .

Si l'on compare ce début d'article avec l'endroit correspondant de Paul Robert cité plus haut, la différence est saisissante. Et Furetière, notions-le bien, se borne ici à enregistrer l'usage de toute son époque, et de tout le XVIIᵉ siècle.

"Faculté, puissance de l'âme qui discerne le bien du mal, le vrai d'avec le faux . . ." C'est exactement ainsi que Descartes, dans les premières lignes du *Discours de la méthode,* en 1637, entendait le terme quand il écrivait que "la puissance de bien juger et distinguer le vrai d'avec le faux, qui est proprement ce qu'on nomme le bon sens ou la raison, est naturellement égale en tous les hommes." Je n'ai pas besoin de souligner que l'équivalence établie par le philosophe ("le bon sens ou la raison") serait proprement inacceptable de nos jours: elle n'en est, à mes yeux, que plus révélatrice!

Treize ans plus tard, Nicole, dans son *Traité de la vraie et de la fausse beauté dans les ouvrages de l'esprit* (1650), écrira:

Il faut avoir recours à la lumière de la raison. Elle est simple et certaine, et c'est par son moyen qu'on peut trouver la vraie beauté naturelle . . .

"La lumière de la raison . . . simple et certaine": cette expression indique à merveille le caractère instantané et incontestable de l'information fournie par la raison: son action est immédiate et sûre, comme celle d'un rayon de soleil passant par la fenêtre qu'on ouvre!

Une quinzaine d'années plus tard, la comédie de *Tartuffe* nous offre deux passages particulièrement intéressants. D'une façon générale, il faudrait souligner l'utilité précieuse de l'oeuvre de Molière pour ce qui est des recherches lexicographiques: d'une part, le poète vise évidemment à se faire comprendre sans aucune peine de tous ses spectateurs, et il est donc conduit à employer les mots dans une acception très largement reçue; d'un autre côté, il pratique volontiers, comme on sait, la redondance et la répétition de la même idée à l'aide de mots différents, et il offre ainsi des synonymes qui éclairent puissamment sur le sens de tel ou tel terme en question. Voici d'abord la déclaration bien connue de Cléante à la scène 5 de l'acte Ier:

Les hommes la plupart sont étrangement faits!
Dans la juste nature on ne les voit jamais;
La raison a pour eux des bornes trop petites;
En chaque caractère ils passent ses limites;
Et la plus noble chose, ils la gâtent souvent
Pour la vouloir outrer et pousser trop avant.

Dans ces vers, la *juste nature* et la *raison* sont manifestement liées entre elles: la juste nature, c'est-à-dire la nature conforme à une certaine mesure, appelle la raison, qui a des bornes qu'il ne faut pas dépasser, au risque de tomber dans l'"étrangeté" (entendez l'extravagance) ou dans l'"outrance." La raison n'est nullement ici synonyme de *raisonnement*, mais d'*appréciation*—ou de *discernement*. Comme W. D. Howarth l'indique très finement, les "raisonneurs" de la comédie moliéresque (et Cléante est un des principaux!) ne raisonnent pas: ils ne font jamais usage de leur *raison raisonnante*, mais seulement de leur bon sens.[6]

J'en viens maintenant à l'autre extrémité de *Tartuffe*, à la tirade de l'Exempt qui fait le dénouement de la pièce; elle commence par ces vers très éclairants pour notre propos:

Nous vivons sous un Prince ennemi de la fraude,
Un prince dont les yeux se font jour dans les coeurs,
Et que ne peut tromper tout l'art des imposteurs.
D'un fin discernement sa grande âme pourvue

Sur les choses toujours jette une droite vue;
Chez elle jamais rien ne surprend trop d'acces,
Et sa ferme raison ne tombe en nul excès.
Il donne aux gens de bien une gloire immortelle;
Mais sans aveuglement il fait briller ce zèle,
Et l'amour pour les vrais ne ferme point son coeur
A tout ce que les faux doivent donner d'horreur.

On remarquera sans peine les quatre couples de mots qui servent également ici à la louange de Louis XIV: *un fin discernement* permet au Roi de jeter sur tout *une droite vue,* c'est-à-dire un regard qu'on ne trompe pas; mais, d'un autre côté, *sa ferme raison* est *sans aveuglement,* elle punit l'hypocrisie comme elle récompense la véritable vertu. En vérité, il serait difficile d'imaginer un parallélisme plus exact ou plus satisfaisant pour l'investigation qui nous occupe. Le seul endroit qui nous paraisse comparable, pour la pensée comme pour le vocabulaire, est ce distique de Corneille (que Molière a dû réciter bien des fois), dans lequel Cinna vante le bonheur qu'un prince éclairé procure à ses Etats:

Avec ordre et raison les honneurs il dispense,
Avec discernement punit et récompense.[7]

La conversation entre Alceste et Philinte qui ouvre *Le Misanthrope* nous offre d'autres emplois très révélateurs du mot *raison.* En premier lieu, quand il s'agit du procès qu'Alceste risque de perdre, le terme désigne la force contraignante de l'évidence à laquelle doit se rendre spontanément tout homme de bonne foi:

Ma foi! vous ferez bien de garder le silence.
Contre votre partie éclatez un peu moins,
Et donnez au procès une part de vos soins.
—Je n'en donnerai point, c'est une chose dite.
—Mais qui voulez-vous donc qui pour vous sollicite?
—Qui je veux? La raison, mon bon droit, l'équité.
—Aucun juge par vous ne sera visité?
—Non. Est-ce que ma cause est injuste ou douteuse?

En second lieu, après avoir noté que l'amour de son ami pour la coquette Célimène est en contradiction avec la haine qu'il manifeste pour "les moeurs d'à présent," Philinte ajoute avec une amicale sollicitude:

—Pour moi, si je n'avais qu'à former des désirs,
La cousine Eliante aurait tous mes soupirs;

Son coeur, qui vous estime, est solide et sincère,
Et ce choix plus conforme était mieux votre affaire.

A quoi Alceste réplique, avec un sourire gêné:

—Il est vrai: ma raison me le dit chaque jour;
Mais la raison n'est pas ce qui règle l'amour.

De toute évidence, le mot désigne, non pas la raison raisonnante, dont on voit mal ce qu'elle viendrait faire ici, mais ce sens des convenances qui est l'apanage de l'homme de la bonne société.

Je voudrais enfin, avant de quitter Molière, rappeler un mot de Chrysale dans *Les Femmes savantes;* c'est le fameux vers par lequel le bonhomme résume l'état déplorable de sa maison abandonnée aux excès d'une science indiscrète:

Mes gens à la science aspirent pour vous plaire,
Et tous ne font rien moins que ce qu'ils ont à faire;
Raisonner est l'emploi de toute ma maison,
Et le raisonnement en bannit la raison . . .[8]

L'antithèse est très significative, entre le raisonnement, qui n'est ici que le signe d'une activité intellectuelle dévoyée et hors de propos, et la raison, cette capacité quasi instinctive de discerner ce qui convient.

C'est toujours ce sens de discernement (j'allais dire de goût) que Boileau donne au mot *raison* quand il s'érige en législateur du Parnasse. Il serait aisé de le montrer d'après les vers que je citais tout à l'heure. Mais je préfère m'arrêter sur un autre passage de l'*Art poétique:*

La plupart, emportés d'une fougue insensée,
Toujours loin du bon sens vont chercher leur pensée:
Ils croiraient s'abaisser, dans leurs vers monstrueux,
S'ils pensaient ce qu'un autre a pu penser comme eux.
Evitons ces excès: laissons à l'Italie
De tous ces faux brillants l'éclatante folie.
Tout doit tendre au bon sens; mais pour y parvenir,
Le chemin est glissant et pénible à tenir:
Pour peu qu'on s'en écarte, aussitôt on se noie.
La raison pour marcher n'a souvent qu'une voie.[9]

Remarquons-le bien, les poètes que ces vers condamnent ne sont pas des esprits faux, qui raisonneraient mal, mais des extravagants qui recherchent une originalité de mauvais aloi, qui affectent une *éclatante folie.*

Boileau ne leur reproche pas d'être de mauvais géomètres, pour parler comme Pascal, mais de chercher à se singulariser par un raffinement contraire au naturel. Cela dit, il vaut la peine de noter aussi que, pour recommander la voie de la raison, notre auteur use d'une image—celle d'une chaussée au milieu d'un marécage—qui annonce curieusement une réflexion de La Bruyère. On lit en effet au début du chapitre *Des ouvrages de l'esprit:*

> Il y a dans l'art un point de perfection, comme de bonté ou de maturité dans la nature. Celui qui le sent et qui l'aime a le goût parfait; celui qui ne le sent pas, et qui aime en deçà ou au delà, a le goût défectueux. Il y a donc un bon et un mauvais goût, et l'on dispute des goûts avec fondement.[10]

Même si ce n'est plus une digue qui est suggérée, mais une ligne qu'il faut atteindre sans la dépasser, les domaines métaphoriques sont voisins, et le mot *goût* relaie de façon très significative le mot *raison*.

Mais on trouve mieux encore dans les *Caractères*. Voici nettement indiquée l'étroite parenté que la raison-discernement possède avec le goût (on voudra bien se souvenir que le bon sens et la raison ne sont qu'une seule et même faculté de l'esprit):

> Talent, goût, esprit, bon sens, choses différentes, non incompatibles.
> Entre le bon sens et le bon goût, il y a la différence de la cause à son effet.[11]

Et voici la raison identifiée à ce que nous appellerions le tact:

> Les belles choses le sont moins hors de leur place; les bienséances mettent la perfection, et la raison met les bienséances . . .[12]

Par un curieux retournement, la raison, dans tous ces exemples, n'est nullement une capacité discursive, mais au contraire une sorte d'intuition qui fait voir la vérité, le naturel, ce qui est de bon goût, ce qui convient. En somme, la *raison,* pour Nicole, Molière, Boileau ou La Bruyère, est très proche de ce que Pascal appelait le *coeur,* et il n'est pas sans intérêt de relever que La Bruyère, quand il évoque l'opération du goût, emploie le même verbe *sentir* qui désigne chez Pascal l'acte du coeur: "Il y dans l'art un point de perfection . . . Celui qui le sent . . . a le goût parfait." De même, quand Boileau tentera, dans sa célèbre Préface de 1701, de définir le beau en littérature, il recourra au même verbe *sentir,* qui dénote une saisie intuitive et rebelle à l'analyse: ". . . un je ne sais quoi qu'on peut beaucoup mieux sentir que dire . . ."

Pascal lui-même, observons-le en passant, ne s'est pas fait scrupule, le cas échéant, de prendre le mot raison au sens de discernement du vrai et du faux. Relisez, par exemple, le célèbre fragment sur l'imagination: vous verrez que l'opposition instituée par moraliste n'est pas entre l'imagination et la raison raisonnante, mais tout bonnement entre l'imagination et le bon sens, le sens des réalités. Autrement, on ne saurait comprendre des phrases comme: "Elle [l'imagination] fait croire, douter, nier la raison," ou comme: "Rien ne nous dépite davantage que de voir qu'elle remplit ses hôtes d'une satisfaction bien autrement pleine et entière que la raison. Les habiles par imagination se plaisent tout autrement à eux-mêmes que les prudents ne se peuvent raisonnablement plaire . . ." [13]

A la lumière des quelques indications qui précèdent, nous pensons être en mesure de mieux comprendre maints passages à la fois célèbres et difficiles de nos grands auteurs classiques, ces endroits que l'on se plaît à citer souvent—en se gardant bien d'en préciser le sens!

Nous nous bornerons, naturellement, à quelques exemples, et nous emprunterons le premier, non pas au XVIIᵉ siècle, mais à Joachim du Bellay. Tout le monde sait par coeur le fameux 31ᵉ sonnet des *Regrets:*

> Heureux qui, comme Ulysse, a fait un beau voyage,
> Ou comme cestui-là qui conquit la toison,
> Et puis est retourné, plein d'usage et raison,
> Vivre entre ses parents le reste de son âge . . .

"Plein d'usage et raison": on peut traduire sans crainte d'erreur "plein d'expérience et de discernement," mais on mesure combien les deux vieux mots sont denses, dans leur brièveté et leur saveur étymologique.

Ouvrons maintenant l'*Astrée* au début de la deuxième partie, et relisons le discours que tient devant Léonide la chaste Célidée, qui est aimée en même temps par le sage Thamire et son neveu l'impétueux Calidon:

> J'ai ouï dire, grande Nymphe, qu'on peut aimer en deux sortes: l'une est selon la raison, l'autre est selon le désir. Celle qui a pour sa règle la raison, on me l'a nommée amitié honnête et vertueuse, et celle qui se laisse emporter à ses désirs, amour. Par la première, nous aimons nos parents, notre patrie et en général et en particulier tous ceux en qui quelque vertu reluit; par l'autre, ceux qui en sont atteints sont transportés comme d'une fièvre ardente, et commettent tant de fautes, que le nom en est aussi diffamé parmi les personnes d'honneur, que l'autre est estimable et honorée. Or j'avouerai donc sans rougir que Thamire a été aimé de moi; mais in-

continent j'ajouterai: pour sa vertu, et que de même j'ai été aimée de Thamire, mais selon la vertu.[14]

La pudique bergère distingue ici les deux formes de l'amour: l'amour-
désir et l'amour "selon la raison." Cette dernière forme d'amour ne saurait être régie par la raison raisonnante, car, comme l'écrira bientôt Pascal, "On ne prouve pas qu'on doit être aimé en exposant d'ordre les
causes de l'amour; cela serait ridicule."[15] Là encore, il faut donner à *raison* son sens de "discernement," car c'est bien de cela qu'il s'agit: pour
aimer quelqu'un, il faut pouvoir découvrir, distinguer en lui *quelque
vertu* qui *reluit;* et cet amour-discernement (nous préférons ce terme à
celui d'amour-sentiment, qui reste ambigu) est bien l'amour généreux qui
animera les héros de Corneille et qui, loin de les asservir, leur apprendra
à bien user de leur liberté pour rester dignes de la personne aimée.

Mais venons à un exemple beaucoup plus difficile: je veux parler de la
fin de la terrible scène 5 de l'acte IV dans *Horace* et des deux vers que
prononce le héros victorieux au moment même où il tue sa soeur Camille:

> C'est trop, ma patience à la raison fait place:
> Va dedans les enfers plaindre ton Curiace.

Que veut dire Horace quand il allègue la raison? Sa raison ne devrait-elle
pas lui représenter que Camille est une jeune fille cruellement meurtrie,
qui vient d'apprendre la mort tragique de son fiancé, que cette jeune fille
est sa soeur, et donc qu'il a précisément mille raisons d'exercer sa patience? C'est la réflexion que nous nous faisons plus ou moins explicite-
ment en entendant ce vers, et nous sommes révoltés et en même temps
déroutés. Mais c'est que nous commettons un grave faux-sens: quand il
prononce le mot de *raison,* Horace ne veut pas parler de sa capacité de
raisonner, qui devrait en effet l'incliner à la mansuétude; il désigne simplement une évidence qui s'impose à lui (la raison, ne l'oublions pas, est
aussi le sens des réalités): Camille est désormais une Albaine, et doit être
traitée comme telle.

Si, du substantif *raison* on peut passer à l'adjectif *raisonnable,* je men-
tionnerais volontiers les premières lignes de la Préface de *Phèdre:*

> Voici encore une tragédie dont le sujet est pris d'Euripide.[. . .] Quand
> je ne lui devrais que la seule idée du caractere de Phèdre, je pourrais dire
> que je lui dois ce que j'ai peut-être mis de plus raisonnable sur le
> théâtre . . .

A première vue, l'assertion a de quoi surprendre, car on ne s'attendait pas à voir qualifier de *raisonnable* le caractère de Phèdre! Aussi bien les commentateurs se sont-ils sentis obligés d'expliquer cet adjectif insolite. "*Raisonnable:* conforme à la nature et à la vérité," indique Henri Chabot dans son édition scolaire de la tragédie.[16] De son côté, le très regretté Raymond Picard écrit: "A n'en pas douter, ce que Racine appelle *raisonnable,* c'est un caractère qui se développe avec rigueur et clarté: or précisément, la progression de Phèdre est marquée avec une netteté subtile qui fait en grande partie la valeur de la pièce."[17] Sans méconnaître ce que ces indications ont de suggestif, je voudrais seulement dire ici que *raisonnable* est à entendre exactement dans le sens où nous avons pris *raison* précédemment; *raisonnable* signifie: conforme au discernement des mouvements de l'âme.

Pour finir, je voudrais proposer une règle toute pratique pour une meilleure intelligence des textes du XVIIᵉ siècle. Chaque fois que nous rencontrerons le mot de *raison* chez un auteur de cette époque, commençons par essayer d'y substituer mentalement "discernement" au lieu de lui donner son sens actuel de "fondement de la démarche scientifique." Notre compréhension exacte de ce que nous lisons y gagnera beaucoup, et même notre compréhension de certaines expressions qui sont demeurées dans notre langue contemporaine. Ainsi, nous saisirons mieux que "perdre la raison" et "perdre le sens" soient synonymes; nous apercevrons aussi que la vieille expression *l'âge de raison* signifie tout bonnement "l'âge du discernement" (comme le suggère l'équivalent anglais—*age of discretion*). Je suis sûr que l'éminent collègue à qui ce livre est offert n'est pas indifférent, loin de là, à ces nuances essentielles.

NOTES

1. *Art poétique,* I, vers 37–38, éd. C.-H. Boudhors (Paris: Les Belles Lettres, 1939), p. 82.

2. Jean Mesnard, *Le Classicisme français et l'expression de la sensibilité,* in *Expression, Communication and Experience* (Cambridge: The Modern Humanities Research Association, 1973), pp. 28–37.

3. *Art poétique,* III, vers 122–23.

4. Ibid., vers 421–23.

5. Lafuma 110–Brunschvicg 282. Cette page est passablement altérée dans

l'édition de 1670; mais les modifications apportées par les éditeurs d'alors ne touchent pas l'emploi du mot *raison*.

6. W. D. Howarth, *Molière. A Playwright and His Audience* (Cambridge: Cambridge University Press, 1982), p. 246–47.

7. *Cinna*, II, 1, vers 505–6, en *Oeuvres complètes* de Corneille, éd. Georges Couton (Paris: Bibliothèque de la Pléiade, 1980), I: 927.

8. *Les Femmes savantes*, II, 7, vers 595–8, en *Oeuvres complètes* de Molière, éd. Georges Couton (Paris: Bibliothèque de la Pléiade, 1971), II: 1013.

9. *Art poétique*, I, vers 39–48.

10. *Les Caractères*, éd. R. Garapon (Paris: Classiques Garnier, 1962), *Des Ouvrages de l'esprit*, no. 10.

11. *Des Jugements*, no. 56.

12. *De Quelques usages*, no. 18.

13. Lafuma 44–Brunschvicg 82.

14. Honoré d'Urfé, *L'Astrée*, éd. Hugues Vaganay (Lyon, 1926), II: 61. Rappelons que le mot *amitié* est souvent mis pour "amour" au début du XVIIe siècle.

15. Lafuma 298–Brunschvicg 283.

16. (Paris: Classiques Larousse, 1933), p. 11.

17. Racine, *Oeuvres complètes*, éd. Raymond Picard (Paris: Bibliothèque de la Pléiade, 1950), I: 1167.

Desmarets's "L'Art de la poésie": Poetics or Politics?

H. Gaston Hall

The text* of Desmarets's "L'Art de la poésie, à Monseigneur le Cardinal-Duc de Richelieu"—established by James Dryhurst from a MS copy in the Bibliothèque de l'Arsenal in Paris—speaks for itself.[1] But after some 350 years it does not by itself fully explain the cultural context in which it was formulated. This ambitious text, though not strictly speaking an *inédit,* since it was incorporated in the text of "L'Excellence et les plaintes de la poésie héroïque" which Desmarets prefaced to the first edition of *Esther* in 1670, is less well known even than his "Discours de la poésie," also dedicated to Richelieu. We do not know exactly when "L'Art de la poésie" was written; but it can de deduced from the dedication that it was written after 1631, when Richelieu was made a duke, and before Richelieu's death in December 1642. Perhaps it preceded the "Discours de la poésie," which was first published in 1633 (along with poems by Maynard, Racan, L'Estoile, Malleville, Baro, Habert, Godeau, and Chapelain) in Boisrobert's anthology *Les Nouvelles Muses* and then republished in Desmarets's *Oeuvres poétiques,* a partial collection of his plays and poems *achevé d'imprimer* by Le Gras on 20 November 1640. That "Discours" stands witness to Desmarets's ambitions in heroic poetry at the time when—already a member of the group of literati incorporated in 1634 as the Académie-Française—he entered Richelieu's personal service, also in 1634.[2] This was evidently the time at which Desmarets began writing *Clovis,* the first and most ambitious of the heroic poems on which he was to work (though not consistently) for over twenty years before it was finally published in 1657.[3]

"L'Art de la poésie" reflects literary theory and literary ambitions somewhat similar to those expressed by Desmarets in his "Discours," which may have superseded it. But I suspect that it was not included in his *Oeuvres poétiques* along with the "Discours" because it was not yet

---

*The text of the poem follows on page 58.

45

written by the end of 1640. Late 1642 seems the likely date of composition. The phrase "au retour des allarmes" in line 5 would appear to have
been prompted by the conspiracy of Cinq-Mars and de Thou and especially by fears for the Cardinal's life as he was brought back to Paris
grievously ill in the fall of that year. The other alarming incidents in Richelieu's career—including the famous *Journée des dupes* of 1630—generally occurred before he was made a duke or else have no obvious
association with a return. Richelieu's death on 4 December shortly after
his return to Paris would account for the fact that "L'Art de la poésie"
was not printed at that time.[4]

Desmarets's involvement with the poetics of heroic poetry is by no
means limited to the period of Richelieu's patronage. Yet what he emphasizes in "L'Art de la poésie" is very much in line with his other literary
preoccupations in the last years of Richelieu's life. The hints of political
allegory from line 101 are compatible with the atmosphere of *Europe,*
first performed in November 1642. The exemplary idealism expounded
from line 81 recalls the no less didactic theory of the novel in Desmarets's
dedication to Richelieu's niece of his unfinished novel *Rosane* (1639).
Here, Desmarets requests that the young princes for whom he was writing *Rosane* (the future Louis XIV and his anticipated brother)

> admirent les exemples parfaits qu'on propose, & se portent avec ardeur à
> les imiter: & pource que la nature produit rarement des personnes par-
> faites, l'art de l'invention supplée à ce defaut. . . .

The art of fiction consists of mixing fable with fact, the entertaining with
the edifying, the marvelous with the educational. The result is not cul-
pable deceit (*feinte, mensonge* in a pejorative sense), but the greatest
imaginative effort of the mind:

> La fiction ne doit pas estre considérée comme un mensonge, mais comme
> une belle imagination, & comme le plus grand effort de l'esprit: & bien
> que la Verité semble luy estre opposée toutefois elles s'accordent merveil-
> leusement bien ensemble. Ce sont deux lumières qui au lieu de s'effacer
> l'une l'autre & de se nuire, brillent par l'esclat l'une de l'autre.

Fiction interacts with fact (*vérité*) on the basis of a perception—doubtless
Aristotelian in origin—that literature is more philosophical than history.
For Desmarets the more fully imaginative works

> sont pleins de feintes parmy la verité, plus ils sont beaux & profitables;
> pource que la feinte vraysemblable est fondée sur la bien-séance & sur la

raison; & la verité toute simple n'embrasse qu'un recit d'accidens humains, qui le plus souvent ne sont pleins que d'extravagances.

Clearly a community of inspiration links this theory of the didactic heroic novel with the poetics of the epic expressed in the "Discours" and in "L'Art de la poésie" and afterwards illustrated in *Clovis* and in Desmarets's other heroic poems. Though no further volume of *Rosane* appeared, this novel must have been in Desmarets's thoughts when he adapted from it his last tragicomedy, *Erigone*—the "comédie en prose" seen at the Palais-Cardinal by guests of Mme de Rambouillet on 19 January 1642.[5] In any case Desmarets's poetics of idealism—the theory by which fact in imaginative works should be ingeniously embellished by fiction—operates on much the same assumptions as those expressed at much the same time by Corneille, who opens his "Abrégé du martyre de Saint Polyeucte" prefaced to *Polyeucte*—a play read or perhaps privately performed for Richelieu shortly before his death: "L'ingénieuse tissure des fictions avec la vérité, où consiste le plus beau secret de la Poésie . . ." Consider also Livie's last lines in *Cinna:*

Et la Postérité dans toutes les Provinces
Donnera votre exemple aux plus génereux Princes
[V: 3]

Throughout Desmarets's practice of the novel, of theater and of heroic poetry runs his conception of literature as an "art merveilleux" (see lines 6, 122, 131, and 142). This conception may have roots in the *merveilleux* of court ballet, in which Desmarets would appear (as Marays) to have distinguished himself as a performer before composing two of the grandest ballets of the age. In "L'Art de la poésie" it is already linked with the "merveilleux chrétien" destined to be so important in *Clovis* and in the Biblical epics which later divided Boileau from Desmarets: note "ce grand Dieu merveilleux" (l. 45). In line 11 the evocation of the beauteous splendors of the heavens and of earth are—however different the implications—clearly reminiscent of Psalms which Desmarets had paraphrased and dedicated to Louis XIII in 1640 before including "Psaumes pour le Roy" in his *Oeuvres poétiques,* beginning with *Coeli enarrant gloriam Dei . . .* (XVIII).

However, if it is correct to date "L'Art de la poésie" to the period immediately following publication of Desmarets's *Psaumes de Davide paraphrasés,* it is all the more curious to note his insistence here on the

thesis that "l'art nous ravit plus que ne fait la Nature" (l. 38). Not that
this attitude is inconsistent with Richelieu's patronage of the arts or with
Mazarin's activity at the time as one of Richelieu's principal collectors of
art works, but because Desmarets later changes his mind more than once.
Just before the mystic experience which may be styled the conversion of
this already deeply religious man, he subordinates art to nature in the
"première promenade" of *Les Promenades de Richelieu* (1653). He dis-
tances himself from the magnificence of the great château (of which he
was then *intendant*) because he prefers "les simples beautez de la riche
Nature"—the works of God—to any works of art "Où les mortelles
mains pretendent trop de part." Not until five years later does he appear
to conciliate his feeling for nature, surely exceptional in seventeenth-century France, with esthetic pleasure derived from works of art, writing in
Les Délices de l'esprit (1658) that "les Arts sont agréables à Dieu & à
l'homme; parce que l'Art est l'ouvrage de l'homme sur l'ouvrage de
Dieu"—a formula reconciling feeling for nature and esthetic pleasure in
the arts both with each other and with religious fervor.

Two strands of imitation theory thus reconciled in *Les Délices de l'esprit* are much more distinct in "L'Art de la poésie," reflecting the ambiguity of the concept *imitation* or *mimesis* associated with the
interpretation of Aristotle's *Poetics*. As Henri Gouhier suggests:

> Le mot [*imitation*] est équivoque. Est-ce l'oeuvre qui imite quelque chose
> ou est-ce l'auteur qui imite quelqu'un? Dans le premier cas, ce qui est
> imité, ce sont les actions des hommes agissant dans le monde; dans le
> second, celui qui est imité, c'est l'auteur présumé du monde dans lequel il
> y a des hommes agissant.[6]

Probably Aristotle meant the former. Desmarets's emphasis on the latter
reflects a Judeo-Christian tradition whereby the Greek verb *poiein*—the
root of such words as *poet, poetry,* and *poetics*—came to be regarded,
through a mutation of concepts, as representing an act of creation,
thereby indicating, as Gouhier puts it, "que l'imitation est celle qui fait
du 'poète' un créateur à l'image du Créateur" (*Ibid.*). In "L'Art de la
poésie" Desmarets (who would publish in 1654 his verse translation of
L'Imitation de Jésus-Christ) blends the duality of imitation theory with
the idealism of didactic exemplarity. By means of imitative (representa-
tional or mimetic) art the writer imitates not only God's creatures (here
relatively disvalued), but His Creation, His creativity (ll. 45–52). Argua-

bly the exemplary "role models" by which the writer then goes on to embellish his fiction are destined to exert a redemptive influence upon the reader analogous to the role of the Savior in the real, historic world corrupted by the Fall of Man. It is ironic, not to say perverse, that in the "Querelle des *Imaginaires*" Pierre Nicole—who took a more radical view of the Fall—would condemn Desmarets's fiction as corrupting although it had been conceived as redemptive.

The serious work of fiction is thus a multiple imitation of God's Creation, combining imitation of the act of Creation with representation of creatures in the fallen state and models for their redemption. In maintaining that "l'Art imitateur est l'ouvrage des hommes, / C'est une créature," Desmarets asserts the concept of creative writing. "L'Art de la poésie" must be one of the earliest texts to do so. But from line 53 "Plus un art à nos sens représente de choses," we are back to the first strand of imitation theory: "l'oeuvre qui imite quelque chose." This strand is developed along the familiar lines of Horace's precept "Ut pictura poesis . . . " with one curious reservation:

La Peinture, embrassant les objets de nos yeux,
Imite tous les corps que l'on voit sous les Cieux.
Mais la Muse divine, à qui tout est possible.
Embrasse tout sujet invisible, & visible

[ll. 55–58]

Literature is argued to have an imaginative dimension somewhat arbitrarily denied to the plastic arts. In the wake of such theorists as the early cubist Albert Gleizes (1881–1953), it is scarcely necessary to repostulate theories by which painting or sculpture may be regarded as creating *objects* rather than as representing *subjects* or to underline the limitations of Desmarets's antithesis on this point. But it is worth noting that the antithesis is not supported by one of his principal illustrators, Abraham Bosse, who derived from the Lyonese mathematician G. Desargues (1593–1662) a theory of perspective serving to represent

sur une surface platte de quelque matiere & inclination qu'elle puisse estre, tous les objets visibles de la nature, & ceux que l'on peut former dans l'imagination.[7]

It is also worth pausing to consider the notion of a "sujet invisible."

An invisible subject may be imaginary, as Bosse suggests; but it may also be doctrinal or allegorical, as in the theological concept that the sun, visible light, manifests God, *lux invisibilis*. It is not Bosse's illustrations of Desmarets's *Ariane* (1639) or his frontispieces for Desmarets's plays published around 1640 that depict invisible subjects so much as the illustrations later engraved by François Chauveau and others for *Clovis* and *Les Délices de l'esprit*. In these texts one may contemplate numerous representations of the imaginary, the allegorical, and the theologically symbolic. Pertinent to the present discussion is the extent to which these beautiful books strive as a whole—text and illustration—to render a sensibility Christian and then modern through forms not only ancient but originally pagan. It is not merely a matter of heroic poetry or the epic privileged by "L'Art de la poésie," but such other forms as the dialogue, the romance, drama, the ode, even the *Ars poetica*. Even if one excepts such devotional works as his recently identified *Lettres spirituelles* and the paraphrased Psalms, the examples set by Saint Paul and by David confirm that Desmarets's literary practice supposes an essential third strand of imitation theory: the imitation of select literary models, mainly from classical antiquity, but also from the Old and the New Testaments. In "L'Art de la poésie" it is possible to show not only general indebtedness to Aristotle and to Horace, but specific inspiration from Virgil. The verse "Des astres nous décrit le réglé mouvement" (l. 59) is unlikely not to have been prompted by Anchises's famous prophesy in *Aeneid* VI: "caelique meatus / Describent radio et surgentia sidera dicent" (ll. 849–50). Here, the thought is imitated; elsewhere, aspects of Virgilian form.

For much of what follows in "L'Art poétique" however, Desmarets appears to imitate a more modern imaginative model: Ludovico Ariosto. To a large extent the imitation is a matter of atmosphere, but at times it seems quite specific. Line 60 "Monté d'un vol hardy dessus le firmament" seems reminiscent of the flights of the hippogriff in *Orlando furioso* and of "Ruggiero, / che scorre il ciel su l'animal leggiero" (VI: 16, but compare also X: 91–92). The view looking down upon wide stretches of the earth from an airborne hippogriff (symbolic among other things of poetic imagination) is not much different from the viewpoint supposed for Virgil's gods, angels or the traditional Christian God. Indeed in *Orlando furioso* "la Bontá ineffabile" gazes down upon threatened France and introduces the allegorical episode with Silence, Fraud, and Discord which Desmarets may have recalled in his lines 102–4. Although Conrart's copyist seems to have neglected the capital letters required for fully allegorical *Erreur* and *Flaterie*, Desmarets does appear to have recalled

Ariosto's Discordia when beginning *Les Promenades de Richelieu:* "Pendant que la Discorde espouvante les loix . . ." Desmarets also from time to time reasserts Ariosto's promise in Canto I, 2, to relate "cosa non detta in prosa mai né in rima."

It is difficult to imagine a more pointed contrast with Malherbe's "aversion contre les fictions poétiques" as reported by Racan. When Malherbe read in Régnier's first *Epître au Roi* "que la France s'enlevait en l'air pour parler à Jupiter et se plaindre du misérable état où elle était pendant la Ligue," says Racan, Malherbe "demanda à l'auteur en quel temps cela était arrivé" because he had not noticed its having occurred during the past fifty years.[8] I wish I could report that Racan replied "in poetry" or "in poetic time." Antoine Adam uses this anecdote (without reply) to illustrate a trivializing influence of Malherbe's famous reform of French poetic diction. Malherbe is said to have reduced the role of the poet, in a land governed by a king and guided by the Church, to that of a mere arranger of syllables, "pas plus utile à la société qu'un bon joueur de quilles" (I: 32).

Not, I think, the whole truth of the matter. But Adam goes on to link Malherbe's reaction against imaginative hyperbole to the cultural impoverishment induced by the Counter-Reformation in France:

La chute que signifie, dans l'histoire de la pensée, la victoire de la Contre-Réforme, s'exprime de façon saisissante dans cet abandon des hautes doctrines de la Pléiade. Elles supposaient un climat de liberté intellectuelle, un affranchissement des traditions, le droit pour l'individu de courir tous les risques et d'oser toutes les audaces. La monarchie, l'Eglise, l'aristocratie ont repris la situation en main, étouffé les efforts de l'esprit pour se libérer. La poésie paie le prix de sa liberté perdue. [I: 32–33]

Desmarets was an important Counter-Reformation personality. He wrote verse exhibited in the Lady Chapel of Notre-Dame Cathedral and later dedicated his verse translation of the *Office de la Vierge* (1645) to the Queen Regent. But the atmosphere of "L'Art de la poésie" is not at all what Adam describes. "Enfin Malherbe vint . . ." belongs to a retrospective part of Boileau's *Art poétique* (1674). Boileau's hostility toward Desmarets, along with that of the Jansenist Nicole and the Protestant Bayle, so influential in the historiography of the seventeenth century, has gravely distorted perception of Desmarets's role and of the cultural patronage of Richelieu. Even Perrault and the Moderns whom Desmarets later did so

much to encourage, lost few opportunities to minimize the achievements
of the period of Louis XIII and of Richelieu in order to maximize a late-
starting "century of Louis-le-Grand"—Louis XIV.

Let me contrast Adam's "chute" with a few passages of Desmarets's
"Discours de la poésie" of 1633, the first of his poems known to have
been noticed by Richelieu, who is straightforwardly advised:

> Si tu veux que ton nom brille aux siècles suivans,
> Chery les vertueux, sois l'appuy des sçavans. . . .[9]

Indeed Desmarets goes on to warn the Cardinal specifically against:

> l'erreur de ces nouveaux critiques
> Qui retranchent le champ de nos Muses antiques,
> Qui veulent qu'on les suive, & qu'adorant leurs pas
> On evite les lieux qu'ils ne cognoissent pas.
> Leur Muse cependant de foiblesse & de crainte
> Pensant se soutenir affecte la contrainte,
> N'ose aller à l'escart de peur de s'esgarer;
> Et parlant simplement croit se faire admirer:
> Elle a peur d'eschaufer le fard qui la rend vaine,
> Et la moindre fureur la mettroit hors d'haleine.

Then Desmarets disparages such "esprits rampans" in favor of a "Muse
sublime"—a term surely worth noticing at this date and a concept contextual for "L'Art de la poésie." For Desmarets proposes a "Muse sublime" with

> un coeur ambitieux,
> Qui d'un superbe vol s'emporte vers les Cieux,
> Et void avec orgueil, marchant dessus la nuë,
> La terre dont le globe à ses yeux diminuë:
> Le Ciel qu'elle apperçoit & plus vaste & plus pur,
> Qui de l'or du Soleil enrichit son azur,
> Luy paroit un seiour digne de son courage:
> Iamais dans un destroit sa grandeur ne s'engage. . . .
> De celeste fureur quelquefois s'animant,
> Elle se sent ravir iusques au firmament . . .
>
>   [80. 5]

Here, as also in "L'Art de la poésie," is an exalted overview reminiscent of Ariosto and of the Pléiade. The neo-Platonist cast of "fureur ce-
leste"—for like the madman, the lover and the mystic, the poet can

through "fureur" attain ecstasy—is intelligible in terms of, for example, Pontus de Tyard's *Dialogues philosophiques*. These last lines may further serve to gloss the "noble furie" of the Muse "des Cieux originaire" invoked in lines 101–9 of "L'Art de la poésie."

The neo-Platonist inspiration of the "Discours" and of "L'Art de la poésie" finds expression also in the activities of the early Académie-Française and of other playwrights associated with Richelieu's patronage. Desmarets in particular was familiar with Pléiade neo-Platonism. In *Les Visionnaires* the "fureur" of the extravagant poet Amidor in Act I, scenes 2 and 3, parodies that aspect of Pléiade poetics, notably Ronsard's ode I, 3 beginning "Je suis troublé de fureur." Poetic "fureur" is complemented by a parody of the lover's "furie" in the role of Filidan, "amoureux en idée" whose inspiration is even more clearly neo-Platonist:

J'adore en mon esprit ceste beauté divine,
Qui sans doute du ciel tire son origine.
[I: 4]

That the parody is firmly grounded in familiarity with neo-Platonist thought is evident in Desmarets's works from the "Discours de la poésie" to *Les Délices de l'esprit,* including his first comedy written for Richelieu *Aspasie* (1636). It must also have been evident in his lost address to the Académie-Française of August 1635 in which he is reported to have argued that Platonic love "a quelque chose de divin." [10]

But Desmarets rejects Plato's notion that literature, being an imitation of ideal reality imperfectly manifested in the world of phenomena, threatens to corrupt its audience. For as we have seen, he envisages a role for the poet not merely as an imitator of things, but as an imitator of divine Creation capable also of introducing redemptive imaginative amelioration into his work. In this way God becomes the guarantor of both the *merveilleux* and the inventive Muse:

Mais alors qu'elle invente une belle aventure
Glorieuse elle suit l'autheur de la Nature;
Et produisant au jour ce qui ne fut jamais,
Imite du grand Dieu les admirables faits
[ll. 113–16]

Ornaments of the *merveilleux* are metaphor and hyperbole—compare with André Gide's observation that "l'oeuvre d'art est exagération." [11] Yet the marvelous remains verisimilar through its relation to fact or to doc-trine—"le fondement, pris sur la verité." By "vérité" Desmarets, who gives scant attention to the technical analysis of rhetoric, seems to mean (in terms of the categories suggested by Aristotle's *Poetics* XXV) not only "things as they were or are," but "things as they are said or thought to be" and "things as they ought to be." This last category strongly favors the redemptive exemplary idealism with which Desmarets is concerned in "L'Art de la poésie" and which he clearly conceives as being compat-ible with verisimilitude. Some thirty years later, in the *Discours pour prouver que les suiets Chrestiens sont les seuls propres à la poësie Hé-roïque* prefaced to the revised edition of *Clovis* (1673), Desmarets argues against the ornamental use of pagan mythology in poetry and associated hyperboles, claiming that "les Chrestiens, qui seuls ont la verité, ont seuls le vrai-semblable."

Because it is so deeply ironic, I hope it is worth repeating that Desmar-ets is sometimes remembered, if at all, only through Nicole's hostile phrase: "Un faiseur de romans et un poète de théâtre est un empoison-neur public, non des corps, mais des âmes des fidèles . . ."[12] For it is forgotten not only how extensive and influential Desmarets's writings were, but that he had been closely associated with the cultural and devo-tional activities of the royal Court itself. Desmarets supplied poems not only for Notre-Dame, but for the statue of Louis XIII in the Place Royale (now Place des Vosges). Doubtless because he had so often danced in Court ballets with the King, it was Desmarets's great *Ballet de la félicité* which was selected to celebrate the birth of the Dauphin, the future Louis XIV; and it was his *Mirame* which was selected to open in 1641 the great new theater in the Palais-Cardinal destined to become Molière's theater and then the Paris Opéra. Though early in his career Desmarets seems to have come close to compromise in the trial of Théophile de Viau, his purpose (as far as I can see) was never to corrupt, but to edify through entertainment. Good intentions do not of course assure success, but ar-guably Desmarets's success was greater than is now appreciated. One can cite the numerous editions and translations into several languages of *Ariane* and *Les Visionnaires*. After his conversion, he was not proud of his early reputation as a star performer in Court ballet, or for the inno-vative staging of *Aspasie* with successive décors and of *Mirame* with transformation scenes which also respected the newly fashionable unities. The innovative illustration of *Clovis* and of *Les Délices de l'esprit* also deserves mention, although the texts (often without illustrations) had numerous reprints, especially the latter. Desmarets was the first to use *Europe* in the title of a separate publication and one of the earliest to use the title and form of the literary *promenade*.[13] He was an early proponent of the critical appreciation of French literature and of what we now call comparative literature in *La Comparaison de la langue et de la poésie françoise avec la grecque et la latine, et des poètes grecs, latins et françois* (Paris, 1670). Neither "L'Art de la poésie," *La Comparaison*, nor any of his other critical writing is strong in detailed analysis of rhetorical theory. But this relative weakness is compensated by a lofty conception of the cultural value of literature and of other arts, including technologies. Above all, he was an early protagonist of the Modern position in the Quarrel of the Ancients and Moderns. As early as 1636 he wrote in his burlesque poem "Les Amours du compas et de la règle" dedicated to Richelieu:

> Et la Muse en riant me conduit par la main
> Où ne marcha iamais le Grec ni le Romain.[14]

Even in this burlesque poem, Desmarets's high purpose stands in sharp contrast both with Malherbe's abdication of high cultural ambitions for literature and with Nicole's hostility toward the liberating innovation of imaginative writing. It involves a sense of post-Renaissance adventure in which, though deeply imbedded in classical forms and Counter-Reformation patterns of thought, he glimpses a new superiority in modern European civilisation and the prospect of establishing within it the cultural hegemony of France. As for Richelieu, this was partly a matter of arms: Desmarets was *Contrôleur général de l'extraordinaire des guerres* and secretary to the French Mediterranean fleet. But it was also very much a matter of diplomacy, of cultural and literary confidence and ascendancy.

One achievement not evident in "L'Art de la poésie" is more or less to have devised the schema through which we divide the study of French literature into separate centuries, through the concept of the century of Louis XIV, which I have discussed elsewhere in relation to Desmarets's *Le Triomphe de Louis et de son siècle* (1674) and to Perrault's *Le Siècle de Louis-le-Grand* (1687).[15] Discussion of his sense of *translatio studii* and of *translatio imperii* would exceed the limits of this presentation. Yet among a growing body of French intellectuals who early in the seventeenth century came to see Bourbon and Catholic France not simply as cyclical successors to such select past periods of greatness as the Empire of Alexander and the Roman Empire under Julius and then Augustus Caesar, but (by an upturn in the cycle) as positively superior in religion, arms, politics, invention, technology, the arts, and literature, Desmarets was clearly one of the more influential. To express a new confidence he often adapted classical forms, as suggested above, but with a different message. Witness the contrast between Anchises's prophesy in *Aeneid* VI, p.847 ff., where Virgil concedes that other nations may excel in the arts and in rhetoric, but Rome will have a dominant political role, and Desmarets's increasing insistence on the superiority of all things French, Catholic and modern. The limitations of such a view hardly need spelling out, and the Quarrel of the Ancients and Moderns did spell them out. But much of this position survives in underlying attitudes long associated with French "classicism," for instance (Catholic dominance excepted) in Voltaire's *Siècle de Louis XIV,* from the explicit *translatio studii* with which it begins, through insistence on cultural as well as military achievements, to Voltaire's general assumption that French literary values are a superior norm even in an increasingly relativist world. Doubtless this oversimplifies, but it scarcely distorts or exaggerates. In any case, it restores some of the credit for the achievements of the later seventeenth century to the foundations laid by Richelieu and by the poet who, in the "Discours de la poésie," addressed Richelieu near the beginning of his ambitious program of cultural patronage in the following terms:

Rends nostre siècle illustre en lettres comme en armes:
Fay qu'un esprit divin descouvre par ses vers
Qu'un LOUIS doit un iour regir tout l'univers. . . .

This is the doubtless still contentious sense in which Desmarets should be considered as "un visionnaire du XVIIᵉ siècle."

NOTES

1. Paris, Bibliothèque de l'Arsenal MS 4116 (Recueils Conrart 4to, XI, 835 seq.). James Dryhurst is the author of a Liverpool University doctoral thesis (1963), *Les Idées de Jean des Marests sieur de Saint-Sorlin (1595–1676).* "L'Art de la poésie" is mentioned on p. 19. I am happy to acknowledge his generosity in placing the text at our disposal and also assistance from the British Academy for related research in Paris.

2. Or so I argue in presenting Desmarets's comedy *Les Visionnaires* (Paris: Didier, 1963), pp. xviii ff. I have since discovered that this was probably the Desmarets who, already in the service of the king at the siege of the château de Caen in 1620, published an account of its surrender, and that it was undoubtedly he who in 1623 was sent by the Parlement de Paris with Bautru to convey complaints to the royal court at Fontainebleau.

3. See Desmarets's *Clovis, ou la France chrestienne,* ed. F. R. Freudmann (Louvain and Paris: Nauwelaerts Edition, 1972), p. 8.

4. Other occasional pieces written by Desmarets after the *Oeuvres poétiques* went to press were added extracollationally to (some) copies left in stock. Such additions include his last play *Europe.* See my papers "Three Illustrated Works of Desmarets de Saint-Sorlin," *Yale University Library Gazette* 33 (1958), pp. 18–23, and *"Europe,* allégorie théâtrale de propagande politique," in *L'Age d'or du mécénat, 1598–1661* (Paris: CNRS, 1985), pp. 319–27.

5. So I deduce from Emile Magne, *Voiture et l'Hôtel de Rambouillet,* 2 vols. (new ed., Paris: Flammarion, 1930), II: 223.

6. H. Gouhier, *L'Oeuvre théâtrale* (Paris, 1958), p. 33.

7. A. Bosse, *La Pratique du trait à preuves, de Mr Desargues Lyonnois* (Paris, 1653), pp. 12–13.

8. Racan, quoted by A. Adam, *Histoire de la littérature française au XVIIe siècle,* 5 vols. (Paris: Del Duca, 1949–56), I: 30.

9. *Oeuvres poétiques,* "Autres oeuvres poétiques," p. 80. The "Discours" is paginated 77–80, 5–6.

10. See *Les Visionnaires,* ed. cit., p. 111n.

11. A. Gide, *Journal* (Paris: Gallimard, 1940), quoted by Gouhier, p. 33.

12. P. Nicole, first *Visionnaire* dated 31 December 1665, quoted by R. Picard, ed., Racine, *Oeuvres complètes,* 2 vols. (Paris: Gallimard, 1952), II: 13.

13. *Les Promenades de Richelieu* was anticipated, on a smaller scale, by *Les Promenades de Saint-Cloud,* a *caprice* by Salomon de Priézac (Paris, 1643).

14. *Oeuvres poétiques,* "Autres oeuvres poétiques," p. 7.

15. The first in a paper of that title in *Actes de Baton Rouge,* ed. S. A. Zebouni (Paris-Seattle-Tübingen: Papers on French Seventeenth-Century Literature, "Biblio 17," no. 25 (1986), pp. 243–53; the second in a paper on Perrault's unacknowledged debts to Desmarets in *D'un siècle à l'autre: Anciens et Modernes,* ed. L. Godard de Donville (Marseilles, 1987), pp. 43–52. See also my *Richelieu's Desmarets and the Century of Louis XIV,* forthcoming from Oxford University Press.

L'Art de la Poesie
à
Monseigneur le Cardinal-Duc de Richelieu

Grand DVC, qui terraçant les monstres de la France,
As couronné ta gloire, en dontant l'Ignorance;
Richelieu, dont le nom courant par l'Univers,
Souffre d'estre porté sur l'aile de nos vers;
Entens un peu parler, au retour des allarmes,   5
De cet art merveilleux dont tu chéris les charmes,
Et de tes hauts pensers tiens le vol en suspens,
Pour goûter ses secrets, qu'au monde je répans.

   De l'esprit des Mortels la douce nourriture,
N'est pas à contempler les faits de la Nature.   10
D'un oeil indifférent nous voyons leurs beautez,
Des moindres feux du Ciel les brillantes clartez,
Du grand Astre des jours la lumière éclatante,
Et le teint argenté de sa soeur inconstante.
L'Homme, de ces beaux corps regarde la splendeur   15
Sans un ravissement digne de leur grandeur.
Il voit des élémens la concorde & la guerre,
Le bel azur des Cieux, & le vert de la Terre,
Des spacieuses mers les écumantes eaux,
Le crystal ondoyant des murmurans ruisseaux,   20
Les flots impetuëux des rivières superbes,
Le vif email des fleurs, & l'oeil riant des herbes,
Les arbres chevelus des rivages voisins,
Les fertiles cotaux où naissent les raisins,
Les épics jaunissants, richesses des campagnes,   25
Et l'abry des valons, & l'orgueil des montagnes.
Il voit de toutes parts mouvoir par l'univers,
Des habitans de l'air le plumage divers,
Il voit des animaux les troupes vagabondes,
Et les peuples muets qui nagent sous les ondes,   30
L'Homme se voit luy même en ce monde logé,

Le Chef-d'oeuvre de Dieu, son portrait abbrégé.
Nous voyons tous les jours tant d'oeuvres nonpareilles,
Sans nous sentir épris de toutes leurs merveilles.
Mais si quelque Mortel d'un habile pinceau,   35
De l'un de ces objets a finy le tableau,
Nous aymons ardemment cette rare peinture,
Et l'art nous ravit plus que ne fait la Nature.
Si quelqu'autre accordant par d'inconnus ressors
La souplesse d'esprit avec celle du corps,   40
Imite une action ou plaisante ou sérieuse,
Cette veuë à nos yeux semble délicieuse,
Sans aymer l'Imité nous aymons l'Imitant.
Ce que l'esprit produit, nous rend l'esprit content.
Ce grand Dieu merveilleux dont nous sommes l'Image,   45
Ayme la créature ainsi que son ouvrage;
Il se plut à l'Instant en ce qu'il avoit fait,
De ses puissantes mains il admira l'effet;
La Nature est de luy, c'est par luy que nous sommes;
Mais l'Art imitateur est l'ouvrage des hommes,   50
C'est une créature, il nous charme les sens,
Et remplit nos esprits de plaisirs innocens.

     Plus un art à nos sens représente de choses,
Plus de perfections là se treuvent encloses;
La Peinture, embrassant les objets de nos yeux,   55
Imite tous les corps que l'on voit sous les Cieux.
Mais la Muse divine, à qui tout est possible,
Embrasse tout sujet invisible, & visible;
Des astres nous décrit le réglé mouvement,
Monté d'un vol hardy dessus le firmament;   60
Elle fuit au delà des lieux imaginaires,
Puis descend aux secrets des effets sublunaires,
D'où naissent les éclairs, l'orage & les frimats,
L'espérance & l'horreur des terrestres climats.
C'est elle qui décrit & Dieu même & ses Anges,   65
Adore son pouvoir, luy donne des louänges,
Dicte les mots sacrez dont on le doit bénir,
Se mêle de savoir le passé, l'avenir;
Pénètre des humains le coeur & la pensée,
Dit ce qu'une ame sent de douleur oppressée,   70
Ou quels sont ses transports nageant dans le plaisir,

Ou s'animant de haine, ou mourant de désir;
Les vices, les vertus, & les humeurs diverses,
Du sort capricieux les biens & les traverses,
Des esprits modérez les jours délicieux,   75
Et les nuits sans sommeil des coeurs ambitieux;
Les douceurs de la paix, les travaux de la guerre,
Et la honte & l'honneur des Princes de la terre.
En fin, d'un vers pompeux, sa verve nous décrit
Tout ce qui reconnoît l'empire de l'esprit.   80

Mais son art qui comprend toute chose imitable,
Sait mêler sagement l'utile au délectable
Par ses charmes flateurs rend le vice abattu,
Inspire adroitement l'amour de la Vertu,
Elle amuse nos sens par les fables plaisantes,   85
Arrachant de nos coeurs les épines nuisantes;
Puis y plante en leur lieu les bons enseignemens;
Comme une Mère entend par des amusemens
A charmer de plaisirs une humeur enfantine,
Cependant que sa main verse la medecine.   90

Dans le vers heroïque, elle forme un guerrier,
Pieux, sage, courtois, vaillant, aventurier,
Patient aux travaux, amateur de justice,
Honnorant les beaux-faits, & punissant le vice;
Tel que doit estre un Roy, de qui les qualitez   95
Font d'un Peuple les maux, ou les felicitez.
Pour dépeindre les Grans, & pour leur estre utile,
Entrant dans leurs palais, elle prend un haut style,
Elle s'arme pour eux de pompe, & de grandeur,
Et fait luire en son front une auguste pudeur.   100
Elle sait s'animer d'une noble furie,
Pour chasser d'auprès d'eux l'erreur, la flaterie,
L'Impiété, l'Envie, & les sales amours,
L'Injustice, & l'orgueil, pestes des grandes cours.
Pour se rendre plus grave, elle enfle sa parole,   105
La docte Métaphore, & la haute Hyperbole,
Sont de ses grans discours les riches ornemens.
Elle se laisse aller aux transports véhémens;
Et pour se faire voir des Cieux originaire,
Dédaigne de parler un langage ordinaire.   110
Car la Muse imitant tout ce que voit l'esprit,

Suit cet art des humains qu'en la terre elle apprit;
Mais alors qu'elle invente une belle aventure
Glorieuse elle suit l'autheur de la Nature;
Et produisant au jour ce qui ne fut jamais,   115
Imite du grand Dieu les admirables faits.
D'abord, en méprisant d'entrer par la barrière,
Elle saute au milieu de sa longue carrière;
Et jette les esprits en ce même moment
Dans l'agréable espoir d'un grand événement.   120
Ayant par le désir attaché les oreilles,
Elle sait les charmer de ses doctes merveilles,
Conduit les grands desseins d'un fil ingénieux,
Ensorcéle nos sens d'un son harmonieux,
Et mêle adroitement d'une veine fertile,   125
Et le faux, & le vray, le plaisant & l'utile.
Puis, pour rendre l'esprit de tout point contenté,
Et ne l'engager pas dedans l'obscurité;
Elle prend aux cheveux les rencontres naissantes,
Pour faire un beau récit des choses précédentes.   130
Ce discours est succinct, clair, doux & merveilleux,
Plein d'accidens divers, de combats périlleux,
De contes inouïs, & de fameux voyages;
Tantôt marquant des mers les dangereux passages;
Tantôt les régions, les ports, & les Citez;   135
Toujours divertissant par ses diversitez.
Enfin, dans ce doux point l'ame se voit conduite,
Qu'elle entend le passé dont elle sait la suite.
Sortant de ce détroit avec tant de plaisir,
Pour savoir le surplus nait un plus grand desir.   140
La Muse avance alors le grand corps de sa fable,
Qui, bien que merveilleuse est toûjours vray-semblable,
Et dont le fondement, pris sur la verité,
Fait qu'on reçoit pour vray tout le faux inventé.
Aux grandes actions, superbe elle s'attache;   145
Des moindres s'en défait, les néglige & les cache;
Elle fait un beau choix, & décrit seulement
Ce qu'elle reconnoît capable d'ornement.
Les querelles des Roys à leurs Etats funestes,
Et du Peuple Innocent les dangereuses pestes   150
Les horribles combats, les siéges, les assauts,
De deux camps ennemis la force & les defauts,

Des plus nobles guerriers la diverse vaillance,
L'un vaillant par vertu, l'autre par arrogance,
Un autre par espoir, ou par nécessité,   155
Par ruse, par exemple, ou par brutalité.

Recueils Conrart 4°, t. XI, p. 835 seq. Ars. MS 4116.

II
Theater

Poetry and the Comic—A Subtle Partnership

Odette de Mourgues

"The English have humor, the French perceive it." This bon mot spring-ing from the well-known gallic arrogance illustrates in a jocular way the possible disjunction between the producer of a discourse and its recipient. It offers a crude similarity, and gives a dismissive thrust, to a delicate question which is at the center of literary criticism and has been much discussed in the past few years: that of the problematic connection be-tween the production of a text (whether conscious, semiconscious, or, as in the French statement mentioned above, supposedly unconscious) and the response of the reader.

I have chosen this lateral opening to the present essay because the alliance of the poetic and the comic in a work of literature not only may require from the author the elaboration of intricate patterns but also may confront the reader with a teasing range of responses. The perception of the comic is by itself a complex operation and the kind of satisfaction suggested by poetry is equally complex and of a different nature. If al-ready a number of people do not expect the comic to have serious impli-cations, many more would find it difficult to conceive that poetic and comic elements could happily blend, each making its full impact on the reader. They might bring as an argument the case in which one of the two elements is entirely subservient to the other, the formal pattern of poetry with its various devices (meter, rhymes, etc.) being used only to produce a comic effect, as in a limerick for instance. This in fact is properly called comic verse, not poetry. It remains that much depends on both authors' and readers' own ideas of what is "poetic." These views are not only influenced by personal idiosyncrasies, literary genres, and, in as far as the reader is concerned, by degrees of competence or application but also historically conditioned by the particular concept of poetry at a given period.[1]

The intricacies of the question are, I think, very noticeable in French classicism and also, up to a point, in English neoclassicism.

The first text I propose to examine is taken from the opening scene of

Molière's *Les Femmes Savantes,* in which the two sisters express their divergent views on marriage:

> Mon Dieu, que votre esprit est d'un étage bas!
> Que vous jouez au monde un petit personnage,
> De vous claquemurer aux choses du ménage,
> Et de n'entrevoir point de plaisirs plus touchants
> Qu'un idole d'époux et des marmots d'enfants!
> Laissez au gens grossiers, aux personnes vulgaires,
> Les bas amusements de ces sortes d'affaires;
> A de plus hauts objets élevez vos désirs,
> Songez à prendre un goût des plus nobles plaisirs,
> Et traitant de mépris les sens et la matière,
> A l'esprit comme nous, donnez-vous toute entière.
> Vous avez notre mère en exemple à vos yeux,
> Que du nom de savante on honore en tous lieux:
> Tâchez ainsi que moi de vous montrer sa fille,
> Aspirez aux clartés qui sont dans la famille,
> Et vous rendez sensible au charmantes douceurs
> Que l'amour de l'étude épanche dans les coeurs;
> Loin d'être aux lois d'un homme en esclave asservie
> Mariez-vous, ma soeur, à la philosophie
> Qui nous monte au-dessus de tout le genre humain,
> Et donne à la raison l'empire souverain,
> Soumettant à ses lois la partie animale,
> Dont l'appétit grossier aux bêtes nous ravale.
> Ce sont là les beaux feux, les doux attachements,
> Qui doivent de la vie occuper les moments;
> Et les soins où je vois tant de femmes sensibles
> Me paroissent aux yeux des pauvretés horribles.[2]

The comic of Armande's speech is, at least at first sight, perfectly straightforward. It lies in the discrepancy between the accepted opinion of a woman's role as a wife and mother and the *précieuse*'s abnormal tenets: refusal of marriage, obsessive yearning for intellectual pursuits. However this feminist attitude—which was partly justified by the condition of women at the time—needed some elaboration to be presented as comic.

The most obvious comic flaw in Armande's rhetoric is its oversimplification. The passage is built on antitheses which constantly oppose mind and matter, spiritual delights and humdrum chores. Keywords underline the opposition: "bas," "grossiers," "vulgaires," "animale" on the one hand, "hauts," "nobles," "charmants" on the other. The dynamic pattern—a succession of rises and falls—translates in its uncompromising verticality the antithetical nature of Armande's overstatements. But the pattern is far from being rigid or mechanical, and is marked by an elegant flexibility. The ascending movement, punctured by objurgations such as "élevez vos désirs," "aspirez aux clartés," comes to a magnificent climax:

> Loin d'être aux lois d'un homme en esclave asservie
> Mariez-vous, ma soeur, à la philosophie,
> Qui nous monte au-dessus de tout le genre humain . . .

Here the absurd analogy, made to stand out through the pauses in the lines, sound like a triumphant clarion call introducing the impressive long period that follows.

The rhymes also play their part, emphasizing the joys of life devoted to study ("désirs"—"plaisirs," "douceurs"—"coeurs"), giving a neat finish to the reminder of an exemplary mother ("fille"—"famille"), magnifying the power of knowledge ("genre humain"—"souverain") in opposition to the downward pull of lower instincts ("animale"—"ravale").

Perhaps one of the most interesting aspects of this speech is the diction which, with very few exceptions, belongs to the grand style characteristic of the literary language of the French classicists. One of the features of this language is the strong tendency to use abstract words with an extensive field of connotations, the blurring of their outlines even increased by the added imprecision of the plural, such as "clartés," "douceurs," "attachements."

Three words, however, do not belong to poetic diction: "claquemurer," "marmots," "idole" (taken here in its seventeenth-century meaning of a dull inert creature, a dolt). But the words are used by Armande more or less in inverted commas as if she were compelled by the violence of her ironical scorn to stoop to such familiar expressions. In any case, the unseemly picturesqueness of "claquemurer" is nicely balanced by the vague grayness of "choses du ménage," "idole" and "marmots" and by the orthodoxy of "époux" and "enfants." The despicable chores of a married woman are thereafter viewed from a great distance and "bas amusements," "sortes d'affaires," and finally summed up in the last line of the passage as "pauvretés horribles."

In comedy, poetic language may take some liberties which would not be possible in tragedy, on the condition of course that it should be done sparingly and with tact. Compare for instance Athalie's periphrasis when referring to Jezabel:

> cet éclat emprunté
> Dont elle eut soin de peindre et d'orner son visage
> Pour réparer des ans l'irréparable outrage.
>
> [II: 5]

and the precise realistic term used by Célimène when talking about Arsinoë to her face in a speech rightly admired for its stylistic elegance:

> Mais elle met du rouge et veut paraitre belle.
>
> [III: 4]

In Armande's lines, quite apart from the intrinsic aesthetic value of the overall effect of the grand style, the very vagueness of this kind of diction is very much in keeping with what we suspect to be the comic vagueness of the *précieuse*'s acquaintance with knowledge. There is also another way in which the lofty terms reveal in Armande a comic discrepancy which will appear more clearly later in the play. The words chosen to convince the *anti-précieuse* Henriette of the delights which a life devoted to higher thinking will offer—the satisfaction of "désirs," the fulfillment of the "coeur," the "charmantes douceurs," "beaux feux," "doux attachements"—are undoubtedly rhetorical overstatements. But, if we remember the lexical range of poetic diction, these terms are part and parcel of the language of love and their sexual implications are subconsciously present in a woman who boasts of despising "les sens et la matière."

Thus the possibilities afforded by a poetic text—rhythm, rhymes, diction—result in a comic discourse which is both forceful in its direct impact and rich in subtle nuances. At the same time the poetic medium is in no way debased and retains its elegant urbanity.

This last point is important when we consider *Les Femmes Savantes* as one of Molière's comedies which has had the misfortune of having been liked or disliked for the wrong reasons. Here, Molière's comic vision of *préciosité* is very skillfully balanced. The refinement of language which we have just seen in Armande's speech—and which historically owed so much to the influence of the *précieux* circles—is not in itself made ridiculous. In fact the *raisonneur*, Clitandre, who stands for good taste, uses the same language as Armande most of the time. But in keeping with the complex pattern of the play, we find variety of tone and diction. And no one better than Molière can show how, in the case of a bad poet, a comic discordance can ruin all the potential poetic value of a piece of verse. Thus Trissotin, in his epigram on the *carrosse* offered to a lady, destroys all the delicate poetic suggestions of the lovely word "amarante" by his deplorable pun:

Ne dis plus qu'il est amarante:
Dis plutot qu'il est de ma rente.

[III: 2]

Such is the flexibility in Molière's use of stylistic devices that if in this last illustration from *Les Femmes Savantes* he can remove the poetic substance from formal verse, conversely he can elsewhere give prose passages a lyrical quality: for instance, Dorante's sophisticated description of an exquisite meal in *Le Bourgeois Gentilhomme* or in the fireworks of Scapin's fanciful inventiveness.

These would deserve close scrutiny but I am concerned here with what in Molière's works conforms to the poetics of French classicism: the mold of the regular alexandrine and the limitations on vocabulary. The restrictions are not a hindrance but an asset when the writer takes advantage of the various connotations of the terms belonging to poetic diction. The choice of the possible implications of a word becomes a question of focus. We saw for instance that in Armande's speech the comic vision of *préciosité* gave a particular significance to the vocabulary of love. A similar vocabulary is also to be found in Tartuffe's declaration to Elmire, but this time the focus is different.

One remembers the two superbly engineered speeches in which Tartuffe displays his rhetoric of seduction, both ending with a neat symmetrical pattern of opposites: the first on the tone of the respectful lover whose diffidence is underlined by the pauses:

Heureux, si vous voulez, malheureux, s'il vous plaît.

[III: 3]

the second with a closely knit pattern which firmly sums up the cynical advantages of his offer:

De l'amour sans scandale et du plaisir sans peur.

[III: 3]

The opening lines of the declaration set the key to the phraseology Tartuffe is going to exploit:

> L'amour qui nous attache aux beautés éternelles
> N'étouffe pas en nous l'amour des temporelles;
> Nos sens facilement peuvent être charmés
> Des ouvrages parfaits que le Ciel a formés.
> Ses attraits réfléchis brillent dans vos pareilles;
> Mais il étale en vous ses plus rares merveilles:
> Il a sur votre face épanché des beautés
> Dont les yeux sont surpris, et les coeurs transportés,
> Et je n'ai pu vous voir, parfaite créature,
> Sans admirer en vous l'auteur de la nature,
> Et d'une ardente amour sentir mon coeur atteint,
> Au plus beau des portraits où lui-même il s'est peint.
>   [III: 3]

This is a variation on the traditional syllogism used by Petrarchan poets with reference to neoplatonic fiction (we must adore Beauty, my mistress is beautiful, therefore I must adore her). The theme here is endowed with an exalted quality rarely to be found in love sonnets. The amplitude of the rhythm strikes a chord of solemnity, particularly when a couple of lines end with polysyllables ("éternelles"—"temporelles") or sonorous rhymes ("pareilles"—"merveilles"). The *beautés éternelles* may conjure up the world of Ideas but the "Ciel" clearly refers to the Christian God, "auteur de la nature" and as such, the maker of a "parfaite créature." The ultimate effect of loftiness comes from the reminder that God created man in his own image, after his likeness:

> Au plus des portraits où lui-même il s'est peint.

Having reached these heights, Tartuffe is able to play with the ambiguities of a rich semantic field in order to assimilate human love and religious fervor.

It has often been remarked that Tartuffe uses terms that belong to the vocabulary of religious mysticism such as "infirmité," "tribulations," "béatitude," "quiétude," adjectives such as "bénigne," "suave." These words with their marked degree of abstractedness, their impressive quality of containing a vast network of evasive connotations fit perfectly into the poetic diction of the speech. They also give a powerful and deeply comic enlargement to the attitude of the traditional Petrarchan lover, almost beyond the customary hyperboles, as well as a different coloring to the poetic substance. The unworthiness of the lover reaches the depths of humility with the Christian implication that only grace can save him as he expects nothing "des vains efforts de mon infirmité." The joys he longs for are on a level with the peaceful contemplation of a soul blissfully attuned to its creator. The religious atmosphere which thus subtly permeates the text affects such conventions of love poetry as the deification of the lady and the invincible power of her eyes so that the line

De vos regards divins l'ineffable douceur

while conforming to the topos suggests the mysterious and ambiguously sensual ecstasy of a saint, as portrayed by a baroque artist.

Boileau also takes up the subject of hypocritical devotion with a portrait of the fashionable *directeur de femme* insisting on the kind of advice he gives to one of his flock, the central point of his comforting doctrine being that

Tout est sanctifié par une ame pieuse
[Satire X][3]

All the moral shortcomings of the lady are justified including her fierce greed and ambition to see all her family grabbing the financial and honorific advantages of high offices at court:

Vostre bon naturel en cela pour Eux brille.
Dieu ne nous défend point d'aimer nostre famille.
D'ailleurs tous vos parens sont sages, vertueux.
Il est bon d'empescher ces emplois fastueux,
D'estre donnez peut-estre à des Ames mondaines,
Eprises du neant des vanitez humaines.
[X]

The comic of this complete reversal of moral values is particularly fine in the last two lines where the grand style adds a solemn emphasis to the preposterous casuistry.

A few lines further on the tone becomes somewhat different when we are given the result of this spiritual guidance:

Sa Devote s'incline . . .

. . . .
Sa tranquille vertu conserve tous ses crimes:

Dans un coeur tous les jours nourri du Sacrement
Maintient la vanité, l'orgueil, l'entestement,
Et croit que devant Dieu ses frequens sacrilèges
Sont pour entrer au Ciel d'assurez privilèges.
Voilà le digne fruit des soins de son Docteur.
Encore est-ce beaucoup, si ce Guide imposteur,
Par les chemins fleuris d'un charmant Quiétisme
Tout à coup l'amenant au vray Molinozisme,
Il ne luy fait bien-tost, aidé de Lucifer,
Gouster en Paradis les plaisirs de l'Enfer.

[X]

We are left in no doubt as to the label to affix onto this comic vision of false devotion. The explicit moral condemnation ("crimes," "sacrilèges," etc.), the precise mention of contemporary religious movements, the stark violence of the irony culminating in the brutality of the final paradox: this is barefaced satire. In Molière's *Tartuffe* the satire was incidental as is almost always the case with him. Vices or foibles, even those seemingly of his own times—the excesses of *préciosité,* the rich *parvenu,* or the *faux dévot*—are a point of departure for a more general criticism of life in the form of a comic presentation of the insoluble problems to be found in human nature. The comic of *Tartuffe* does not lie in being a take-off on a contemporary *dévot* (they were more subtly clever than he is) but in the contradiction between his assumed saintly appearance and the only too visible reality of his gluttony and lechery. Moreover Tartuffe is part of a more intricate comic picture in which his maneuvers and utterances light up and conversely are colored by the reactions of the other characters.

Boileau is a satirist. And with satire the alliance of the poetic and the comic faces a particular difficulty. Satire is a hybrid form of the comic. Pure comic to be perceived requires an attitude of detachment which basically seems impossible in the case of satire. The satiric mode tends to bring out in the reader immediate reactions of his sensibility such as disgust, indignation, even painful bitterness and loathing.[4]

Yet with Boileau the perception of the comic is safe. The main subject of his attacks is not one likely to upset the reader's sensibility. Occasionally, as in the satire against women from which I have just quoted a passage, he may treat a conventional topic; however, what he is primarily concerned with is not an aspect of human conduct but a more intellectual problem: the aesthetics of poetry. What he attacks is not men but books, words: not Chapelain the man but Chapelain the poet as in Satire IX. The violence in him takes the form of "la haine d'un sot livre" (IX) and what he has so wittily and rightly called in his preface to Satire XII "une espèce de colère poëtique." This focus undoubtedly implies limitations. The sphere of his satire has nothing in common with that cruel tussle with evil which is the hallmark of great satire. But his singleness of purpose gives him a very special place in the pantheon of formal satire. His achievement can be considered, for the greater part, as an original and remarkable contribution to a very close partnership of the poetic and the comic—poetry being at the same time the tool and the material in producing the comic effect.

The revaluation of Boileau in the second half of the present century has brought to the fore his qualities as a poet and I shall have the pleasure of referring to some aspects of this most stimulating approach.[5] A number of Jules Brody's remarks are especially relevant to the present essay, as when he very finely delineates the kind of response—an active participation—Boileau's text must elicit.[6] This invitation on the poet's part to "collaborate" (to borrow Brody's word) implies both curiosity and sympathy from us. This should be the most rewarding, given the attractive complexity of Boileau's own attitude toward poetry, because for him poetry is fun and is also the most serious thing in the world.

The strict requirements of verse form may appear to him at times the curse of his life:

Maudit soit le premier dont la verve insensée
Dans les bornes d'un vers renferma sa pensée.
[Satire II]

And yet when praising the King's victories in Holland what enjoyment he derives from next to impossible rhymes and from his feigned inability to deal with names in essence unpoetic!

Et qui peut, sans fremir, aborder Woerden,
Quel Vers ne tomberoit au seul nom de Heusden?
Quelle Muse à rimer en tous lieux dispozée
Oseroit approcher des bords du Zuiderzée?
. . . .
Et par tout sur le Whal, ainsi que sur le Leck,
Le vers est en déroute et le poëte à sec.
[Epistre IV]

These last two rhyming monosyllables sound like a sharp tap on the Muse's fingers.

More subtle than this juggling with difficult rhymes is the sustained *jeu poétique* which presides over the fundamentally serious content of Satire IX, and gives it its pattern. The poem is *par excellence* Boileau's apologia for satire. As Maynard Mack has shown in a brilliant essay[7] it is necessary for the satirist to make his ethical position clear and convincing by presenting himself in a favorable light, worthy of being trusted. Hence the importance of the persona he assumes. In Satire IX we witness the acrobatics of the fictitious persona who, endowed with a split personality, embarks on a mock duel from antithetical positions: for or against the right to satirize. The successive twists in the exchange or arguments— some of these cleverly self-defeating—result in a great variety of tones— reproachful, sarcastic, falsely naive, irritated, humble—and multiply through the skillful maneuvers of the duelists the number of thrusts, at times pleasantly unexpected, which directly or indirectly are aimed at the satirist's victims.

The victims are of course the bad poets of the period but the virtuosity of this attack transcends its contemporary character and thus escapes the fate of short-lived topical satire.

Et qui sçauroit sans moi que Cotin a prêché?

A joke but also a prophetic statement. Cotin and the other writers whom Boileau has ridiculed exist for the modern reader as protagonists in a poetic comedy we can appreciate for itself. But if the original features of these personages have faded into a kind of timeless transparency, it remains that, as is the case with Molière, the reader's active response to Boileau's text must take into account the conventions of seventeenth-century literary language. They affect in a rather interesting way the classicist's handling of metaphors.

Here are a few lines from *L'Art Poétique* where Boileau, referring to Scudéry, makes fun of the descriptive technique of an author who never knows when to stop:

S'il rencontre un Palais, il m'en dépeint la face:
Il me promène après de terrasse en terrasse.
Icy s'offre un perron, là règne un corridor,
Là ce balcon s'enferme en un balustre d'or:
Il compte des plafonds les ronds et les ovales,

Ce ne sont que Festons, ce ne sont qu'Astragales.
Je saute vingt feuillets pour en trouver la fin,
Et je me sauve à peine au travers du jardin.

[Chant I]

The passage undoubtedly relies on figurative language for its comic and poetic effect. Paradoxically, the slow, boring reading of a tedious description undergoes a lively transformation. Verbs of motion sketch the haphazard and dull method of the author: chance encounters, leisurely meandering, exhaustive survey of niggling details, and the swift desperate escape of the reader. Inanimate objects acquire a life of their own through the interplay of denotations in verbs like "s'offre" and "règne," the finest semi-personification being that of the "balcon" with the "s'enferme" which suggests a gesture and a mental attitude of proud disdain. All these suggestions are light touches and their rapid succession while stimulating our imagination does not leave us with lasting pictures. We have here that impression of evanescent metaphors to be found as well in other classical writers.[8] The two elements of the narrative, the actual and the imaginary, are nicely fused at the end of the passage in the juxtaposition of the impatient flipping through the pages of a book and the panic-stricken flight through the grounds of the mansion.

The imagery of motion, conspicuous in these lines, plays a very important part in Boileau's poetry.[9] It was perhaps a subtle way for a classicist to re-introduce unobtrusively a concrete element in a literary language which was so cut off from a realistic representation of the world. We find it equally in La Bruyère with a similar comic and poetic value.

We may also notice another paradox in the passage. Although the surcharge of ornaments in the description is ridiculed, the line which expresses such unnecessary sophistication has a sophisticated beauty of its own ("Là ce balcon s'enferme en un balustre d'or") so that even the quotation from Scudéry, inserted almost immediately after, strikes a note of pleasurable luxury, mostly with the sonorous and lovely word *Astragales* which sounds (quite wrongly as far as its etymology and meaning are concerned) like a display of starbursts.

It is not the only time that we find in Boileau the device of incorporating a quotation from another poet into his own text, thus illuminating both with a lateral shaft of light. It may be a quotation from a poet he admires as when the lines he borrows are, at several degrees removed, from Malherbe:

Irai-je dans une Ode, en phrases de Malherbe,
Troubler dans ses roseaux le Danube superbe:
Délivrer de Sion le peuple gemissant;
Faire trembler Memphis, ou paslir le Croissant:
Et passant du Jourdain les ondes alarmées,
Cueillir, mal à propos, *les palmes Idumées?*

[Satire IX]

This is obviously a little dig at Malherbe's slavish imitators, but the verse
retains a Malherbian nobility and the amusing twist at the end sets off
the exotic allusiveness of the Idumaean palms while inviting the reader to
share in the joke of the anticlimax.

Literary borrowings from the classics are another matter. Here too one
has to remember that imitation was still a principle of art in the seventeenth century. The Horatian flavor of a great deal of Boileau's poetry is
well known. Imitation of the classics gave an ennobling patine to a poem.
This could not fail to be an important consideration for him:

Quoyque vous écriviez, évitez la bassesse.
Le stile le moins noble a pourtant sa noblesse.

[Art Poétique I]

He would never allow the comic to debase the poetic language. When we
think of the two traditional genres that established ready-made patterns
for the alliance of the poetic and the comic, it is significant that he did
not choose the burlesque, which he abominated, but its very antithesis,
the mock-heroic, (which raised a subject taken from low life onto a
higher and nobler plane) and composed *Le Lutrin.*[10]

One of the most precious legacies of Greece and Rome was the mythological atmosphere which had been the privileged domain of French
poetry since the Renaissance. Among other advantages, it provided a dec-
orative imagery for the poet's creative process. Boileau finds it useful to
render his own harassing experience of the search for perfect rhythm,
perfect rhymes and rich expressiveness:

Sans cesse poursuivant ces fugitives Fées,
On voit sous Les Lauriers, haleter les Orphées.

[Epistre XI][11]

(These two lines with their seemingly effortless harmony and their sug-
gestive power giving the lie to the implied statement.)

Some of the most obvious mythological figures linked with poetic inspiration were equally convenient for self-mockery; and even more so for satirizing incompetent poets:

Phébus a-t-il pour vous applani le Parnasse?
[Satire IX]

Mythology had lost a great deal of its evocative quality by the time of French classicism. Boileau manages more than once to infuse a breath of life into a world frozen by convention. This he achieves by using once more images of motion but tactfully, with a great lightness of touch, so as not to upset the accepted connotation of the mythological element. This careful process can be seen very clearly in the way he expresses the clumsy attempts of the *poète sans art:*

Sa Muse déreglée, en ses vers vagabonds
Ne s'élève jamais que par sauts et par bonds
[Art Poétique, III]

The incongruous movements of the Muse in her abortive flight upwards are comic but within the harmony of the verse the jerkiness is poetically controlled. Note also that the concrete element is kept in check. The word "déreglée" which qualifies the muse can only apply to an abstraction (for "Muse" read "inspiration"). We move smoothly from abstract to concrete through the "vers vagabonds." As a result of this delicate balance there is no danger of a burlesque picture of the muse.

Elsewhere in the *Art Poétique* a pompous and insensitive poet is ridiculed for metaphorically sounding a clarion in the middle of a gentle eclogue. The effect of this loud discordant noise is rendered by the graceful flight of rustic deities:

De peur de l'écouter, Pan fuit dans les roseaux,
Et les Nymphes d'effroi se cachent sous le eaux.
[II]

Mythology had not lost its charm entirely and could at times give a delicate coloring to Boileau's comic sketches.

When we see the pastoral landscape thus lending its scenery to the comic vision without being debased in any way, we may well think of another poet, English this time, Pope, who also took advantage of the same tradition, mostly in his milder satiric vein.

Here are a few lines devoted to the pretentious garden of a wealthy man:

His Gardens next your admiration call,
On ev'ry side you look, behold the Wall!
No pleasing Intricacies intervene,
No artful wildness to perplex the scene;
Grove nods at grove, each Alley has a brother,
And half the platform just reflects the other.
The suff'ring eye inverted Nature sees,
Trees cut to Statues, Statues thick as trees,
With here a Fountain, never to be play'd,
And there a Summer-house, that knows no shade.
Here Amphitrite sails thro' myrtle bow'rs;
There Gladiators fight, or die, in flow'rs;
Un-water'd see the drooping sea-horse mourn,
And swallows roost in Nilus' dusty Urn.
                    [Epistle IV: ll. 114–26][12]

The comic here might appear as a caricatural description of a garden where everything is wrong, the amusing effect increasing with the enumeration and variety of the examples which testify to false art, including the absurdity of a fountain without water and a useless summerhouse.

The unrelenting symmetry of the landscaping emphasized in several lines by the caesura gives the features of the garden preposterous human attributes (a nod or a brother) and makes its strongest impact with the pattern of line 120 where the mutilation of nature and coarsening of art are translated with superb compactness through the comic inversion of the normal order of things:

Trees cut to Statues, Statues thick as trees,

The placing of the statues—these destined to add the refinement of classical culture to the grounds—is in complete contradiction with the attributes of the figures they represent and may well seem the most grotesque aberration in the design of the park.

And yet I think I was not right in using the word caricatural. This would not take into account the poetic character of the passage which is particularly marked in the last four lines. Strangely, the classical figures by being seen in unexpected surroundings recapture a lost evocative power. Amphitrites appear more lovely, if less conventionally regal, sailing through bowers of myrtle which one thinks should have been destined to Aphrodite. The gladiators, no longer petrified as *Gladiator Pugnans* and *Gladiator Moriens,* assume, even in their dying fall, a lissom grace against a flowery background. The line that depicts the fate of the sea-horse starts with an elegant syntactical inversion and is made to sound as a long, drawn out pathetic plaint and the last line, with its pleasant alliteration and its swallows, brings renewed life to the dusty emptiness of the urn held by the river god.

Here perhaps the response of the modern reader would be to connect in his imagination the charm of the pastoral suggestions with the haunting and subtle beauty of those old, long-neglected formal gardens where fountains are for ever silent and nature has with random artistry invaded what is left of former statuary.

This last remark might suggest that the postromantic reader would more easily find Pope's lines poetic than he would the illustrations from Molière or Boileau I have given. This may be the case. Pope is obviously a very great poet. But we must remember that if English neoclassicism had a great deal in common with French classicism, there were also important differences; for neoclassicism incorporated a much wider tradition. Most important of all, whatever the presence of a poetic diction which Wordsworth was to attack later on, the literary language was not restricted by the limitations inherent in the poetics of seventeenth-century France. A poet could couple the nobility of the grand style with the crisp raciness of a rich vocabulary, as Pope did, for example when satirizing, like Boileau, the boring long-winded writers:

Still humming on, their drouzy course they keep,
And lash'd so long, like tops, are lash'd asleep.
    [*An Essay on Criticism*, ll. 600, 601]

It remains that with Molière and Boileau as with Pope the comic impact with all its nuances is inseparable from the poetic achievement. In the case of these French seventeenth-century writers, the author-reader (or listener) relationship may happen to be a very close one, with a self-effacing attitude on the part of both, given the respect of the first for the poetics of his time and for his audience and, as far as the second is concerned, the willingness to enjoy the *plaisir du texte* according to a certain code.

It does not necessarily follow that all the readers will oblige. I have mentioned some specific reactions of the twentieth-century reader. And my pleasurable response to the word *Astragales* may be an unjustified personal one. But, in spite of some inevitable variations in the way our imagination reacts, the kind of text I have illustrated in this essay keeps the quality of uniqueness in the handling of literary language, characteristic of classicism, which gives it its highly rewarding, if somewhat exacting, appeal.

There was, incidentally, at the same time another French poet whom I have not yet mentioned whose works show in the most exquisite form how subtle the partnership between the comic and poetry could be: La Fontaine.

But that, Best Beloved (if I may so address the Muse of Comedy) is another story.

NOTES

1. See on this point the very interesting essay of Jane P. Tomkins, "The reader in history: the changing shape of literary response," in *Reader-Response Criticism* (Baltimore: The Johns Hopkins University Press, 1980).

2. The quotations from Molière are taken from *Oeuvres Complètes*, 2 vols., ed. R. Jouanny (Paris: Gallimard, 1962).

3. The quotations from Boileau are taken from *Oeuvres Complètes*, ed. Françoise Escal (Paris: Gallimard, 1966).

4. The point is strongly emphasized by Alvin P. Kerman in his essay "A Theory of Satire" in *Modern Essays in Criticism*, ed. R. Paulson (Englewood Cliffs: Prentice-Hall Inc., 1971).

5. Jules Brody and Bernard Beugnot have played a most important part in this revaluation. A useful bibliography as well as a clear historical account of Boileau's fortunes will be found in *Boileau, visages anciens, visages modernes*, Bernard Beugnot and Roger Zuber (Montreal: Presses de l'université de Montréal, 1973). Since then Jules Brody has added to his previous work on Boileau a brilliant paper "Boileau et la critique poétique," *Colloques Internationaux du C.N.R.S.*, No. 557 (Paris, 1974). There has been a very interesting attempt by Gordon Pocock to reach a unifying picture of Boileau in connection with problems of doctrinal attitudes in *Boileau and the Nature of Neo-classicism*, (Cambridge: Cambridge University Press, 1980). Susan W. Tiefenbrun has given an original and lively essay "Boileau and his Friendly Enemy: a Poetics of Satiric Criticism," in *Signs of the Hidden* (Amsterdam: Edition Rodopi, 1980), pp. 115–140.

And it is a great pleasure here to make special mention of two excellent articles by Hugh Davidson: "The Literary Arts of Longinus and Boileau," in *Studies in the Seventeenth Century Literature Presented to Morris Bishop* (Ithaca: Cornell University Press, 1962), pp. 245–62; and "The Idea of Literary History in the *Art Poétique* of Boileau," in *Symposium*, 1964, pp. 264–71.

6. Brody, "Boileau," pp. 240–41.

7. See "The Muse of Satire" in *Modern Essays in Criticism.*

8. I am very much interested in this type of metaphor and in the interplay of abstract and concrete in seventeenth-century literary language and have made some brief comments on the subject in "Quelques paradoxes sur le classicisme," Zaharoff Lecture (Oxford: Clarendon Press, 1981).

9. See the very perceptive remarks of Nathan Edelman on the poetry of motion in Boileau, particularly with reference to Satire IX in "L'Art Poétique: 'Longtemps plaire et jamais ne lasser,'" in *Studies in the Seventeenth Century Literature,* pp. 229–44.

10. *Le Lutrin* deserves more than a passing mention. We are, however, very fortunate to have a recent very good article by Michael Edwards, "A Meaning for Mock-Heroic," in *The Yearbook of English Studies* 15 (1985). The article deals with *The Rape of the Lock* as well as *Le Lutrin* and shows through subtle and convincing analyses how the transformation of the real into poetry operates in both poems.

11. The word was used to mean any fantastic being, including the muses. There is no question of Boileau introducing here an allusion to the national folklore.

12. The quotations from Pope are taken from his *Poetical Works,* ed. Herbert Davis (Oxford: Oxford University Press, 1966).

Corneille, Oedipus, Racine

Terence Cave

Anyone who inserts the name of Oedipus between Corneille and Racine can nowadays hardly help inserting a note of anxiety into what is otherwise a classic and indeed banal parallel. Opposition, even conflict, was of course always there, but in the form of a reassuring antithesis: Corneille Jesuit, Racine Jansenist; Corneille optimistic, Racine pessimistic; Corneille political, Racine psychological; Corneille heroic, Racine passionate; even Corneille boring, Racine interesting. The interference of Oedipus puts the twins, or the father and the son, in an uneasy relation with one another, a relation in which difference and identity are not easily disentangled. Both, in the texts I shall be considering, seem to grapple obscurely and anxiously with a complex topos of poetics, the topos jointly constructed by Aristotle and Sophocles. It is thus in the first instance on their authority—Sophocles' and Aristotle's—rather than Freud's that Oedipus appears in this paper; but by the very nature of the subject, the question of authority will remain an open one.

My point of departure is a simple chronological observation: Corneille's *Oedipe*, published in 1659, was immediately followed (in 1660) by his *Examens* and *Discours,* whereas Racine's first tragedy, *La Thébaïde,* was written only some three years later.[1] The grouping may be accidental, but accidents of that kind invite interpretation. For example, Corneille in his reflections on tragedy writes *against* the Sophoclean *Oedipus* as a paradigm, dissociating himself sharply from Aristotle, yet at precisely the same time he writes his own version; Racine, who as a young playwright must have been acutely aware of the threat posed by Corneille's monumental reputation, chose as his first subject the sequel to the story of Oedipus. At the center of the configuration is the question of tragic recognition (Aristotle's *anagnorisis*) as a theme of poetics with which the story of Oedipus is deeply bound up, and the principal object of this paper is to approach from that angle the rather delicate issue of the relationship between neoclassical theory and practice.[2]

One precautionary remark is needed about the definition of "recognition." In the course of the history of poetics, the term becomes extremely elastic: in fact, the period in question is a crucial test of its elasticity. But it is important to emphasize that the authority of *Oedipus* as Aristotle's chief example as well as in its own right leads virtually all commentators of the sixteenth, seventeenth, and eighteenth centuries to restrict the use of the term primarily to instances where *persons* are recognized: other possibilities, such as the recognition of a state of affairs or of a hidden psychological truth, are only marginally admitted to the canon.[3] It is necessary to make this point, as some of the more influential modern commentaries on the *Poetics* have adopted a far more catholic view,[4] and one therefore risks begging an important historical question, the question of the apparent decline of recognition.

It is not difficult, in fact, to show that neoclassical poetics, in France at least, is uneasy about tragic anagnorisis. D'Aubignac, whose *La Pratique du théâtre* is after all the most substantial and complete treatise of the period, has little to say about the topic except in relation to the question of suspense;[5] Boileau makes no specific reference to recognition in the *Art poétique;* and Dacier, writing in 1692, claims that "Nos Poëtes Tragiques ont peu fait de dénoüemens par la reconnaissance."[6]

Yet the fact remains that spectacular recognitions could draw in the crowds until late in the seventeenth century, as is shown by the notorious success of Thomas Corneille's *Timocrate,* first performed not long before *Oedipe* was written; as another example, one might cite Claude Boyer's *Le Fils supposé,* published in 1672, when Racine was in mid-career. Dacier himself claims that Rotrou's *Venceslas* of 1647 continued to be popular because its recognition scene was technically an improvement on the Sophoclean model.[7]

Such discrepancies and oscillations already suggest a pervasive tension between theory and practice, or indeed within theory and practice. The tension is certainly perceptible in Corneille; the case of Racine is slightly different, since his theoretical writings are marginal in comparison with Corneille's, but the underlying question remains the same: the question on the one hand of a recurrent anxiety about *Oedipus* as a model and, on the other, of the recognitions in which such anxiety seems most critically to be invested.

Corneille's attitude to anagnorisis ("agnition") in his theoretical writings appears to be consistently negative. The one instance in which he allows it as a possibility (a dénouement in which a character may discover that he is of noble birth) is mentioned in the context of comedy. As far as tragedy is concerned, the key passage occurs in the second *Discours*. Having enumerated Aristotle's classes of tragic dénouement (from *Poetics* 14), he notoriously reverses the Aristotelian order of priority, placing the cases in which the character is fully conscious of his deeds and acts openly ("à visage découvert") above those in which he is in ignorance.[8] The result is that recognition plots are relegated to an inferior status, and Corneille goes on to say: "Je sais que l'agnition est un grand ornement dans les tragédies: Aristote le dit; mais il est certain qu'elle a ses incommodités." For Corneille, sustained emotional dilemmas and conflict are preferable to the single outburst afforded by recognition scenes. *Le Cid* and *Rodogune* are far more moving than *Oedipus*.[9]

The phrase "á visage découvert" is an interesting one in that it recalls the romance tradition of knights in disguise rather than the tradition of poetics. It certainly illustrates the extent to which Corneille's critical language attempts to excise what is covert or hidden, what is not the object of conscious knowledge. One could illustrate the same point in relation to his treatment of *hamartia*: he knows the word can mean "error," but he excludes this reading in favor of a moral one, which has the further effect of separating hamartia from anagnorisis.[10] The question of tragic ignorance or knowledge seems to be marginal for Corneille, in his theoretical writings at least.

The consequence, when it comes to Oedipus, is that a good deal in the paradigm is rejected, treated abrasively, or suppressed. What is rejected first of all is contrivance: Sophocles' play is mentioned as an example of how the ancients, in their recognition scenes, made use of an extraneous character appearing fortuitously, an error which Corneille says he has corrected in his version; he also speaks of the way he has tidied up the story of Oedipus' killing of Laïus and other implausibilities. These are of course problems arising from the need to sustain and motivate Oedipus' ignorance. In more general terms, Corneille treats very gingerly the question of the horror of the play, its monstrous transgressions. In his discussion of catharsis, he points out that no spectator of *Oedipus* would "craindre de tuer son père ou d'épouser sa mère"; the play would be more likely to purge the desire to have recourse to predictions, since these may make us fall into the very misfortune we seek to avoid.[11] This is the first time that Oedipus' patricide and incest are explicitly referred to in the *Discours,* and Corneille wraps them up in a kind of pre-Voltairean joke. In the *Examen,* he remarks that he has suppressed the horror of the subject:

Je tremblai quand je l'envisageai de près. Je reconnus que ce qui avait passé pour merveilleux en leurs siècles [sc. ceux de Sophocle et de Sénèque] pourrait sembler horrible au nôtre; que cette éloquente et sérieuse description de la manière dont ce malheureux prince se crève les yeux, qui occupe tout leur cinquième acte, ferait soulever la délicatesse de nos dames, dont le dégoût attire aisément celui du reste de l'auditoire; et qu'enfin, l'amour n'ayant point de part en cette tragédie, elle était dénuée des principaux agréments qui sont en possession de gagner la voix publique.[12]

What Corneille perceived when he looked at it closely, then, was that the horror of Oedipus' recognition exceeded the bounds of contemporary taste. It is no doubt worth noting that, while claiming that the play is defective in love interest, Corneille succeeds in omitting any reference to Oedipus' incest. The blinding, which Corneille treats as if it were (again) a kind of embarrassing joke, serves perhaps as a metaphorical substitute for sexual wounding. The other topic that is visibly missing is recognition itself:[13] the plotting of monstrous ignorance and the threat of unspeakable transgressions are both relegated to the margins, hidden from the delicate view of the audience. In his theoretical writing, Corneille attempts to tackle Oedipus and his problems *à visage découvert,* but only at the cost of averting his gaze.

One might well ask why Corneille wrote *Oedipe* at all, given his strictures on both the form and the subject of the classical model. It seems likely that his preoccupation with poetics at this stage in his career led him to undertake an exercise which, like much of his theoretical writing, pays homage to Aristotelian authority while marking a critical difference from it: Nadal is I think right to point out that *Oedipe* is a critique of *Oedipus.*[14] On the other hand, there was also a demand for the subject: Fouquet commissioned the play, giving Corneille a choice of three possible subjects, and the King subsequently rewarded him for his work. Given the status and stature of Corneille, the very existence of the play implies a desire on the part of contemporary audiences to see the monster paraded again on the stage, decked out in *agréments* which hide his bleeding eyes and his sexual misdemeanours.

This desire was both acknowledged and (predictably) deplored by d'Aubignac in his 1663 *Dissertation* on *Oedipe.*[15] D'Aubignac returns almost obsessively to the impropriety of imposing on the audience an action reeking of incest and parricide, accompanying this with an equally predictable attack on the wholesale lack of plausibility in the plot (the implausibility is of course once again located in the continued ignorance of Oedipus and other characters). He recognizes that Corneille has tried to "rectify" the errors of Sophocles in this respect, but takes the view (as Voltaire will also) that he has only tinkered with the surface, leaving all the main problems intact. What d'Aubignac in fact does in this polemical document is to magnify Corneille's own strictures and thus display more prominently a difficulty which is already inherent in the project of rewriting *Oedipus* in mid-seventeenth-century France. D'Aubignac's censorship is the sign of an anxiety which he shares with Corneille; their difference, in the sense of *différend,* is produced by a concealed identity.

Oedipe is in various ways an oddity in Corneille's dramatic output, almost a *hapax.* Written after a period of seven years in which Corneille had produced no writings for the theatre, *Oedipe* emerges from the silence, a circumstance which lends it a no doubt spurious air of mystery. Yet it is possible to discern a group of earlier experiments having something like a "recognition plot" and belonging to the phase of Corneille's career immediately preceding the silence. I am thinking here in particular of *Héraclius* and *Don Sanche,* in which both the recognition structure and the Oedipal themes of parricide and incest are used uneasily, critically, with embarrassment as it were: censorship and seduction alternate in their themes and presentation. They are also examples of generic uncertainty, mingling questions of classical poetics with materials from tragicomedy and romance.

A more detailed treatment of these plays is not possible within the compass of the present study.[16] For reasons that will become apparent later, it is, however, necessary to make a brief excursion still further back in Corneille's career, to *Rodogune*. Corneille classed *Rodogune* as a play in which the tragic deed is undertaken consciously, no doubt because Cléopâtre knows perfectly well what she is doing. The classification, however, fails to account for certain central aspects of the play. Although its subject is nonclassical, it is distinctly reminiscent of the classical family plot: there are echoes, for example, of *Medea* and the *Oresteia*, and parricide is an ever-present possibility realized in the murder of Séleucus.[17] More particularly, these elements are conjugated with a plotting dependent on uncertainties, on the withholding of knowledge: Rodogune refuses to say which twin she prefers; the death of Séleucus places Antiochus between two women either of whom may be guilty; and the issue of primogeniture—which of the twins has the marginally superior right to the throne?—hovers unresolved over the whole plot. From the beginning of the play, these elements are explicitly placed in relation to a textual memory: Séleucus reminds his twin that, being rivals in both love and political ambition, they risk repeating the disasters of Thebes and Troy, tragedy and epic. More specifically, the allusion to Thebes recalls the story of the twin sons of Oedipus, Eteocles and Polynices; it thus provides the exact counterpart of the resolute friendship of the twins, which withstands their double rivalry and the attempts of Cléopâtre to make trouble between them.[18] The memory of Thebes is a memory of Oedipus, and of *Oedipus Rex,* a memory which *Rodogune* is already trying to rectify.

D'Aubignac, in his *Dissertation,* was the first to make in public the perhaps all-too-obvious point on which most of the following discussion of *Oedipe* is based, namely, the splitting of the plot between the love-episode and the Oedipal episode. D'Aubignac goes so far as to say that what one would nowadays call the "romance" element—the ultimately happy love-affair between Thésée and Dircé—supplies the main plot, with the story of Oedipus and his recognition serving only as a secondary episode.[19] This duality or split epitomizes the problem of the play as an attempt to rectify or evade the monstrosities of the Sophoclean version. By regarding it as a simple error, which could have been overcome either by greater dramatic skill or—better—by complete censorship, d'Aubignac remains trapped in what one might call the politics of evasion. In repeating the analysis (and it is, in part at least, a repetition), I would hope to show that the error is a complex one, in the sense that Corneille's play itself draws on and thematizes a difficulty which Corneille explicitly recognized in his theoretical writings. The "confusion" which is produced by the generic and structural ambivalence of *Oedipe* is not an accidental but an intrinsic effect, and in this sense the play already goes beyond d'Aubignac's strictures.

The play opens, flamboyantly enough, with romance: Dircé, daughter of Laïus and Jocaste, exhorts her lover Thésée to leave Thebes before he is struck down by the plague. The Oedipal question itself is not fully raised until I.5, where the oracle is reported to have refused to speak, thus giving rise to uncertainty and anxiety among the characters. From this point on, the plot is sustained by a series of false inferences and thus false recognitions. In II.3, the ambiguous reply of Laïus' ghost is at once taken by everyone to mean that Dircé will have to be sacrificed to lay the ghost (i.e., the name of Dircé is recognized as the solution to the riddle posed by the metonym "mon sang" in the oracular speech of the ghost). In III.4, Oedipe reports a rumor that Jocaste's exposed infant survived; Thésée now pronounces himself the son of Laïus and hence the brother of Dircé, much to Jocaste's surprise (line 1183: "Quoi! vous seriez mon fils?"). In IV.4, Jocaste, then Oedipe, discover that Oedipe is the murderer of Laïus, the story of the robbers having been shown to be a fiction. The guilt is now divided, it seems, between Oedipe and Thésée (1546: "Je suis le parricide, et ce fils est l'inceste"), although Thésée has already admitted to Dircé, and thus to the audience, that he himself started the rumor as a ruse to prevent her from becoming the victim. Finally, in V.2–3, with the arrival of the messenger from Corinth, the various pieces of the story come together and full recognition is achieved.

The first thing to note here is that recognitions proliferate, initially at least, in order to imprint their mark on the love-intrigue. The balance only gradually swings from the note of heroic offers of self-sacrifice (from Dircé and Thésée) towards the blinding of Oedipe. Meanwhile, the relationship between these generically different elements remains an awkward one, and is marked as such when, in III.4, Oedipe first shows signs of serious anxiety: he remarks that, having previously wanted to prevent the lovers' marriage, by force if necessary, he now—"sans savoir pourquoi"—would like them to go away and consummate their passion "loin de [s]a vue," out of sight and out of mind. "J'admire," he says, "un changement si confus que le mien" (1048), as well he might.

Such moments, where textual tensions are exhibited in the anxiety of characters, recur later in the play: the imperfect accommodation of dark desires and monstrous acts with fragments of a romance discourse is in an important sense what *Oedipe* is "about." Around this central uncertainty may be grouped other signs of displacement and would-be rectification, beginning with the passages which remove or supplement Sophoclean "defects" such as the story of the several robbers who are said to have killed Laïus (see IV. 2). These passages are the direct echo within the play of Corneille's theoretical strictures, functioning as a rectification of the logic of Sophocles' version.

The term "rectification" in cases like this is however equivocal, since the trace of commentary designed to erase the play's implausibilities creates new tensions, skewing the text in sometimes surprising ways. One of these is the move by which Oedipe's title to the throne—his ability to solve the riddle of the Sphinx—is demoted by Dircé to the level of mere wit: "J'ai vu ce peuple ingrat que l'énigme surprit / Vous payer assez bien d'avoir eu de l'esprit" (451–52). Voltaire would have appreciated the joke; so, no doubt, would Freud. It might appear to be only a local instance, but the same satirical note is evident elsewhere, particularly in certain passages where the implied motivation of *Oedipus Rex* is called into question. Every time the possibility of a recognition—however spurious—comes into view, the character concerned hastens to motivate her or his "crime." Dircé accuses herself of being the occasion for Laïus' death (643–55). Thésée accepts the mild imputation of unwitting and unconsummated incest with his "sister" but cannot swallow the monstrous allegation that he has killed his "father" (1198–1200); he also argues that anyone ought to be able to recognize a king, even one disguised as a peasant, so that ignorance is no excuse (1348–50).

In these ways, the problem of Oedipus' error and punishment is scathingly explored by the characters in the play, much as if they were personifications of an issue in poetics. The most flamboyant instance is undoubtedly Thésée's tirade at the end of Act III in favour of free will and moral responsibility as against arbitrary predestination: the kind of fatality normally associated with the case of Oedipus is repudiated, again with scorn (1167: "D'un tel aveuglement daignez me dispenser"). As a representative of romance and its habit of poetic justice, Thésée inevitably comes into conflict with the topoi of tragedy. Thésée, however, has a right to complain, since he is a character from another kind of fiction who suddenly finds himself without a passport in the troubled lands of tragedy. Oedipe is a displaced person in a rather different sense: however the play is rewritten, he cannot rid himself of his transgressions or of the expiation they require, so that the tension and the anxiety in his case are self-evidently greater.

One might first note that his culpability is established in advance by other characters in various ways—once again, the mania for motivation. Thésée's argument about the obligation to recognize kings at all times whatever their guise clearly covers Oedipus' case; Dircé, disapproving of his consultation of the dead, associates this "insolence" with his tyrannical behavior toward the whole family of Laïus, accuses him of usurping the throne, and predicts that the dead will punish him for his violence and the gods for his impieties (553–60).

Despite this evidence, Dacier was to claim that Corneille's Oedipe failed to answer to the Aristotelian *juste milieu* because he is a virtuous man who falls into misfortune. This view is no doubt a consequence of

Oedipe's reaction to the recognition of his guilt, which closely corresponds to Thésée's speech on free will (1820–40, 1988–94). When Oedipe finds out who he is and what he has done, he disowns his crime and
thus turns recognition into a scandal, a meaningless error, to be faced out
with stoic constancy and contempt: to put it in another way, hamartia
reverts here to the sense of "error" (see for example 1919), and thus,
according to Corneille's own theory, loses all claim to meaning. There is
in fact a major shift in the *ethos* of Oedipe in the course of the play: he
begins by behaving like a standard Cornelian tyrant and usurper and
ends by behaving like a standard Cornelian hero. In *Héraclius,* the tyrant
Phocas can be done away with, leaving the characters to sort out the
problem of identity to their own satisfaction. But Oedipe is another matter: he can't simply be ejected from the plot. So Dircé in the end has to
take back everything she had earlier said about his tyrannical behaviour
and claim that she had said it *à contre-coeur* anyway (1799–1812). Indeed, it rather neatly proves to be the case that if Oedipe is the son of
Laïus, he is the rightful king of Thebes, not a tyrant and usurper: he goes
out complaining of the tyranny of the *gods* (1991–94), so the irony can
hardly be overlooked.

Oedipe, then, loses a voluntary guilt and acquires an involuntary one
for which he can therefore disclaim responsibility. What is recognized, in
this sense, is that Oedipe is a hero like Thésée:

> Mon souvenir n'est plein que d'exploits généreux,
> Cependant je me trouve inceste et parricide,
> Sans avoir fait un pas que sur les pas d'Alcide,
> Ni recherché partout que lois à maintenir
> Que monstres à détruire et méchants à punir.
>   (1820–24)

By a curious twist in this notoriously twisting plot, Oedipe shows himself
to be entitled to cross the boundary into tragicomedy and romance, the
land of heroic monster-killers. The moment at which he begins to cross it
can be exactly pinpointed: it is the moment referred to earlier when he
mysteriously changes his mind about Thésée and Dircé and wishes them
safe and sound from the contamination of Thebes. He begins at that moment to feel a nostalgia for romance.

All this could be stated in terms not only of Corneille's hesitations and
defensiveness but also of the way the audience might be expected to react

to textual memories. To speak of the characters as if they personally had feelings on the matter is of course simply a convenient fiction (although it's true that the best fictions are usually the convenient ones). The play engineers an accommodation between the romance plot and the Oedipal plot: the unacceptable face of the Oedipal recognition has to be disguised or repudiated, compensation being provided by the *éclat* of heroic discourse, the appeal of *admiration*.

Despite the showy Cornelian "miracle" of the last scene, the mixture remains an uneasy one, the sign of a profound difficulty in the rewriting of the master-text. Knowledge may be re-established through recognition and a schema for its interpretation may be imposed; yet the question of knowledge remains problematic as the curtain falls. After Thésée's confident pronouncement that there can no longer be any doubt about the choice of a victim by the gods, Dircé gloomily adds: "Un autre ordre demain peut nous être donné" (2007). Consequently, an element of doubt hovers over the ending, a doubt which seems to point proleptically toward the story of Oedipus' progeny, toward the yet unwritten *La Thébaïde*. It is also not difficult to show that the criteria which characters use to determine the truth in the course of the action are all uncertain or fallible. Nature speaks through "le sang," and may retrospectively be seen to be right, but it doesn't speak clearly enough to prevent Oedipe from killing Laïus or marrying Jocaste, or to enable Jocaste to be quite certain Thésée isn't her son. *Raison* allows some distinctions to be made and some positions secured, but it is constantly undermined by states of confusion, passion and desire, and all too easily ramifies into spurious logic and false inference. Corneille makes virtually no use of the themes of blindness and insight characteristic of *Oedipus Rex,* but "obscurité," "confusion" and other vocabulary of this kind circulates throughout the play. Dircé herself, despite her commitment to uncontaminated romance values, is seduced by the sexual ambiguities of the Oedipal plot:

> L'amour pour les sens est un si doux poison,
> Qu'on ne peut pas toujours écouter la raison.
> Moi-même, en qui l'honneur n'accepte aucune grâce,
> J'aime en ce douteux sort tout ce qui m'embarrasse,
> Je ne sais quoi m'y plaît qui n'ose s'exprimer,
> Et ce confus mélange a de quoi me charmer.
>
> (1255–60)

The 'confus mélange' is in fact a temptation that all the characters—and surely the audience—find hard to resist, shocking as that no doubt seemed to d'Aubignac.

In these ways, the play seeks constantly but unsuccessfully to disguise its own transgressions. Generic transgressions: the mingling of romance and tragedy; transgressions of *ethos*: the figure of the usurper first becomes confused and then turns into a hero; transgressions of *bienséance*: Corneille's decision to unveil the monster before a polite but distinctly interested audience. In the end, the naturalization of the acceptable yet seductive master-plot actually draws attention to the means by which it is naturalized, creating an unease which can't be erased (as the so-called errors of Sophocles might be erased) from the tragic recognition. *Oedipe* betrays the anxiety of a text confused about its title and origins, a text groping for an identity and finding only difference.

In several senses, Racine's first tragedy was composed in the shadow of Oedipus. Its subject is the fatal enmity of the twin sons of Oedipus and Jocasta; its action, like that of *Andromaque,* is the reverberation of a disaster which has already become notorious. The play is preceded, *extra fabulam,* by the paradigm of all recognitions: its action is saturated, thematically and diegetically, with knowledge of Oedipus' transgressions. The presence of Jocasta alone, resurrected from the noose of *Oedipus Rex,* would be enough to ensure this effect, since Jocasta is herself knowledge incarnate. All the transgressions have passed through her body, and in Racine's version she is not inclined to let the other characters (or the audience) forget it. References to her womb and breast are insistent to a degree matched by neither Euripides nor Rotrou—Racine's principal models.[20] So, for example, the mutual hatred of Eteocles and Polynices is in Racine's version exclusively congenital: in Euripides' version, it was at least in part brought on by Oedipus' curse, to which there is no reference in *La Thébaïde.* More strikingly still, for the first time in Racine's play the brothers are *twins,* already fighting before they left their mother's womb. Or at least they become twins in a late variant (four lines added in 1697):[21] Racine brings out in retrospect a symmetry or identity which can be regarded as latent in the first version. Despite what Jules Brody says about the moral superiority of Polynice,[22] it seems to me in fact that Racine has made the brothers much less different than they are in either Euripides or Rotrou. They appear, especially with the endorsement of the variant, as identical twins, and like other identical twins, they perfectly and absolutely *know* one another, except that their likeness is manifest in hatred, in their *différend*: they reach agreement only on the decision to fight to the death in single combat.[23]

In the face of this flood-tide of knowledge, there seems little room for the uncertainties and enigmas that compose the recognition plot. Certainly no contemporary critic or theorist would have dreamt of using the term anagnorisis in connection with this play. Corneille himself could not have complained that Racine's characters act any less *à visage découvert* than the characters of his own plays. Yet knowledge is still a question in *La Thébaïde,* and the question is raised already by the decision in I. 3 to consult the gods, which leads to the quotation of an ambiguous oracle in II. 2. Predictable as this oracle and its ambiguity may be, the device is exploited structurally by Racine in a way that is much closer to *Oedipus Rex* (or *Oedipe*) than to *The Phoenician Women* or Rotrou's *Antigone,* in both of which the function of the oracle is local and episodic. The characters—in particular Jocaste and Antigone—are led at a crucial point (Act III) to believe erroneously that the oracle has been fulfilled by the voluntary, heroic death of Ménécée, who seems to have paid the price of all sins and all crimes; it also gives Créon the chance to pretend that he has been converted by the death of his son, and thus to foster Jocaste's illusion that the meeting of her sons will heal the rift.

In this way, the play is plotted towards a climactic and decisive scene (IV. 3) which Russell Pfohl has confidently (rather over-confidently for my taste) called a "magnificent recognition scene."[24] It begins with Jocaste triumphantly proposing a reconciliation and ends with her renouncing natural maternal affection. The twins meet not in order to recognize one another, to discover that they *are* twins (as in the *Comedy of Errors*), but to disclose irrevocably their enmity. Jocaste nevertheless, in her opening speech, invites them to recognize one another as brothers, as if they had forgotten or were ignorant of the fact. This gesture shows that the lapse in her knowledge is due not only to oracular indirection but also to a nostalgia—even in this context—for the natural and the plausible.[25]

The Oedipal plot, then, is not present in *La Thébaïde* as an inquisition or a guessing-game or a perpetual riddle-solving narrative. It appears as the last delusive glimmer of the possibility that the monstrous might be staved off; or, more accurately perhaps, of the constant desire to avert one's gaze from an intolerable breakdown of the conventions that make the world comprehensible. Oedipus, master and victim of the inquisitorial plot, had similarly averted his gaze from the evidence presented to him by Tiresias and others, as Racine in his notes on Sophocles' play had himself observed.[26]

La Thébaïde is in this sense the inversion of a recognition play; the meeting of Eteocles and Polynices is the identical yet opposite twin of anagnorisis. The difference between the brothers is, as Rotrou if not Racine keeps reminding one, a *différend*, a conflict which cannot be resolved by appeal to a higher authority. There are no higher authorities in the post-Oedipal world, only predators like Créon who wait for their adversaries to destroy one another. Indeed, one might well be tempted to accept Poulet's view that Créon is the central figure in *La Thébaïde*, the figure who attempts to efface the past (the story of Oedipus, the death of his own sons) in order to become an absolute and arbitrary authority in the present:[27] in this sense, he repeats the ethos of Oedipe as tyrant and usurper, but sustains it throughout the play. His ambition, too, will collapse (it is after all the kind of ambition for which collapse is an ever-present possibility), so that anomy prevails both politically and epistemologically; the question of knowledge is fractured and scattered throughout the action. The Oedipal plot, which in Aristotle and Sophocles is phrased as an ignorance ultimately supplanted by knowledge, operates in reverse. The monstrous is already known, and its presence can now only be called into question again in the form of a fitful nostalgia for ignorance.

One may at this point revert to the Corneille–Racine parallel by citing Bénichou's rather curious contention that *La Thébaïde* is written predominantly in the Cornelian mode.[28] It is certainly true that Racine tackles Corneille on his own ground, but it looks rather as if the similarity is chosen expressly in order to bring about a difference. Indeed, the intertextual *lice* provided by *Oedipus* and its aftermath could hardly be more precisely circumscribed. So, for example, in her attempts to persuade Polynice to hold off, Jocaste—desperately averting her gaze—urges him to go and prove his status as a hero elsewhere:

> Soyez, mon Fils, soyez l'ouvrage de vos mains.
> Par d'illustres exploicts couronnez vous vous-mesme,
> Qu'un superbe laurier soit vostre Diadéme;

Regnez & triomphez, & joignez à la fois
La gloire des Heros à la Pourpre des Roys.
      (1266–70; 1697 ed. 1138–42)

Don Sanche might have taken the point, but not Polynice, who dismisses Jocaste's suggestion as "chimères." The irrelevance of heroism is in fact one of the principal things the play seems to be about: it is instructive and even diverting to watch Racine demolishing heroes so efficiently in 1663. Ménécée goes first, a paragon of innocence and virtue, sacrificing himself uselessly to a misreading of the oracle (in Euripides, his suicide did in fact guarantee the peace of Thebes; in Racine, the gods meant something else, although of course they were after Ménécée, too). He is followed in due course by his brother Hémon, who on the instructions of Antigone tries to separate the twins in their final combat: if one were to pursue the game of personifications, he could be said to represent gaze aversion, the unwillingness to accept that hereditary kinks can never be straightened out by a normal clean-living youth. The good brothers destroy themselves like the bad brothers, only a bit sooner.

So much for heroes. In a preface written some twelve years after the play, Racine expressed regret at having allowed love-interest to intervene in such a bloody story.[29] The remark sounds like a delayed riposte to Corneille's claim that *Oedipus* was a subject sadly deficient in love-interest; likewise, if the Antigone-Hémon episode "imitates" the Dircé-Thésée episode, it does so *à contre-coeur*, reversing its sense. In *La Thébaïde*, love and heroism go under hand in hand, whereas in *Oedipe* they survive the contamination of knowledge.

A further feature of the parallel is the presence in both plays of passages embodying critical reflection on the themes and motivation of *Oedipus Rex*. Alongside the examples I have already given from Corneille, one might place Jocaste's speech in III. 2 on the scandal of divine injustice, which works in much the same way as a defensive preface. Racine, like Corneille, is aware of the difficulties of the paradigm, and the embarrassment shows. But whereas in *Oedipe* the defensive move alters the whole course of the dénouement, in *La Thébaïde* the questions raised by such passages remain suspended as the action progressively and ruthlessly eliminates all the characters. The scandal, in Racine, is allowed to run its course.

Finally, in drafting the "twin" motif into *La Thébaïde*, Racine neatly

inverts the terms of *Rodogune:* the textual memory of Thebes which Corneille's play evokes and then attempts to rectify is resurrected in its most
anxiety-ridden form, and will be rehearsed by Racine in *Britannicus, Ba-
jazet* and *Mithridate,* all plays concerning murderous rivalry between
brothers.[30]

In such ways, the textual engagement of *La Thébaïde* with *Oedipe*
already displays a mythical symmetry which will recur in later phases of
the combat between Corneille and Racine: *Britannicus* exactly inverts the
imperial theme of *Cinna,* while the story of the twin versions of *Bérénice*
is too well known to need repeating here (except to note that there too
the question of primogeniture is unresolved). The elaboration of "parallels" between Corneille and Racine, from La Bruyère to Barnwell, has
enshrined the symmetry—or at least the antithesis—as a critical commonplace, so that it becomes easy to rephrase it. One could say, for example, without too great a risk of hyperbole, that the rivalry and enmity
of the two dramatists are already figured in the story of Eteocles and
Polynices as Racine rewrites it; or that, in removing representatives of
effective authority, Racine's play attempts to erase Corneille's monumental reputation; or again, conversely, that Racine himself renewed for Corneille the threat of *Oedipus.* However one puts it, Oedipus always seems
to intrude between Corneille and Racine, turning the parallel into an
episode and its indeterminate sequels. These critical myths represent no
immediate historical reality, although one could no doubt construct a
historical context for them.[31] Nor can the somewhat asymmetrical parallel I have been drawing be said to lay bare the psyches of the playwrights—Corneille and Racine are here always used as labels for groups
of plays and other writings. The mythical parallel in this case has what is
primarily a heuristic value in sketching out the figure of a complex intertextual relation: the relation between *Oedipe* and *La Thébaïde;* between
Racinian tragedy and Cornelian tragedy; between instances of poetics
and instances of dramatic practice; and between the modern corpus and
the ancient corpus.

At the center of this construction, what is at issue is the articulation in
tragedy of something called knowledge. Something *called* knowledge because it attracts the rhetoric and the vocabulary of inquiry, uncertainty
and recognition, but leaves the object of knowledge always in some measure in abeyance. Tragedy doesn't and can't answer questions; but in
Sophocles' *Oedipus* it presents the mirage of an answer to a question so

persistent that it can't be avoided. Ever since Aristotle framed *Oedipus* as the paradigm of tragedy, and thus made recognition itself a central question in poetics, the mirage has continued to be reflected and refracted in the rival discourses of tragedy and poetics. One of the consequences is that *Oedipus* has become impossible to rewrite. Later versions already know too much, whether directly or through poetics (those two routes being barely distinguishable). Racine and Corneille, like Eteocles and Polynices, know all too well, in one sense, what they are doing; they agree in advance on the impossibility of recognition tragedy, so that their fight to the death with each other and with the master-text takes place *à visage découvert.*

On the other hand, the intervention of Oedipus or of *Oedipus Rex* always casts a shadow, the shadow of what cannot, despite all repetitions and reformulations, quite be said. In this sense, the aftermath of *Oedipus*—Euripides, Rotrou, Corneille, Racine, *et bien d'autres encore*—may be imagined as a series of ricochets, or as the ever-increasing débris of a chain reaction. Or again, it could be described as the interminable retelling of a story which will always retain a margin of secrecy, despite the apparent answering of the Oedipal question in the authorized version of Sophocles.

What I mean in this context by saying that the story always retains a margin of secrecy, or by speaking of the shadow of something that can't quite be said, is that it is impossible to assign a definitive content to the knowledge such plays seek unsuccessfully to conceal and to reveal. The truth brought to light by Oedipus and his progeny is not an ethical or a metaphysical scandal, though themes of that kind may surface in the plays; it is not an authentic self, stripped at last of its masks and self-deceptions; it is not a transcendent Hegelian synthesis; nor is it a repressed desire to kill the father and have sex with the mother. These predicates are all pretexts invented plausibly by and for each cultural milieu in which the question is posed. I am tempted to suggest that, in the current cultural milieu, the predicate might best be described as a hoax: Oedipus discovering that he's been taken for a ride, though a very long and absorbingly interesting one.

There seems in any event to be little point in trying retrospectively to lay down the law for the "true" paradigm of recognition. I have been using the word "paradigm" all along in connection with *Oedipus Rex,* for reasons that are self-evident, but it is now time—high time, at the last moment—to question that assumption. The trick worked by Sophocles could perhaps only work once, despite Aristotle's inveterate habit of moving to the universal from the particular; *Oedipus Rex* would then not be a paradigm but a *hapax*. If that view is accepted, all of its progeny are doomed to endless particularity and to endlessly unresolved conflict. Oedipal tragedy and Oedipal poetics become the joint search for a recognition which always comes too soon (Oedipus got there first) or too late (we've added it ourselves).

NOTES

1. Other dates, in a more detailed analysis, would rapidly present themselves: Thomas Corneille's *Timocrate* (1656–57); d'Aubignac's *La Pratique du théâtre* (1657) and—in particular—his *Dissertation sur Oedipe* (1663) (see below).

2. The configuration of texts studied here is discussed in relation to the question of simplicity of plot (and thus the question of poetics) by H. T. Barnwell, *The Tragic Drama of Corneille and Racine: an old parallel revisited* (Oxford: Clarendon Press, 1982), pp. 134–37.

3. An interesting exception is J.-F. Sarasin's *Discours de la tragédie* (1639). Sarasin claims that the moral illumination of Tyridate in Scudéry's *L'Amour tyrannique* meets the requirements of Aristotelian anagnorisis.

4. A striking and influential example is provided by F. L. Lucas, *Tragedy: serious drama in relation to Aristotle's 'Poetics'* (London: Chatto and Windus, 1981) (first published 1928), p. 113, note 1: "We associate the word too closely with the narrow sense of discovering a *person's* identity, whereas *anagnorisis* may equally well signify the discovery of *things* unknown before." The point becomes crucial in relation to E. Vinaver's widely accepted hypothesis that Racine consciously shifts the sense of anagnorisis from a material to a psychological level (*Racine et la poésie tragique*, 2nd ed. [Paris: Nizet, 1963], chaps. 6 and 7). For a general account of "peripety and discovery" in the tragedies of Corneille and Racine, see Barnwell, *Tragic Drama*, chap. VI. John A. Stone, *Sophocles and Racine* (Geneva: Droz, 1964), stresses the importance for Racine of the Sophoclean intertext, and in particular of Sophoclean "scenes of revelation"; the relationship between these and Aristotelian anagnorisis is however not elucidated.

5. D'Aubignac, *La Pratique du théâtre*, ed. P. Martino (Algiers and Paris: Champion, 1927), pp. 95, 134, 274, 295.

6. A. Dacier, *La Poétique d'Aristote . . . Traduite en françois, avec des remarques critiques sur tout l'ouvrage* (Paris: Claude Barbin, 1692), p. 155.

7. Ibid., p. 226.

8. P. Corneille, *Oeuvres complètes*, ed. A. Stegmann (Paris: Seuil [L'Intégrale], 1963), pp. 833–34.

9. Ibid., p. 834(b). Corneille actually says that Chimène and Antiochus

arouse stronger feelings than the character Oedipe in his own version of *Oedipus: Oedipe* as a whole may be more moving, but only because of the pathos of Dircé's situation. It may be inferred from this analysis that Sophocles' *Oedipus,* having no character equivalent to Dircé, cannot compete with *Le Cid* and *Rodogune* in this respect.

10. Ibid., p. 831(b). The exclusion of the reading "error" ("une simple erreur de méconnaissance"), which throws doubt on *Oedipus* as a tragic paradigm, flows from Corneille's moral interpretation of catharsis.

11. Ibid., p. 832(b).

12. Ibid., p. 567.

13. Unless one sees it displaced into Corneille's own "recognition" of the horror of the subject ("je reconnus que . . .").

14. O. Nadal, *Le Sentiment de l'amour dans l'oeuvre de Pierre Corneille* (Paris: Gallimard, 1948), pp. 236–37.

15. The *Dissertation* may be found in vol. 2 of F. Granet, *Recueil de dissertations sur plusieurs tragédies de Corneille et de Racine* (Paris: Gissey and Bordelet, 1739).

16. I have suggested a reading of *Héraclius* in "Recognition and the reader," *Comparative Criticism,* 2, ed. E. S. Shaffer, Cambridge University Press, 1980, pp. 56–62. A more extended treatment of the topic as a whole is provided in my book *Recognitions: A Study in Poetics* (Oxford: Clarendon Press, 1988). Oxford University Press has kindly given permission for me to reproduce materials from the book in the present essay, which was originally expected to appear before the book was published.

17. On the classical intertext of *Rodogune* and *Nicomède,* and the constraints imposed by the *bienséances* on the representation of parricide, see Corneille's second *Discours* (*Oeuvres complètes,* pp. 836–37).

18. *Rodogune,* lines 169–200.

19. See *Dissertation,* pp. 40ff. The point is also made by Nadal and Barnwell. The notion of "rectification," to which I revert below, is insistent in d'Aubignac's discussion of Corneille's adaptation of the Oedipus story (see for example *Dissertation,* pp. 17, 21).

20. A detailed account of the textual relationship between *La Thébaïde,* Euripides' *The Phoenician Women,* Rotrou's *Antigone* and other plays is given by R. C. Knight, *Racine et la Grèce* (Paris: Editions Contemporaines, n.d.), pp. 248–63. See also Jules Brody, "Racine's *Thébaïde:* an analysis," *French Studies* 13 (1959): pp. 199–213; Brody is dismissive of any significant connection between *La Thébaïde* and Corneille's tragedies.

21. M. Edwards, *La Thébaïde de Racine: clé d'une nouvelle interprétation de son théâtre* (Paris: Nizet, 1965), p. 160. The relevant lines are 1017–22 in the first edition, 917–26 in the 1697 edition (in almost no other case did Racine *add* lines in the later versions). Knight, Edwards and other commentators appear not to have noticed this significant tightening of the fraternal relationship; for Edwards' commentary on the variant, see pp. 83–84.

22. Brody, "Racine's *Thébaïde*," pp. 205–7.

23. See R. Barthes, *Sur Racine* (Paris: Seuil [Collection Points], 1963), pp. 63–65: Barthes brings out forcefully the way in which the brothers fight for the space of the womb, the throne, and the battleground or *lice*.

24. R. Pfohl, *Racine's 'Iphigénie': literary rehearsal and tragic recognition* (Geneva: Droz, 1974), p. 211.

25. The vocabulary of recognition is indeed insistent here: "que chacun de vous reconnoisse son Frère" (1080); "Sur tout que le Sang parle & fasse son office" (1083). The same unwillingness to accept parricide and incest as natural or *vraisèmblable* is evident in other characters, particularly Antigone: see for example II. 3, where Antigone accuses Polynice of failing to "recognize" her: "La nature pour luy n'est plus qu'une chimère; / Il méconnoist sa Soeur, il mesprise sa Mere"; Polynice ripostes: "Je vous connois tousjours & suis tousjours le mesme" (*ed. cit.*, p. 139, ll. 591–92, 607). In the first edition, Antigone's speech ends with the following lines, later deleted: "Je ne vois point mon Frere, en voyant Polynice; / En vain il se presente à mes yeux éperdus, / Je ne le connois point, il ne me connoist plus" (596–98).

26. Racine, *Oeuvres complètes*, ed. R. Picard, vol. II (Paris: Gallimard [Bibliothèque de la Pléiade], 1966): 855.

27. G. Poulet, *Etudes sur le temps humain* (Edinburgh: Edinburgh University Press, 1949), pp. 140–41.

28. P. Bénichou, *Morales du grand siècle* (Paris: Gallimard, 1948), pp. 215–16.

29. See Barnwell, *Tragic Drama*, p. 139.

30. For Barnwell (*Tragic Drama*, p. 135), the closest parallel for *La Thébaïde* among Corneille's plays is *Horace*. The symmetry of the conflict between the Horaces and the Curiaces, with messengers appearing breathlessly on the scene to report the progress of the battle, is indeed countered by the still more deadly and intimate symmetry of the duel between Etéocle and Polynice.

31. For example, it is evident that the chronological configuration I began with falls precisely in the aftermath of the Fronde, in the period when Louis XIV began to establish absolutism on a hitherto unprecedented scale and when the influence of Port-Royal on secular literature was just beginning to be felt.

A Theatrical Reading of *Cinna*

Judd D. Hubert

In interpreting *Cinna,* not only do I favor a metadramatic approach, but I go so far as to postulate that a given character's so-called tragic flaw coincides with performative failure, or sometimes self-defeating success, as dramatist, director, actor, spectator.

Auguste, in substituting Cinna and Maxime for Maecenas and Agrippa, has hardly shown skill in casting. He has picked as advisers the leaders of a conspiracy against his life; he has substituted for his way-ward daughter a firebrand eager to destroy him. Grown weary of the imperial role he himself had imposed, he wishes to abdicate and thus cease altogether to function as dramatist.

Emilie fares no better, for her part as lover constantly interferes with her star role as avenger. Inevitably, she lapses into a state of confusion, akin to the bewilderment of her beloved Cinna, that reluctant assassin who would gladly accept his casting as chief counselor in the imperial establishment. In Maxime, we find a character repeatedly upstaged and outperformed by every one, including his own confidant Euphorbe whose trite plotting generically belongs to comedy. Paradoxically, Corneille's re-markable success as playwright depends on these performative shortcom-ings of his dramatis personae—but naturally not on inadequacies on the part of his actors and actresses.

Metaphorically, exchange, as Jacques Ehrmann has shown,[1] domi-nates the play; while dramatically the big switch, as Susan Tiefenbrun has proved, operates throughout, even to the point of turning the political world upside down.[2] Finally, the often repeated motif of sacrifice relates equally to exchanging and switching; by reason of ambiguity, it contains within itself all the dynamics of reversal.

Cinna plans to kill the emperor during the religious ceremony, thereby conveniently substituting one sacrificial victim for another. The emperor's punishment would thus fit his numerous and well-documented crimes against the citizens of Rome. Cinna, Emilie, and even Auguste frequently describe the proscriptions and massacres of the civil war in terms of sac-

rificial immolations, a metaphorical switch conducive to dramatic reversal. The entire play lends itself to a Girardian interpretation; indeed,
Corneille has dramatized a sacrificial crisis similar to those described in
La Violence et le sacré.[3] One might even claim that the denouement of
Cinna shows how Auguste puts an end to this crisis, not by a sacrifice but
by the imposition of a new order based on law, relegating violence and
religion to an inoperative past. But from a theatrical standpoint, Auguste
has assumed a new role and assigned specific parts to his subordinates
who must henceforth perform according to his script. Instead of rewriting chronicles, they face with equanimity a rigorously programmed future. Corneille, a thoroughly modern dramatist, not to say legal mind,
dispenses altogether with scapegoats—not only here but even in his *Oedipe*. The emperor's achievement at the denouement may provide a *mise-
en-abyme* of Cornelian drama, for he succeeds in imposing a workable
order on the world, an order reflecting the efficacy expected of a well-
made and professionally staged play. Auguste's historical triumph, which
ends the tragedy, appears to arise from and reflect on Corneille's theatrical mastery.

The play opens with Emilie's dramatically complex soliloquy. She gen-
erates a plurality of voices pertaining to two conflicting personifications
or, if you prefer, actants, each one striving for domination: revenge and
love. Reversal operates from the beginning, for revenge, clearly defined
as duty, arrogates the vocabulary of Eros: *désire, séduite, ardents transports* as well as such metonymies as *enfants* and *naissance*. Conversely,
love, deprived in part of its usual terminology and forced to fall back on
the vocabulary of duty, uses terms indicative of subordination or morality
such as *sers, céder, honte, gloire, généreux*. Emilie reaches paradoxical
heights in stating:

> Au milieu toutefois d'une fureur si juste,
> J'aime encore plus Cinna que je ne hais Auguste,
> Et je sens refroidir ce bouillant mouvement
> Quand il faut, pour le suivre, exposer mon amant.
> [17-20]

Coldness pertains to love; boiling and fury to the self-imposed duty of
avenging her father. As she no longer knows what role to perform or
what play to write, she exhorts the warring factions within her to exchange their parts. In other words, she requires an impossible perform-

ance that would reflect not only her own predicament but also the proneness to reversal so characteristic of the play as well as the sacrificial crisis that undermines all action.

Stylistically, Emilie keeps at a distance the competing and alienating personifications she has herself set in motion. By thus combining displacement with presence, elusion with illusion, she automatically condemns herself to failure in everything she undertakes. Her own statements, in so far as we can distinguish them from the voices she puts into play, involve the related themes of evaluation and exchange, which we can also consider as metaphorical equivalents of her initial displacement and elusion. Exchange and evaluation, however, have very little in common with love or with the kind of generosity which, at the end, will impose an acceptable order. Indeed, they can only lead to blackmail and a perpetuation of the sacrificial crisis: ". . . des mêmes présents qu'il verse dans mes mains / J'achète contre lui les esprits des Romains" (79–80). Auguste's material generosity will, by reversal, lead to his own undoing. But Emilie here and elsewhere advocates a moral switch, similar to the exchange of terminology between love and revenge: "Pour qui venge son père il n'est point de forfaits, / Et c'est vendre son sang que se rendre aux bienfaits" (83–84), and later: "Je fais gloire, pour moi, de cette ignominie" (973). Duty, through this reversal, assumes all the verbal characteristics of crime.

Unlike the secretive Emilie, Cinna, according to the narrative of his meeting with his co-conspirators, knows how to manipulate an audience:

> Au seul nom de César, d'Auguste, et d'empereur
> Vous eussiez vu leurs yeux s'enflammer de fureur,
> Et dans un même instant, par un effet contraire,
> Leur front pâlir d'horreur et rougir de colère.
> [159–62]

Cinna's imaginary audience, by thus achieving a physionomical impossibility in responding to an identity, leaves far behind Corneille's real audience which, at that moment, can hardly feel hatred against an emperor who gave his name to a century. Moreover, this imaginary audience serves as a magnifying mirror for both Cinna's and Emilie's postures:

> Tous s'y montrent portés avec tant d'allégresse
> Qu'ils semblent comme moi servir une maîtresse;

Et tous font éclater un si puissant courroux,
Qu'ils semblent tous venger un père, comme vous.
[149-52]

In this manner, Cinna, even before he addresses them, has transformed
the conspirators into performative extensions of himself and Emilie.
Their behavior as audience leads from the beginning to an impossibility,
as the models he provides for avenging a father and serving a mistress
would seem to exclude one another no less than joy and wrath. Perhaps
the behavior of the conspirators reflects the contradictions inherent in
both Cinna and Emilie. Moreover, Cinna, in order to spellbind his audience, merely narrates the past; and the conspiracy against the emperor's
life, by adding just another sacrifice and immolation, will do no more
than repeat what has happened so frequently in the recent history of
Rome.

Although Corneille may not have entrusted Cinna with his own super-
lative intelligence and imagination as dramatist, he has given him a keen
sense of the spectacular and a remarkable understanding of his various
audiences—the conspirators, Emilie, and the emperor. Like Emilie, he
shows a weakness for personified abstractions:

Ma vertu pour le moins ne me trahira pas:
Vous la verrez, brillante au bord des précipices,
Se couronner de gloire en bravant les supplices,
Rendre Auguste jaloux du sang qu'il répandra,
Et le faire trembler alors qu'il me perdra.
[312-16]

Unlike Emilie, he makes his abstraction act in a spectacular and heroic
manner. His narrative, written in the future tense, brings about another
dramatic reversal, for it shows Auguste behaving like a craven victim and
Cinna like an intrepid hero. The conspirator resembles La Fontaine's
milkmaid Perette, even though he pitches his rhetoric on a somewhat
higher plane. But recourse to rhetoric, particularly in the future tense,
makes one suspect that Cinna does not exactly coincide with the heroic
posture he intended for Emilie. In a sense, he sorely needs to limit himself
to *vertu*, Roman of course, in the same way that Emilie has to exclude all
but filial revenge. Both of them personify abstractions, perhaps because
neither one has discovered a valid part to play or a suitable drama in
which to perform.

Cinna achieves his greatest theatrical triumph in convincing Auguste to change his mind and continue to perform as emperor. Auguste had spoken of his political power in the vocabulary of personal, almost erotic, gratification, using such terms as *aimer, beautés, jouit, déplaît, assouvie, charmes, plaisirs, désir, possession.* He has thus operated a lexical reversal not unlike Emilie's, between personal and collective values. To convince Auguste of his error, Cinna reinstates the emperor's public image and the idea of glory or, in theatrical terms, his spectacular role in the universe as opposed to his private identity. Cinna's strategy consists, so to speak, in reasserting the positive values and attitudes prevalent in practically every serious play Corneille ever wrote. Although Cinna expresses opinions at variance with those he had advocated in his fiery statements to the conspirators, he nonetheless reasserts the compelling influence of the past, whereby he differs from the emperor who sees only the present. Theatrically, these two opposed standpoints express the relationship between immediacy and historical representation, between presence and fable. Cinna paradoxically reaffirms the historical perspective of the audience off-stage against the very statesman who had shaped the historical events! These events appear in three different perspectives: Auguste views them from the vantage point of personal gratification; Cinna, in his speech to the conspirators, as a pure unfolding; and, in his advice to Auguste, from the perspective of an admiring historian—after the fact and with an eye to the results:

Si le pouvoir suprême est blâmé par Auguste,
César fut un tyran, et son trépas fut juste,
Et vous devez aux Dieux compte de tout le sang
Dont vous l'avez vengé pour monter à son rang.
[429–32]

According to this advice, only a positive political attitude toward power can give meaning to the past. Corneille's Cinna, a prize pupil of the Jesuits, justifies the emperor in terms of an implicit declaration of intentions. He himself had merely redirected his own intentions in moving from one audience to the next. In both instances, he provides his listeners with precisely the ideas they wish and expect to hear. Although he knows how to appeal to any audience, he does so in the manner of a catalyst rather than a dramatist. Worse still, he falls under the spell his own words have cast.

In attempting to counter Cinna's argument, Maxime also invokes the judgment of posterity, but in terms of personal transcendence rather than history:

> Votre gloire redouble à mépriser l'empire;
> Et vous serez fameux chez la postérité
> Moins pour l'avoir conquis que pour l'avoir quitté.
> Le bonheur peut conduire à la grandeur suprême;
> Mais pour y renoncer il faut la vertu même.
>
> [474–78]

By following Maxime's advice, Auguste would admire his own transcendent image in a sort of self-perpetuating immediacy. Maxime fails because the emperor must situate his role historically and perform actively rather than contemplatively in front of a vast and changing audience. Nonetheless, both Cinna and Maxime advocate complementary aspects of Cornelian drama: historical representation and heroic admiration, here given as antithetical, but that Auguste will reconcile and combine in the final scene.

In clinching the argument, Cinna associates two apparently antithetical concepts: finance and, surprisingly, pity, an inconspicuous commodity in Octave's rise to power:

> Que l'amour du pays, que la pitié vous touche;
> Votre Rome à genoux vous parle par ma bouche.
> Considérez le prix que vous avez coûté.
>
> [605–7]

How can Auguste possibly resist the touching spectacle of himself as leading man in a historical love duet with suppliant Rome? By comparison, Maxime's abstract images of virtue and generosity would hardly hold the stage.

Cinna, both in his address to the conspirators and his counsel to the emperor, merely catalyzes a mixture already present. He does not even possess a theatrical presence that he can claim as his own. His role in the imperial establishment derives from the emperor's miscasting, and his part in the conspiracy from Emilie's dramatization of past events. In both these contradictory capacities, he functions as a deputy, as an extension of competing playwrights, Auguste and Emilie.

Torn between the two of them, he has recourse to a reversal, to a lexical switch, whereby the beloved Emilie assumes all the characteristics of a tyrant, while Auguste, because of his appreciation of Cinna, deserves only love and service. In a sense, his advice to the emperor, based, or so he tells Maxime and Emilie, on deception, untruth and illusion, has convinced him as much as it has Auguste. He thus becomes an admirer, so to speak, of his own discourse, which happens to coincide with political truth, circa 1640. Through his mediation, the emperor has at last understood the value of historically motivated performance.

Caught between his newly discovered monarchical zeal and his oath to Emilie, or, if you prefer, two mutually exclusive scripts, Cinna once again falls back on a narrative written in the future tense:

> Vous le voulez, j'y cours, ma parole est donnée;
> Mais ma main, aussitôt contre mon sein tournée,
> Aux mânes d'un tel prince immolant votre amant,
> A mon crime forcé joindra mon châtiment,
> Et par cette action dans l'autre confondue
> Recouvrera ma gloire aussitôt que perdue.
> [1061–66]

The two irreconcilable texts will coincide, thanks to Cinna's imagination, in a spectacularly sacrificial display, hardly acceptable to Emilie or even the emperor. And like Auguste, Cinna combines, by means of illusion, the roles of sacrificer and victim.

Once he has discovered the conspiracy, Auguste, like Emilie and Cinna before him, hesitates between incompatible roles of revenge and clemency, but finally combines the part of victim with that of executioner in a spectacular narrative where Rome's sacrificial crisis reaches a climax:

> Meurs; mais quitte du moins la vie avec éclat;
> Eteins en le flambeau dans le sang de l'ingrat;
> A toi-même en mourant immole ce perfide;
> Contentant ses désirs, punis son parricide;
> Fais un tourment pour lui de ton propre trépas,
> En faisant qu'il le voie et n'en jouisse pas.
> Mais jouissons plutôt nous-même de sa peine,
> Et si Rome nous hait, triomphons de sa haine.
> [1179–86]

Auguste's narrative provides the same spectacular features as Cinna's, but stresses erotic, not to say sado-masochistic, gratification rather than heroic gesture and replaces the future tense by the imperative, in keeping with the speaker's rank. Moreover, Auguste reverts to the private world from which Cinna's counsels had momentarily dislodged him, for once again he views power, punishment and sacrifice in terms of personal re-action. Clearly, he has not yet succeeded in putting his role, his act, and his play together. He too compounds elusion, for he describes himself as a "Coeur irrésolu / Qui fuit en même temps tout ce qu'il se propose!" (1188–89).

Another kind of discrepancy or displacement resulting from personal feelings occurs in Emilie: "D'où me vient cette joie? et que mal à propos / Mon esprit malgré moi goûte un entier repos!" (1288–89). And she adds: "A chaque occasion le ciel y fait descendre / Un sentiment contraire à celui qu'il doit prendre" (1292–93). It would seem that no character in the play can maintain any kind of unity of focus. A civil war rages within every one of them, leading to betrayal and self-betrayal.

Emilie's use of the word "descendre" may provide a clue to these dis-crepancies. Ascent and descent throughout the play appear equally favor-able or unfavorable. Emilie cannot accept Cinna as a gift from the emperor, for this downward movement would bring shame and servi-tude, while an upward thrust on the part of Cinna, by immolating Au-guste, would win her hand. However, Octave's usurpation of power, with its accompaniment of proscriptions, had certainly followed an upward movement, as the emperor himself suggests in a famous line: "Et monté sur le faîte, il aspire à descendre" (370). Perhaps the trouble derives from the inevitability of displacement and from the tendency to confuse iden-tity with position or role.

Despite these contradictory feelings and movements, Auguste will nevertheless discover a solution acceptable to all, but only after he has uncovered the full extent of everybody's betrayal, proof of his descent into hell. Indeed, the downward movement must reach rock bottom be-fore the resulting upward thrust can take over. Auguste exclaims:

> Je suis maître de moi comme de l'univers;
> Je le suis, je veux l'être. O siècles, ô mémoire,
> Conservez à jamais ma dernière victoire!
> Je triomphe aujourd'hui du plus juste courroux
> De qui le souvenir puisse aller jusqu'à vous.
> [1696–1700]

The emperor, speaking authoritatively in the present tense, finally puts his personal reactions and the world on precisely the same footing, with the full knowledge that he must impose his will both inside and outside. He realizes that these personal reactions had mattered even more, perhaps because they could do more damage, than all the conspiracies arrayed against him. Indeed, he insists on his triumph over his wrath, without even mentioning his victory over the conspirators. He has laid the past to rest and takes charge of posterity. History, finally made meaningful, or suitable for representation, fills the stage at the moment the curtain drops.

NOTES

1. Jacques, Ehrmann. "Les Structures de l'échange dans *Cinna*," *Les Temps Modernes*, 246, November 1966, pp. 929–60.

2. Susan Tiefenbrun, *Signs of the Hidden* (Amsterdam: Rodopi), pp. 181–208.

3. René Girard, *La Violence et le sacré* (Paris: Grasset, 1972).

"Docere et delectare": Richesses de l'*Avare*

Marie-Odile Sweetser

L'*Avare* n'a pas beaucoup attiré l'attention de la critique au cours des dernières décennies, alors qu'elle continue à connaître un succès soutenu à la scène, car elle fournit un rôle de premier plan, celui d'Harpagon, dans lequel se sont illustrés bien des acteurs célèbres.[1] Si l'*Avare* n'a suscité ni à l'époque de sa création ni de nos jours les controverses passionnées dont l'*Ecole des Femmes, Tartuffe, Dom Juan,* le *Misanthrope* ont fait l'objet, on peut à bon droit supposer que Molière s'est précisément employé à les éviter. Son théâtre, traitant de sujets brûlants: droits des femmes dans une société patriarcale, escroquerie pratiquée sous le voile d'une fausse dévotion, libertinage de moeurs et d'idées d'un "grand seigneur méchant homme," réussite mondaine liée à l'hypocrisie, lui avaient attiré des ennemis acharnés dans presque tous les camps. Le parti dévot continuait à s'opposer à la représentation de *Tartuffe.*

En attendant la décision royale qui devait lui permettre de jouer cette pièce qui lui tenait tant à coeur, Molière doit, pour faire vivre sa troupe, remplir son théâtre. Mais plus encore qu'une exigence économique, il s'agit pour un dramaturge de créer et de maintenir un rapport avec son public, comme Hugh Davidson l'a très bien montré. L'homme de théâtre, plus que tout autre créateur a conscience de l'échange qui a lieu entre le poète, l'oeuvre et les spectateurs. Cette situation se trouve renforcée au XVIIᵉ siècle par des facteurs économiques et sociaux.[2]

La société à laquelle Molière s'adresse, à laquelle il doit plaire et dont, dans l'ensemble, il obtient l'approbation et la complicité chaleureuse, comporte essentiellement deux volets, la cour et la ville.[3] Le dramaturge venait en 1668 de satisfaire la cour en lui fournissant des divertissements faits pour lui plaire: *Amphitryon,* comédie à sujet mythologique, transposant dans un registre fabuleux l'atmosphère galante de Versailles. On sait, en effet, depuis la grande thèse de Jean-Michel Pelous, que le climat mondain était passé de la préciosité à la galanterie dans les années 1660–1670. Pourtant Molière avait su doser galanterie et comique avec les scènes où paraissait Sosie. De nouveau, pour les fêtes du Grand Divertissement Royal de Versailles en juillet 1668, il présente avec *George Dandin* un divertissement où la farce traditionnelle du "Mari confondu," reprise de *La Jalousie du Barbouillé* alterne avec des intermèdes d'un tout autre style, relevant de la pastorale, si bien que Jacques Morel a pu déclarer: "*George Dandin* n'est pas en vérité l'histoire d'un homme qui est berné par sa femme; c'est le dialogue d'un genre littéraire et d'un autre . . ."[4]

Pour satisfaire la ville, Molière allait monter peu après, en septembre 1668, l'*Avare,* sa première grande comédie de moeurs et de caractère depuis le *Misanthrope.* L'insuccès de la pièce du vivant de Molière a été largement compensé par plus de deux mille représentations depuis la fondation de la Comédie Française en 1680. On a généralement attribué cet échec initial au fait que la pièce était écrite en prose. Puisqu'il s'agissait d'une grande comédie en cinq actes, le public se serait attendu à une pièce en vers. Pourtant, Molière avait tenté l'emploi de la prose dans *Dom Juan;* selon Hallam Walker, il aurait poursuivi l'expérience dans l'*Avare.*[5] Il s'emploiera d'ailleurs à se renouveler jusqu'au bout de sa carrière, comme les comédies-ballets en font foi.[6] L'emploi de la prose accélérait le mouvement, noté dès 1661 par La Fontaine, à l'occasion de la représentation des *Fâcheux,* vers le naturel:

Nous avons changé de méthode:
Jodelet n'est plus à la mode,
Et maintenant il ne faut pas
Quitter la nature d'un pas.[7]

En composant l'*Avare,* Molière a certainement songé à ne pas donner prise à ses détracteurs habituels, les dévots et les doctes. Pour satisfaire ces derniers, il puise dans une source classique, l'*Aulularia* de Plaute dont il venait d'utiliser l'*Amphitruo.* Du côté des dévots, il pouvait s'estimer à couvert, puisque l'Ecriture avait proclamé: "Radix omnium malorum cupiditas" (Epître de Saint Paul à Timothée, I, 6, 10). Les dévots ne pouvaient donc accuser Molière d'impiété ou d'immoralité, comme ils l'avaient fait pour l'*Ecole des Femmes, Tartuffe* et *Dom Juan.* Au contraire, les prédicateurs ne cessaient de rappeler aux riches leur devoir de charité, d'encourager les bonnes oeuvres: on pense à St. Vincent de Paul, à Bossuet prêchant sur "L'Eminente dignité des Pauvres dans l'Eglise" (1659). L'avarice était le vice qui s'opposait à la vertu chrétienne fondamentale, la charité, conçue dans son sens le plus large d'amour des autres. Harpagon qui ne pense qu'à son or pêche donc contre la charité. La condamnation de son vice et de ses conséquences ressort du tableau d'une famille en train de se désintégrer. La perte du respect, le dégoût et l'horreur ont remplacé tout sentiment filial chez les enfants qui abandonnent leur père à son or. Harpagon contrevient à la morale familiale et sociale, s'exprimant au XVIIᵉ siècle dans les règles de conduite de "l'honnêteté." L'honnête homme devait éviter tout excès, observer la règle du juste milieu, aussi éloigné de l'avarice sordide accompagnée de marchandages honteux et de prêts à taux usuraires que de la prodigalité des grands seigneurs libertins, dissipant leur patrimoine, tel Don Juan.

Harpagon, de toute évidence, son train de maison l'indique clairement: gouvernante, domestiques, chevaux, équipage et surtout intendant, appartient à la bourgeoisie bien nantie.[8] Normalement, s'il était un père prudent et sage, un chef de famille éclairé, doué d'une légitime ambition, songeant à l'avenir de ses enfants et des futures générations, il s'emploierait à doter sa fille, favorisant ainsi une alliance avantageuse qui permettrait à la famille de s'élever; il procurerait à son fils les "offices" qui aideraient l'ascension sociale de celui-ci et de ses descendants. L'égoïsme d'Harpagon, illustré par une absence de vision d'avenir, est donc total. Lorsqu'il prévoit pour chacun de ses enfants un mariage avec un partenaire beaucoup plus âgé: une riche veuve pour son fils, le seigneur Anselme pour sa fille, non seulement il s'oppose à leur bonheur personnel attaché à un libre choix, mais à l'avenir même de son lignage, par absence probable de descendance[9] et par un refus implicite du schéma d'ascension sociale courant sous l'ancien régime. La réaction indignée de Cléante se trouve donc justifiée:

> Voilà où les jeunes gens sont réduits par la maudite avarice des pères; et on s'étonne après cela que les fils souhaitent qu'ils meurent.[10]

On retrouve la même attitude chez les domestiques qui ne peuvent plus respecter un maître ayant perdu tout sens des convenances, de sa dignité, au point de ne pas leur fournir de livrées décentes ni d'exercer envers eux la protection attendue dans un système paternaliste, ni de leur montrer la confiance d'un bon maître vis-à-vis des gens de sa maison: il les soupçonne de le voler, les accuse sans preuve et se montre prêt à les livrer à la justice. Au point que La Flèche se voit lui aussi justifié: s'il volait Harpagon, ce ne serait pas par désir de gain ou pour récupérer les gages qui lui sont dûs, mais par une réaction morale, pour le punir de son avarice sordide, moralement condamnable:

Il faut avouer que le vôtre [votre père] animerait contre sa vilanie le plus
posé homme du monde. Je n'ai pas, Dieu merci, les inclinations fort pati-
bulaires . . . mais à vous dire vrai, il me donnerait, par ses procédés, des
tentations de le voler; et je croirais, en le volant, faire une action méri-
toire. [II: 1, 535]

Le vol de la cassette, dans cette perspective, apparaît non seulement
comme un procédé dramatique utile au développement de l'intrigue, mais
comme un juste retour des choses de ce monde: Harpagon qui, par sa
tyrannie et son vice, tend à étouffer les besoins vitaux de ceux qui l'entou-
rent, enfants et domestiques, se voit dérober ce qu'il considère aussi précieux que la vie, son or. Ce premier châtiment comique est donc
proportionné à son vice. Puisqu'il s'agit d'une comédie, le "vol" restera
un procédé destiné à supprimer les obstacles et à amener un dénouement
heureux. Un autre châtiment, plus durable, beaucoup plus grave, sera
toutefois réservé à Harpagon: la solitude, l'exclusion de la vie familiale
et sociale qu'il a reniée, la réification. Il y a donc bien une prise de position morale de la part du dramaturge sous les réjouissances traditionnelles du dénouement.[11]

D'autre part, les doctes ne pouvaient traiter Molière de simple farceur
puisqu'il se réclamait d'un des plus célèbres poètes comiques de l'anti-
quité. Il avait probablement utilisé des éléments pris dans des pièces et
dans la réalité contemporaines. On cite *La Belle Plaideuse* de Boisrobert
(1655), *La Dame d'intrigue* de Chappuzeau, le meurtre du lieutenant de
police Tardieu et de sa femme, avares célèbres, par des voleurs, exemple
utilisé également par Boileau dans sa *Satire X*. Il montrait ainsi qu'il était
sensible à l'actualité. Surtout, il se souvenait d'expériences personnelles
avec les usuriers. A l'époque de l'Illustre Théâtre, dans les dures années
1645–46, il avait désespérément cherché de l'argent pour faire face aux
dépenses courantes et devait finir en prison pour dettes.[12] On imagine
facilement les couches successives d'expérience, livresque et vécue, qui
rendent compte de la genèse de la pièce.

Du point de vue de la tradition comique, on retrouve la même abondance, la même structuration en couches superposées. Le dramaturge
tente de marier, d'harmoniser plusieurs types de comique. Cette tentative,
selon certains critiques, aurait échoué et expliquerait l'insuccès initial de
la pièce, le romanesque servant de hors d'oeuvre et de dessert à un plat
de résistance constitué par une forte comédie de moeurs et de caractère,
épicée de farce et de commedia del arte.[13] Au contraire, selon d'autres,
cette alternance est de toute première importance et ce serait mutiler la

pièce, refuser d'accepter les intentions du créateur que de la négliger. Un historien de la littérature, Antoine Adam, et un homme de théâtre, Charles Dullin, sont d'accord pour souligner l'équilibre recherché par Molière entre la comédie romanesque et sentimentale, et la comédie de moeurs et de caractère. Et Dullin, grand interprète du rôle d'Harpagon, condamne les mises en scène qui privilégient ce rôle au détriment des autres personnages.[14] Comme le remarque Jacques Morel à propos du mélange des genres dans *George Dandin:* "Il faut bien voir que l'artifice est qualité d'artiste, et que dans une fantaisie théâtrale les rapports d'opposition peuvent être source d'harmonie."[15]

Récemment, la critique moliéresque a fait appel aux données de l'anthropologie culturelle et à celles de la psychanalyse pour éclairer la nature du comique.[16] Northrop Frye distingue deux types de comédie: la comédie de caractère et la comédie romanesque; la première serait essentiellement celle de Molière, la seconde, celle de Shakespeare. Frye a certainement raison de distinguer les deux types de comique, mais dans le cas de Molière, il convient de reconnaître qu'il n'a pas négligé, même dans une pièce située en milieu bourgeois et qui s'appelle l'*Avare,* l'élément romanesque, les amours contrariées, les épreuves touchantes des jeunes premiers qui luttent contre un formidable obstacle, représenté par le père et son vice, afin de réaliser leur désir naturel de bonheur dans l'amour et le mariage. L'intrigue romanesque débute avec l'évocation d'Elise, sauvée des eaux par Valère, amoureuse de lui à la fois par reconnaissance et par inclination mais craignant

> l'emportement d'un père, les reproches d'une famille, les censures du monde; mais plus que tout, Valère, le changement de votre coeur . . .
> [I: 1, 516]

Valère, non seulement a montré une "générosité surprenante" en risquant sa vie pour sauver celle d'Elise, mais de plus, accepte pour rester près d'elle de "négliger et parents et patrie": nous assistons donc au triomphe de l'amour tendre, "Omnia vincit amor". Le jeune gentilhomme accepte aussi de se déguiser en domestique, humiliation insigne pour un homme de son rang qui fournit ainsi une preuve indéniable d'amour à sa bienaimée. Valère se voit obligé de s'abaisser à flatter le vice d'Harpagon pour gagner sa confiance, si bien que dans la fameuse scène du "Sans dot" (I: 5), la satire de l'avarice s'allie au paradoxe comique de l'amoureux prônant le mariage de la femme aimée avec un autre.

Molière continue à établir les jalons essentiels de l'intrigue romanesque par un procédé de parallélisme qui montre combien il soignait la
construction de ses pièces: Cléante avoue à sa soeur, Elise, son amour
pour la charmante Mariane, aimable mais sans fortune. Le frère et la
soeur se heurtent au même obstacle, celui d'un père tyrannique, cruel,
inhumain et de plus, dans un autre paradoxe comique, amoureux, lui
aussi, de Mariane. Le conflit familial entre le père et le fils, rivaux en
amour, se révélera inévitable. Par suite, les jeunes premiers ici sont beaucoup moins stéréotypés, moins fades que l'on pourrait s'y attendre, certainement plus individualisés que les "adolescentes" de Plaute ou de
Térence.

Harpagon remonte à l'archétype du "senex amans," du vieillard
amoureux de la tradition comique, généralement amoureux d'une très
jeune fille qui aurait l'âge de sa propre fille, par suite saisi d'une passion
contraire à la nature et ridicule dans ses manifestations: on se souvient
des scènes d'un comique appuyé touchant à la farce où Harpagon fait la
cour à Mariane qui éprouve une révulsion évidente devant l'horrible vieillard (III: 4 et 5).

Les jeunes premiers ne pouvant faire entendre raison à un père endurci
dans son vice et dépourvu de tout sentiment paternel, devront avoir recours à la ruse, à une série d'artifices et de mesures désespérées. La première sera la tentative d'emprunt faite par Cléante dans des conditions
de plus en plus exorbitantes à un prêteur anonyme qui ne sera autre
qu'Harpagon. La confrontation entre le père usurier et le fils aux abois
provoquera une série de reproches et d'insultes réciproques, scène
comique par l'effet de surprise et l'outrance des propos, sérieuse dans la
dénonciation de l'usure et de ses conséquences néfastes. En se livrant à
un commerce honteux pour un homme de son rang, Harpagon compro-
met l'honneur de sa famille, se déclasse:

> Ne rougissez-vous point de déshonorer votre condition par les commerces
> que vous faites? de sacrifier gloire et réputation au désir insatiable d'en-
> tasser écu sur écu . . .

et s'abaisse à un niveau moral véritablement criminel:

> qui est plus criminel, à votre avis, ou celui qui achète un argent dont il a
> besoin, ou bien celui qui vole un argent dont il n'a que faire. [II: 2, 537]

La seconde manifestation du conflit fondamental entre les générations
tourne autour de la rivalité amoureuse. Le vieillard, arrivé à l'hiver de sa

vie, proche de la mort par conséquent, veut empêcher l'arrivée et le triomphe du printemps, de la jeunesse et de la fécondité.[17] Mais Harpagon,
quoique désireux d'épouser une très jeune fille, ne renonce pas à l'avarice
par amour: il n'y a en lui aucun sentiment humain, ni affection pour ses
enfants, ni amour pour Mariane. Au moment de recevoir cette dernière
chez lui à souper, Harpagon cherche par tous les moyens à économiser
sur les frais de boisson et de nourriture. Il recommande à ses valets de
donner à boire "seulement lorsque l'on aura soif, et non pas selon la
coutume de certains impertinents de laquais, qui viennent provoquer les
gens et les faire aviser de boire lorsqu'on n'y songe pas" (III: 1, 545); à
Maître Jacques qui souhaiterait montrer ses talents de cuisinier en servant
un repas somptueux:

> Il faudra de ces choses dont on ne mange guère, et qui rassasient d'abord;
> quelque bon haricot bien gras, avec quelque pâté en pot bien garni de
> marrons. [III: 1, 548]

Dans un contraste comique, Cléante a recours à la ruse pour assurer
une collation élégante. Il a fait venir, au nom et aux frais de son père
"quelques bassins d'oranges de la Chine, de citrons doux et de confi-
tures" (III: 7, 556). Il parvient même à forcer Mariane à accepter un
diamant porté par Harpagon. La signification symbolique de ce cadeau
met en valeur le contraste entre Cléante et son père vis-à-vis de Mariane.[18]
Sur des soupçons éveillés par la vue de son fils baisant la main de la jeune
fille, Harpagon va, lui aussi, avoir recours à la ruse pour découvrir les
véritables sentiments des jeunes gens. Nous sommes donc en plein dans
"l'ère du soupçon," chacun se voit obligé de jouer un rôle, de pratiquer
méfiance et tromperie.

Le père ayant appris par la ruse que son fils est son rival en amour, il
s'ensuit une seconde scène de confrontation, avec échange comique de
répliques accusatrices. Elle se termine en un mouvement de farce, voire
de guignol, Harpagon menaçant son fils de coups de bâton: le tragique
est donc évité. La situation de rivalité amoureuse entre père et fils, utilisée
dans la tragédie, subit dans la comédie un traitement différent selon
Charles Mauron. La situation angoissante de la tragédie montrant le fils
rebelle ou le parricide châtié se trouve renversée: c'est le père s'opposant
à l'amour des jeunes gens qui est éliminé.[19] C'est le cas pour Harpagon
qui renonce à ses projets matrimoniaux pour récupérer sa cassette, véritable "objet" de son amour.

Le bouleversement psychique causé par la perte de son or donne lieu à des scènes d'une grande force comique et dramatique. Harpagon, traitant sa cassette comme un objet d'amour prépare la personnification de cette dernière, donnant lieu au quiproquo comique au cours duquel Valère parle d'Elise et proteste de la pureté de ses intentions, alors qu'Harpagon parle de sa cassette qu'il l'accuse d'avoir volée (V: 3). L'attitude d'Harpagon aboutit réciproquement à la réification des personnes. Dans un article récent, Ralph Albanese met en valeur l'aspect socio-culturel de la pièce en le reliant à son aspect moral: ". . . l'argent, qui semble à première vue se prêter aussi mal à l'esthétique comique que la religion—tous deux engendrent des vices dangereux en puissance—possède en fait une efficacité théâtrale réelle." [20]

Harpagon, "à la fois thésauriseur et usurier" va clairement contre la politique d'expansion économique et commerciale qui est celle du roi et de son ministre, souvent désignée sous le nom de "colbertisme" ou de mercantilisme. John Cairncross avait noté que "la bourgeoisie à cette époque était une force bien jeune et se laissait séduire par le prestige et le faste des aristocrates. De fait, elle tendait à renoncer à la tâche utile de donner un essor à l'économie du pays et cherchait à s'anoblir." [21] Cette vue se trouve confirmée par les travaux récents des historiens. Ces travaux montrent que les efforts de Colbert dans la création de manufactures et de compagnies commerciales comme dans les constructions navales avaient rencontré bien des obstacles et surtout se heurtaient à la mentalité d'une bourgeoisie "attachée aux offices royaux et aux revenus terriens": "une mutation 'capitaliste' était impossible, faute de gros capitaux à investir et faute d'une mentalité d'entreprise." [22]

Harpagon, par son usure, ruine les fils de famille qui ont recours à ses services. En amassant de l'or et en l'enfouissant dans son jardin, il le retire de la circulation et le rend improductif. Le vice d'Harpagon va donc à l'encontre de la politique d'expansion économique de Colbert, soucieux d'enrichir l'Etat. En ridiculisant et en condamnant implicitement l'avarice, Molière avait certainement l'intention de plaire au roi, son protecteur, qui offrait, dans un but nettement politique, des spectacles à Versailles. Comme le note Hugh Davidson:

Selon d'Aubignac, le théâtre remplit une fonction politique bien définie . . . Après les exploits, les divertissements . . . On ne nous parle pas, cependant, de simples passe-temps. Ces plaisirs publics se chargent bientôt, dans la pensée de d'Aubignac, d'un ensemble de valeurs morales.[23]

Le sens psychologique et moral de la comédie se trouve renforcé par l'emploi structurel de figures rhétoriques de base, antithèse et paradoxe: puissance destructrice de l'argent, le possesseur possédé. L'avare se déshumanise en traitant en objets les êtres les plus proches, ses enfants, la jeune fille qu'il voudrait épouser sans l'aimer. La cassette devient objet d'amour, comme une personne dans le célèbre monologue:

> Hélas! mon pauvre argent, mon pauvre argent, mon cher ami, on m'a privé de toi; et puisque tu m'es enlevé, j'ai perdu mon support, ma consolation, ma joie . . . sans toi, il m'est impossible de vivre. [IV: 7, 569]

La dernière réplique est probante: Georges Couton souligne que "la pièce se termine véritablement par ces retrouvailles d'un homme et d'une cassette, et que le dernier mot est *cassette*." [24] Harpagon s'identifie ainsi à l'objet de sa passion, se réifie. Son aliénation est totale: il est seul en face d'une famille nouvellement constituée qui aurait pu être la sienne, mais qui se groupe autour d'un père vraiment humain lui, bon et généreux, soucieux de remplir sa fonction sociale qui consiste à assurer l'avenir de ses enfants et de substituer la réciprocité à l'égoïsme. [25]

Molière se montre, lui aussi, généreux dans cette comédie sur l'avarice, diversement qualifiée de pièce noire, âpre et grinçante, rosse, de drame bourgeois. On a tenté d'en dégager les nombreux niveaux d'expressivité et de signification: la comédie romanesque et sentimentale, agrémentée, comme chez Shakespeare, de naufrage, sauvetage, déguisement, séparation, retrouvailles et double mariage; la grande comédie de moeurs et de caractère se jouant dans le cadre d'une famille bourgeoise déchirée; les drôleries et jeux de scène de la farce et de la commedia del arte. Molière, comme dans une pièce montée, n'hésite pas à utiliser en couches superposées toutes les grandes traditions comiques, la réalité contemporaine et sa propre expérience. Le dramaturge fait flèche de tout bois, mais combine, repense, réinvente les données traditionnelles, y ajoute du sien et remplit ainsi le double but de plaire et d'instruire.

NOTES

1. Maurice Descotes, *Les grands rôles du théâtre de Molière* (Paris: P.U.F., 1960), pp. 135–36.
2. Hugh M. Davidson, *Audience, Words and Art. Studies in Seventeenth-Century Rhetoric* (Columbus: Ohio State University Press, 1965), p. 143.

3. Ibid., p. 163.

4. "Le Modèle pastoral dans l'oeuvre de Molière," dans *Le Genre pastoral en Europe du XVe au XVIIe siècle* (Publications de l'Université de Saint-Etienne, 1980), p. 342.

5. *Molière*, TWAS 176 (New York: Twayne Publishers, 1971), p. 146.

6. Robert Garapon, *Le Dernier Molière* (Paris: SEDES, 1977); Gérard Defaux, *Molière ou les métamorphoses du comique: de la comédie morale au triomphe de la folie* (Lexington, Ky.: French Forum Publishers, 1980); Claude Abraham, *On the Structure of Molière's Comédies-ballets*, Biblio. 17, no. 19 (Paris, Seattle, Tuebingen: Papers on French Seventeenth-Century Literature, 1984).

7. La Fontaine, *Lettre à M. de Maucroix* du 22 août 1661 dans *Oeuvres diverses*, Pléiade, éd. Pierre Clarac (Paris: Gallimard, 1958), p. 526.

8. Voir sur ce point l'excellente analyse de James F. Gaines, *Social Structures in Molière's Theater* (Columbus: Ohio State University Press, 1984), pp. 170–80.

9. Ibid., pp. 173–74.

10. Molière, *Oeuvres complètes*, Pléiade, éd. Georges Couton (Paris: Gallimard, 1971), II: 535. Toutes les citations de Molière renvoient à cette édition.

11. G. Defaux, *Molière*, estime que la première période dans l'oeuvre de Molière se termine avec le *Misanthrope*, en 1666. Selon lui, Harpagon n'est pas puni, par suite la pièce ne serait pas morale: voir p. 189.

12. G. Couton, *Notice* de l'*Avare*, dans *Oeuvres complètes*, II: 509–10.

13. James Doolittle, "Bad Writing in *L'Avare*," *L'Esprit créateur*, vol. 6, no. 3 (Fall 1966): 197–206.

14. Antoine Adam, *Histoire de la littérature française au XVIIe siècle* (Paris: Domat, 1956), III: 373; Charles Dullin, *Présentation* de *L'Avare*, Collection Mises en scène (Paris: Seuil, 1946), p. 11.

15. J. Morel, "Le Modèle pastoral," p. 342.

16. Voir M.-O. Sweetser, "Domaines de la critique moliéresque," *Oeuvres et critiques*, VI, 1 (Eté 1981), pp. 9–28.

17. Northrop Frye, *Anatomie de la critique*, trad. Guy Durand (Paris: Gallimard, 1969), "Mythos du printemps: la comédie," pp. 199–226; et "Le mythos de l'hiver: ironie et satire," pp. 272–91; Francis L. Lawrence, *Molière: The Comedy of Unreason*, Tulane Studies in Romance Languages and Literature, no. 2, 1968, pp. 18–19; Marcel Gutwirth, "The Unity of Molière's *L'Avare*," *PMLA* 76, no. 4 (September 1961): 366.

18. James F. Gaines, *Social Structures*, pp. 177–78.

19. Charles Mauron, *Psychocritique du genre comique* (Paris: José Corti, 1964), pp. 14, 19.

20. Ralph Albanese, "Argent et réification dans *L'Avare*," *L'Esprit créateur*, Sociocriticism 21, no. 3 (Fall 1981): 35.

21. John Cairncross, *Molière bourgeois et libertin* (Paris: Nizet, 1963), pp. 39–40.

22. Hubert Méthivier, *L'Ancien Régime en France. XVIe, XVIIe, XVIIIe siècles* (Paris: P.U.F., 1981), p. 352.

23. Hugh M. Davidson, "Pratique et rhétorique du théâtre: étude sur le vocabulaire et la méthode de d'Aubignac," dans *Critique et création littéraires en France au XVIIe siècle* (Paris: CNRS, 1977), pp. 169–70.

24. G. Couton, *Notice,* II: 514.

25. J. Gaines, *Social Structures,* p. 180.

III
Fiction

Doubling and Omission in the Text of Anne Ferrand/Bélise

Charles G. S. Williams

Anne Ferrand's anonymously published novel, *L'Histoire de Cléante et Bélise* (1689, 1691),[1] and the love letters included with it (1691) capped with scandal a notoriety that had begun in 1686, when her husband, the magistrate Michel Ferrand, instituted legal separation from his wife after ten years of marriage. Keys to manuscripts, letters, and other public notices show that contemporary readers connected fiction with lawsuit and read the novel as the inside story of Mme Ferrand's affair with Louis-Nicolas Le Tonnelier de Breteuil, begun in 1680 and ended, the letters imply, some two years before the court action. A thousand persons know of the affair, remarks one of the novel's narrators, and that figure was increased, in a 1696 manuscript note, to an expressive if hyperbolic 10,000.[2]

The scandal of Mme Ferrand's writing brought some exclusions, especially from the society over which Mme de Maintenon held sway. "Je trouve les femmes plus méprisables dans la dévotion que dans la galanterie" (72), Bélise had written and was no less direct about herself: "Je n'ay ny le bonheur ny la foiblesse de devenir dévote, & vous pouvez vous asseurer que vous ne me verrez jamais que philosophe amante & fidelle . . ." (27–28). For at least one key-supplying reader of *Les Caractères*,[3] and enterprising publishers for over a century,[4] Anne Ferrand's letters put her into another company, that of Heloise and the narrator of the *Lettres portugaises*. Bélise's desire had already found this community: "Qu'une véritable passion est noble, & qu'elle inspire des sentimens élevez! Si jamais je parviens à avoir quelque mérite, je le devray à la mienne. Je suis touchée d'émulation pour toutes les femmes qui en ont" (38).

Recent attention, almost exclusively to the technical and historical features of Anne Ferrand's single published novel, has separated the constitutive letters and *récit* of what may be a historically unique text.[5] Like the earlier biographical tradition which conflated the Bélise of the text with the historical Présidente Ferrand, this new criticism also separates the writer Anne Ferrand/Bélise from other texts, later extant writings left in manuscript during her long life (1657?–1740). My intention here is to bring these texts together and with them the image of the woman to be found in legal documents that gave Anne Ferrand a place among the curiosities of legal history. The resulting interplay of textuality points finally in her writing to a central drama obscured by traditional interpretative scenarios of the *femme abandonnée* and/or *mal-mariée*. With this disclosure comes, I believe, clarification of what the act of writing meant for this woman who first wrote about her life during five years of confinement enforced by *lettres de cachet*.

1. A femme forte

Shortly after Mme Dacier's death, Anne Ferrand wrote a lengthy and detailed letter about her.[6] Distinction as a scholar initially seemed, she confesses, good reason for not making Mme Dacier's acquaintance. But friendship and admiration followed the surprise of meeting a remarkable woman "qui ne faisoit jamais sentir le Moi" (184)—happy and devoted in marriage and motherhood, practical in management and an idealist of firm commitment, as sensitive in conversation as in her love of music. The fullness of Anne Lefèvre Dacier's life, different from her own in so many way, captivated Anne Ferrand and elicited in her letter a response of friendship remarkable in its fullness. When the easy tone of the letter changes, as it does three times during its reminiscences, much is revealed about the writer Anne Ferrand. To one of these changes, especially significant for the writer's sense of difference, I shall return in my concluding section; the other two, related as they are, suggest a strategy fundamental to her writing.

Evoking the "prétendues fautes" other scholars found in Mme Dacier's "excellents ouvrages," Anne Ferrand launches a general denunciation of male vanity: "Je n'ai pû m'empêcher de soupçonner les hommes de voir d'un oeil d'envie la science dans les femmes, et que ce ne soit à eux que nous devions nous prendre la puérile éducation que l'on nous donne." Continuing to meditate combatively, she describes the triumph of Mme Dacier as that of a style containing the best that men have to offer and going beyond it. Mme Dacier's writing has, she judges, "la force et l'exactitude du stile des hommes, jointes à une certaine douceur propre aux femmes, qui rendoit sa manière d'écrire supérieure à tout autre" (184^v).

This judgment's independence—from the emerging cliché that in polemics Mme Dacier's prose was the "best man's"—suggests Mme Dacier had won a reader in the always self-taught Anne Ferrand. She may well have begun at the beginning with what she calls the "excellent works" prepared with special pedagogical care and skill for another restive reader (the Dauphin). There *douceur* was evident both in Mme Dacier's desire to address her text to an adolescent and to convey filial piety in her continuation of the pedagogical and scholarly work of her father; "forcefulness and exactness," in the establishment of text, in her self-assurance in annotation, and in at least one, uncharacteristic denunciation of male educators that Anne Ferrand echoes.[7]

The *dédoublement* Anne identifies, with its particular authority/superiority, speaks a long-cherished desire at work in the writings collected in view of a never-finished volume of memoirs recently begun when the letter on Mme Dacier was written.[8] The intention of that project of writing, evident in part 1 of the papers, is a defense of Colbert that would be polemical as well as historical. Anne Ferrand applies the lesson taken from Mme Dacier's style in an experiment of her own with *dédoublement*. She plays the stylistic game of hiding grammatical indicators of a nonmale narrator.

After a brief, conventional justification of "eye-witness" history, Mme Ferrand attacks the recently published *Histoire d'Henriette d'Angleterre* by Mme de Lafayette[9] (sects. 7–20) and the abbé de Choisy's *Mémoires* (sects. 21–36).[10] Both are heatedly denied credibility for their misrepresentations of the minister's character, actions, and historical stature. Choisy's writing is simply gossip; Mme de Lafayette's—significantly for the orientation of the sometime novelist now apprentice historian—a bad imitation of her novel *La Princesse de Clèves*.[11] Commentary on these sources, to the end of the larger project, is subordinated to a shrewd historical analysis (sects. 2–6) of the anti-Colbertian feeling that they illustrate and unjustly continue.

Intelligent as she was, Anne Ferrand could not long have supposed that third-person narrative might shield the historical subject; nor could she have been unaware of its fundamental contradiction with the desire to speak her own truth. Although political subjects (and a recent unfounded implication in the Cellamare conspiracy)[12] might make it seem desirable, the narratorial "il" is less a strategy of clandestinity than one of a double, enforcing the historian's authority already evident in the vigor of its criticism. Other "titles" are prepared to the same end in the two series of reflections assembled in the shorter part 2 of the papers. Placed like "justificatory pieces," a series of moral reflections (sects. 38–55) professes an unassailable belief in God's order as the basis of all morality. This might be reassuring to anyone associating the writer with her son Antoine (d. 1719), who had frequented the circle of the Temple.[13] The closing sentence of part 2 could be equally so to any reader who remembered Bélise's extravagance and disruptiveness: "Il y a en toutes choses une abondance vicieuse: le 'ne quid nimis' me paroît le chef-d'oeuvre du discernement."

The *ne quid nimis* topos here appears to be a kind of memorandum by the writer to herself for a closing "in beauty" she would need in the finished volume. At this stage of writing its conventional wisdom remains at war with the immediately preceding notes on satire, with the aggressive tone of earlier criticism, even with the moralist's assertive statements of principle. Few direct appeals to or use of authoritative sources occur; general allusions, like those to Pascal on humility, also seem notes for the future ornaments of a finished work.[14] They soon give way, as do generalized principles, to the more congenial anecdotes and pointed questions of social comedy, as the *moraliste* considers the subjects of conversation, confidentiality and gossip, promises and lying, the proper spirit of almsgiving. The signs of authority summoned for the "je," engaging combat on several fronts, mobilize a special talent for spying out the ridiculous. This part of Anne Ferrand's voice (not unlike that of the fifth *Provinciale*) doubtless kept Rémon among others in her "salon" and prompted the comtesse d'Uzès to put a young kinsman to finishing school there.[15]

The notes on satire reveal a woman still *insoumise*,[16] issuing a double warning: "La piété, mal entendue, est dangereuse" (531) and "Il faut entendre raillerie." Indeed she wishes Mme Dacier had had one more lesson to teach her. Her desire specifically to go La Bruyère one better is inscribed as discontinuous reflections that pursued insistently assert her mind's right to free movement:

[56.] Dissertation sur le ridicule—Il me semble que c'est une curiosité raisonnable que celle qui nous porte à vouloir connoître la cause de nos sentiments. Aussi, après avoir joui du plaisir de voir, sur le théâtre et sur la scène du monde, beaucoup de différents ridicules, j'ay essayé de démêler en quoi consiste le *ridicule*.

Il y a longtemps que j'ai souhaité que l'illustre Mme Dacier n'eût pas dédaigné de nous instruire . . .

[57.] Les Caractères de La Bruyère sont bons, et l'on ne peut douter qu'il n'eut de l'esprit; mais, je crois qu'ils pourroient être encore meilleurs. Il allonge ses descriptions sans nécessité, il semble qu'il veut faire voir qu'il sait les termes de l'art; affectation puérile, quand ces termes ne sont pas nécessaires pour l'intelligence du lecteur. [537]

To defend Colbert was also to defend François Bellinzani, Anne's father, who had risen to prominence through Colbert's patronage, then fallen into disgrace for alleged peculation after Colbert's death.[17] At the heart of the "memoirs" is the daughter's account of attempts to visit her father (521), successful only through the offices of the duchesse d'Aumont. Success came too late: "le pauvre M. Bellinzani" was dead when his daughter reached Vincennes. The potentially Greuzian narrative is marred by no *sensiblerie*. And nothing detracts from the accusation of royal injustice to which it leads. "Sa majesté ne fut point susceptible du scrupule d'avoir causé la mort d'un homme qui avoit bien servi, et la ruine de sa famille, sur une fausseté" (522). Through her defenses, Anne's writing becomes a renewed act of friendship extended to Colbert's family. She retained ties, with Mme de Menars,[18] and kept Colbert's daughters in a special place of reverence in her memories of difficult times. It was they, she confides, who had inspired her in her own grief to emulate courage.[19]

The project of memoir-writing centers finally around a commemoration of Anne's friendships with women who had been kind to her. She returns that kindness to special friends and in her critical appraisal of sources defends others—like her mother's friends Mlle de la Vallière and the comtesse de Soissons—against a variety of thoughtless allegations, from the distortions of gossip to those made by historians mistaking their proper names. "Touchée d'émulation pour toutes les femmes" as Bélise once professed herself, the memoir-writer's community is one of friendship, rather than passion, which opens with "douceur propre aux femmes" to her own mother (née Louise Chevreau).

"*Ma* mère," Anne writes, giving away the stylistic game (510–11). And if the writer's fantasy had been to do La Bruyère one better, it could well have been for this additional defense that came with writing. La Bruyère, readers believed, had ridiculed Mme Bellinzani in the character of the parvenue Arfure.[20] Filial piety had not earlier been available for her, as Mme Ferrand's novel had shown the world that knew her mother. At the point of writing the "memoirs," however, it extends to the woman who was absent when needed by her daughter and for her own safety had fled to Brussels "déguisée en homme."

> [32.] Les Le T[ellier] ne s'étoient pas contentés d'avoir fait périr en prison un homme, qui n'avoit rien à dire, mais qui auroit parlé s'il en fut sorti,— ils craignoient le courage et le ressentiment de Mme de Bellinzani, qui n'étoit pas moins bien instruite que son mari; on résolut de l'arrêter [. . .].[522]

By giving Louise Bellinzani her place in the adversity they had shared, the once-abandoned daughter who became Bélise rights with this writing, after her mother's death (1710), at least one wrong born with the creation of the *dédoublement* Anne Ferrand/Bélise.

2. *A femme abandonnée*

The distinguishing feature of Anne Ferrand's novel, technically and historically, is its shifting point of view. The text enacts an experiment, in *dédoublement*, largely unrecognized because of the unclear relationship of its parts. No sources have yet documented the exact moments, between 1684 and 1691, when the four segments of the text were composed nor the way they were combined for the Rouen printers who published the novel both in 1689 and 1691 without permissions and under false imprints. Like Anne Ferrand's later writings, however, this text inscribes its own desires for publication.

In part 1 of the *Histoire* an older and sadder Bélise recounts to Zélonide, one of a series of older *confidantes,* the adventures of her early adolescent attraction to Cléante and its history over almost a decade before it was shared. On the one hand, passion was allowed to become the driving force of her life—reason for self-cultivation as compensation for a lack of physical beauty, for her movements in society and at home, finally for the spontaneous "pledge" of a gift to him of *Il pastor fido*— while on the other, she fought passion by flights from home, refuge in convents, counsel sought from older women. "Quelle honte pour une femme de dire la première qu'elle aime!" (19). Part 1 ends with the intervention of a suspicious mother and a father who "m'aimoit trop pour se résoudre à me perdre pour toujours." In her interest they abandon their daughter to an arranged marriage, sealing the "cruelle destinée" of the *mal-mariée* told in part 2 when Bélise has recovered from the memory of that moment of abandonment (25).

Bélise again attempts to find shelter from passion, since "la vertu ... jusques là ne m'avoit pas encore abandonée" (28). Even in her family, through an unwelcome suitor, she discovers that she is not free from the pleasure of love with Cléante she had fantasized. Pleasure and vanity are clearly identified at the outset of the continuing confession of the abandonment of all virtue. It was she who pursued Cléante, largely through letters, overcoming his physical repugnance and moral distaste for her. In the retelling, moments of the shame of "indigne ardeur" alternate with a rekindling excitement as obstacles once sought now give way. Love comes alive again, indeed seems never to have been otherwise, as Bélise concludes—"Je l'ay toûjours aimé & l'aime encore avec une ardeur qui n'eut jamais d'égale" (42).

As the *femme abandonnée* pursues her seduction, and the narrator gives herself to it, settings are rapidly noted, details of plots elided; other actors are at best bit players until their insistent presence forces her to take greater notice of them. "Mon père sur tout plus éclairé & plus jaloux qu'un autre. . . . et la violence dont il étoit sur tout ce qui me regardoit, l'aveugla . . ." (52). With this new abandonment by the father who had remained physically and financially present in his daughter's household, the adolescent is audible. "Il m'ôta mon équipage & me fît garder à vuë. . . ." Henceforth the father is reduced to the common enemy, the "jaloux," as Bélise's mother unnamed in part 2 had already been. The rest of the family has no specified characterization apart from the importunate other. Bélise's narrative ends with her triumph over this other by "persévérance et vivacités." Again overcome, she abandons her friend and subsequently society itself, with the promise that the end of her tragic affair will be revealed to Zélonide in "la pluspart de mes Lettres."

Part 3, which ends the 1689 printing, shifts to Cléante, though neither he nor Bélise is directly present. After "quelques années," it is a friend of Zélonide (told Bélise's story despite vowed confidentiality) who seeks the denouement and learns it at second hand from a very knowledgeable friend of Cléante (who also breaks confidence). What was once known only privately is now public record for others to examine and judge. And judgment is the question. The tone changes with an early signal of male point of view given by an allusion to the story of the matron of Ephesus.[21] That story becomes the framing exemplum for the completed narrative of the would-be heroine Bélise. Finally fixed as the subject of a cautionary tale, and meriting no better, Bélise's "bizarre aventure" becomes "un portrait si terrible de la mauvaise foy de la pluspart des Dames" (59). Final judgment is thus humiliation.

Repeated airings of injured male honor for which Cléante is given moral justification necessitate a thickening of plot in part 3. Bélise is now seen as the fickle lover faithlessly abandoning Cléante as she had the husband in whose house, it is added, she had repeatedly hidden her lover. First from boredom during Cléante's two-year absence for a diplomatic mission—when Bélise wrote to him some of her finest letters (64)—then brazenly after his return, she conducted an affair with the grotesque rival of a "Pédant"—"ce petit colet!" (85).[22] Moving in the direction of the contemporary *nouvelle* (of the "désordres de l'amour" variety), and away from the earlier narrative's confessional directness, Cléante's highly plotted story, within its third-person scaffolding, sets at a distance of severe moral judgment all those things most important to Bélise.

The letters that were the direct record of passionate life are reduced to the wit and art of an "artificieuse Bélise." Passion itself proclaimed in them as eternal becomes nothing more than time-bound, intermittent "emportements" of a violent temperament. Already reduced to the adversary in Bélise's scenario, her family is further humiliated. Its "affaires fort fâcheuses"—Bellinzani's fall—are held only to be a pretext for Bélise's "chagrin" (65). Subsequent alarm over surveillance (now without her father), like pleas to Cléante for discretion or even temporary separation, are viewed only as strategies to cover the new affair. Changes in circumstances that allow Cléante to visit her are now put down simply to Bélise's inexplicable caprice, to the point that Cléante's patience breaks in "la lettre la plus outrageante que le dépit & la rage puisse jamais dicter" (85). Bélise's unabashed admission of "preuves de son crime" justifies Cléante's decision to abandon Bélise "pour jamais à toute l'horreur de sa mauvaise conduite" (88). The closing paragraph of the *Histoire* justifies this judgment and apparently gives the last word to Cléante.

As promised, Bélise's letters are added, in the 1691 printing, seemingly as evidence for Cléante's case. The selected letters have an order of their own (as did most probably those circulated before the novel's publication).[23] They neither correspond to the letters evoked in part 2 nor include any of those cited in part 3 as most incriminating Bélise during the last stage of the lovers' relations. The seventy-two letters, mostly short, all undated, now close with the separation of Cléante's voyage. The ending "in beauty" was prepared in part 3 by praise of the letters of separation and has succeeded in its rhetorical intention for recent readers like Maurice Lever.[24]

Bélise's last adieu and solitude as she is abandoned, by a lover whose ambitions prolong absence, and abandons herself to silence and death are not without echoes of the *Lettres portugaises*.[25] But like Racinian overtones they are fleeting. The dominant register is resolutely practical and briskly orders the course of the story the love letters memorialize. With unrelenting clarity about herself, physically and morally, and no illusions about the "naturalness" of her passion, Bélise typically refuses Cléante's idealizing portrait. "On se connoît toûjours malgré les efforts que fait l'amour propre pour nous tromper . . . je ne suis pas belle" (57–58; again, 63). Vanity is savored—"J'en jouis avec . . . plaisir" (49)—and Cléante is more than once warned against its power to blind as he is against other weaknesses. He has more than ample warning of Bélise's special pleasures—"Je suis une amie difficile et une maîtresse glorieuse" (65) and "N'admirez vous point la foiblesse des femmes & leur legereté?" (72).

The *dédoublement* of a male voice, as the letter writers themselves would hear it, is evident, in a letter on Cléante's ambition worthy of a Cornelian father (no. 47). But that voice's intermittent presence gathers cumulative strength throughout the letters: in the aggressiveness of the seduction pursued in the first grouping (nos. 1–25) as in the willful abandonment to pleasure of those at the center that celebrate mutual love (nos. 26–54). "Si j'étais homme . . ." (43) is often assumed.

Enjoyment of passion is at first fearful, inhibited in the temporary security of the eluded gaze of the family. "Je puis m'abandonner toute entière aux movemens de mon coeur, je suis délivrée de tout ce que je hais." But sensual abandon radiates through the letters at the heart of the published collection. "Peut-on mieux faire que de travailler à se rendre heureux & peut-on l'être sans s'aimer . . . ?" (39). It is a repeated total gift of self that Bélise's passion demands. Her desire remains inscribed in the commemorative closing letter and in her last words of part 2 before her withdrawal from society:

Je m'abandonne à vous & à la tendresse, sans réserve, & sans crainte . . . Jouissez de cette victoire, mon cher Amant. (35)
Abandonnons nous sans réserve à l'amour pendant le peu de jours qui nous reste à nous voir. . . . (55)

Cléante too is to be judged in terms of this absolute during separation and by inference after the reader's separation from the text:

> Si vous m'aviez bien connuë, vous ne m'eussiez point abandonnée pour elle [ambition]. (78)

> Vous renoncez à des plaisirs ... Savez que quand on veut être plus qu'un homme, on devient beaucoup moins quelquefois. Thésée fut moins blâmé d'avoir été sensible aux charmes d'Ariane, que de l'avoir abandonnée. (80)[26]

The return to Bélise and the first-person of the letters reinforce the already striking differences that distinguish part 3 from the first two parts of the *Histoire*. But rather than see in part 3 Anne Ferrand's inventiveness in constructing a typical male narrative, looking forward uniquely in its time to relativist experiments (Jules Romains's *Psyché*, say, or Montherlant's Andrée Hacquebaut, whom Bélise sometimes curiously resembles), a continuing male critical tradition has without external evidence contested her authorship. At one point, the hypothesis goes, Breteuil/Cléante intervened and through a hired author—Fontenelle?—inserted the last word on Bélise.[27] Part 3 is held to be the man's writing, marked as it is by judgment; 1–2, with its passionate first-person, the woman's (*a fortiori* an Italian woman's). In the perspective of Anne Ferrand's later writings, and the letters as published, these lines of argument cannot be taken seriously. "Il faut entendre raillerie," she warned, and engaged it through *dédoublement*. Irony is the weapon of a desire for vengeance that began with a renewed self-affirmation found in writing.

Irony, and self-punishment with it, is initially audible in the name chosen for Anne Ferrand's persona. The inescapable association with Bélise is Molière's character, in *Les Femmes savantes,* whose delusion is that all men are courting her.[28] Angry and disabused, the woman who later moved from particular "ridicule" to the question "en quoi consiste le ridicule" and reflected on La Bruyère may have found Molière's staging of Bélise's ridicule irresistible grounds for reflection. "Tu l'as voulu, Bélise" (to change plays) is as probable as any other response of Anne Ferrand's alert mind as she revised the letters for publication in 1691, and with freedom in sight, a fuller settling of accounts. That irony may be seen focused in the changed title of 1691, in which the older Bélise then writing excised the special pleading of the first title's "jeune Bélise." "On a peine à comprendre qu'une femme, peu éprise de son mari, dans un âge

où l'on prend la vanité pour la gloire . . . ne fut point touchée de sa prétendue passion," Anne reflected in her memoirs (524). In the clarity of
loss, with the dark days of 1686–87, the distance for the same judgment
on herself—through Cléante—could have been hers as probably as
another's.

Critical readers have from 1880 to the present invariably preferred
Bélise's letters over Cléante's narrative. By comparison it has seemed conventional, wooden; Cléante himself, self-righteous and lacking in generosity. The placement of the letters as "justificatory pieces" by the
ordinary legal logic of a writer surrounded by judges (as Anne Ferrand
literally was in her husband's family) turns against Cléante. The letters in
fact force dissatisfaction with part 3, a questioning of its devices of story-
telling, even a search for Cléante's errors. Vanity rather than honor? Belief in gossip and appearances rather than an abiding love? Surely love
could have seen through the Pédant, in the circumstances of the Bellinzani
débâcle? Or if the scenario were different, could not love with its old
teasing spirit of complicity have seen through a new ritual testing? The
worst of Bélise gleaned in the letters is made literally true in part 3 and
used against her to the point of overshadowing the fact that the worst of
Cléante—his vanity and weakness—also if more insinuatingly appears
there. Cléante's final "moral portrait"—offered at second hand—elicits
retrospectively from the reader of Bélise's letters a response not unlike
that Prévost invites with Des Grieux's ambiguous "perfide Manon," "per-
fides larmes." The accounts closed by the writer in 1691 are balanced by
a "femme forte qui se retire du monde." Through Cléante's final severity,
as through Bélise's raised tones, there remains an insinuating doubt: "Et
cet Amant qui crie qu'on l'abandonne est *peut-être* tout prest à m'abandonner" (57).

In Anne Ferrand's letters, as Bernard Bray suggests, there is a pure
melody of pleasure.[29] But there is also an edge of nastiness, particularly
in dealing with the "hated family," not only the all-too-present-husband
but also the absent mother. Exulting over foiling their surveillance, Bélise
covets a satirist's revenge: "Disons leur pour nous venger" (42). And
when her husband waxes "galant," she promises it—"la vengeance est
certaine" (72). The promise is raised to a solemn oath: "Que l'union qui
sera désormais entre nous serve de punition à ceux qui me persécute, &
qu'elle me venge de tout ce qu'ils me font souffrir" (47–48). With calculated self-interest "young Bélise" restrained this desire to avenge "les cha-

grins que me cause la bizarrerie de ma famille": "Si je ne me contois pour beaucoup, j'agirois d'une manière que je leur ferois bien voir que je les conte pour rien" (62). After the death of her father, and with the destruction of her past in 1686–87, the desire is no longer restrained. The transgressive writing of the four parts of the text of 1691 is a self-affirmation that settles more than accounts with Cléante/Breteuil.

3. Mother and Daughter

As Anne Ferrand lingers over intimate scenes between Mme Dacier and her daughter, who died prematurely, her tone changes dramatically. Her own loss of a daughter and with it the difference of her own life from Mme Dacier's break the text. Solitude had been her lot rather than the consolation friends and family offered Mme Dacier, "bonne mère, après avoir rempli les devoirs de fille."

> Cet endroit de ma lettre me rapelle le souvenir de mes propres pertes. Quelle douleur de voir périr ce qu'on a aimé, quand l'estime publique s'accorde avec notre tendresse! M^d Dacier mêloit ses larmes avec celles d'une autre elle-même; et ce qui sembloit augmenter son affliction servoit à l'adoucir; mais mes larmes avoient tant de différentes causes, que je ne puis comprendre comment j'ai résisté à une situation si cruelle. Je suis presque honteuse de vivre. [f. 187]

The time of recollection in this moment of emptiness and lack is not simply that of the death in 1698 of Anne's elder daughter, who died at twenty-one in Riom, far from her mother. The multiple causes of grief and shame reactivate the loss and solitude of the year 1686 and the following years of internment (at the abbey L'Eau-Notre Dame south of Chartres). Legal documents begin to show that Anne's memories did not exaggerate.[30]

Michel Ferrand made no secret of the "rixes" between spouses, mainly relating to Bellinzani's disgrace, that raised his fear of more violence. Nor did he hide the fact that he could no longer tolerate life with the "daughter of a criminal."[31] Although a separate establishment in the rue du Bac was legally stipulated, the Ferrands' son remained with his father. If their two daughters lived with their mother at all, it could only have been briefly. The moment was right for them, at ten and twelve, to board at the nearby Filles de Sainte-Marie. There the younger remained. With the elder's betrothal during her exile, Anne Ferrand in fact lost both daughters in 1686–91.

When the letter on Mme Dacier was written it was thus too late for Anne Ferrand to have with her own daughters the friendship so valued in her writings. And so it seemed too with her own mother, by transference, as Anne made amends to Louise Bellinzani: the daughter, the *Histoire* indicates, had not sought her friendship in adolescence and could not in 1686 when exile separated mother from daughter. Turning to writing during exile—rather than to devotion—the daughter had effected an act of independence from her mother. But her daughters are the major omissions of that text. They are cruelly subsumed by the generalized other, then again displaced by the "mon enfant" incongruously lavished on the lover Cléante.[32] Like the *dédoublement* Bélise-Cléante at the moment of writing, the "mon enfant" becomes with this second displacement of memory a synecdoche of writing, now the shame of having written.

"Bélise" is born fully armed with the literary transformation of the letters to Breteuil, that of the *épistolier* into *auteur-épistolier*. Stylistic corrections, re-ordering, excisions, occasional rewritings all appear in the Arsenal manuscript.[33] Typical of these procedures is the reworking of the last letter, admired by Maurice Lever for raising the *femme abandonnée* from melodrama to the tragic. But beyond excisions and other alterations of levels of style, emendation has special significance at this climactic moment.

> 1691: Je n'ai jamais été heureuse, et je meure encore plus malheureuse que je n'ai vécu. *Si ma mort ne peut mettre ma gloire à couvert,* et que ceux qui me haissent veulent, pour se venger de moi, publier ce qu'ils ont pu découvrir de mon adventure [. . .] Asse, 155–56 [fac. ed., 89; emphasis added]
>
> MS: Je n'ay vescu que pour vous. Je n'ay jamais vescue heureuse et je suis encore plus que je n'ay vescu *si ma mere ne peut mettre ma gloire a couvert* et [. . .] [f. 14ᵛ]

Whatever is lost in revision, the suppression of the mother is gained. Following failure to forestall publication alluded to here, and with the felt abandonment of 1687–91, *se venger* is defiantly enacted by writing *for* publication (Cléante is of course also served as Bélise herself preempts her challenge to him—"publiez mes lettres si . . ."). This closing letter, originally part of the earliest sequence charting the course of the love,[34] translates Louise Bellinzani from a point of usefulness in it (revealingly, since this role is elided in the *Histoire*) to the climactic instance of failure. The apparently semic link *mère/mort* at this moment of lack and abandonment again opens into the present particular events of 1686. Anne Ferrand in her last years was forced to dwell on them and to relive the association mother/death with new cruelty.

Seven months after separation from her husband, in November 1686, Anne Ferrand gave birth to a third daughter. The baby was taken from her for nursing, it was later revealed, and was not returned to her before her exile. In 1725, in the wake of Michel Ferrand's death (1723), a thirty-nine-year-old woman appeared claiming her part in the estate as the Ferrands' last and indeed long lost daughter. Mme Ferrand and collateral heirs contested, then appealed the judgment won for the plaintiff by the illustrious Cochin.[35] The legal documents of what became twelve years' litigation, as complicated as any novel, afford a last dramatic view of Anne Ferrand—unable or unwilling to find in this woman the daughter and friend she desired for her own advanced age, unable as well perhaps to maintain the "reprieve" of Louise Bellinzani the dutiful daughter granted in the first stages of memoir-writing.

Her mother, Anne's testimony divulges, had lied to her: "She informed me that the baby had died."[36] Evidence was produced and sustained that Louise Bellinzani had in fact had the infant christened as a foundling, then arranged through servants for pensions under a variety of assumed names through a succession of convents. Taking on what she supposed were her mother's charities, Anne testified, she continued support of this girl, who was identified to her as the illegitimate offspring of her younger, wayward brother. That birth had been hidden, after Bellinzani's death, to avoid further troubles for the family that he then at least nominally headed (after leaving his monastery at eighteen).

Whether or not Anne Ferrand finally accepted that her mother had lied to her about her youngest daughter's death, she could not have avoided reflection on the possibility. And she could not have escaped some painful reflection on the inextricably linked relationships she had had with her own daughters. Having outlived immediate family, Anne Ferrand retired to the convent du Cherche-Midi for the last year of her life. Accounts with Breteuil and with Michel Ferrand had long been closed, the drama of the *mal-mariée* closed by her own writing and by litigation.[37] But the *femme abandonnée* again alone had yet some dramatically unsettled accounts on which to reflect in the final shelter of the convent that she had once upon a time so clamorously sought.

Notes

1. 1689 title: HISTOIRE / NOUVELLE / DES AMOURS / DE LA JEUNE / BELISE / ET DE CLEANTE. / Divisée en trois parties, / Par Mʳ D.***/ Suivant la copie imprimée à Paris. Eugène Asse's ed. (Paris: Charpentier, 1880) has not been replaced; for convenience all references are to the facsimile presented by René Godenne (Slatkine, 1979).

2. B.N. MS. fon. fr. n.a. 4040, f. 58ᵛ.

3. Praise is given to epistolary style. See *Caractères,* ed. Servois, I: 418 and F. Deloffre, ed., *Les Lettres portugaises* (Paris: Garnier, 1962), p. vi.

4. Reprinted in 1696 (The Hague); 1699 (Amsterdam); 1701 (The Hague); 1702 (Amsterdam); 1714 (Brussels); 1716 (The Hague); 1721 (Rotterdam); 1725 (Amsterdam); 1738 (Anvers); 1760 (London); 1777 (London).

5. See Bernard Bray, ed. *Lettres portugaises . . . et autres romans d'amour par lettres* (Paris: Garnier-Flammarion, 1982), p. 181; R. Godenne, "Présentation," pp. vi–vii; Maurice Lever, *Le Roman français au XVIIᵉ siècle* (Paris: PUF, 1981), pp. 233–36.

6. Arsenal MS. 5346, f. 182–87ᵛ: "Lettre de Madᵉ la P.F. à Monsʳ l'abbé R. Doctʳ de Sorbonne. à Paris le 21. janvʳ 1721." Partial publication by Paul Bonnefon, *RHLF* 13 (1906): 326–31; Fern Farnham, *Madame Dacier.* 2nd ed. (Monterey: Angel Press, 1980), pp. 195–98.

7. On Mme Dacier's lack of militancy, see Farnham, pp. 50–51 and passim. The exception is the dedication to her Delphin ed. of Callimachus.

8. The MSS. have seemingly disappeared from public domain. Published with minimal textual annotation by Marcel Langlois, *RHLF* 32 (1925): 497–528. On the basis of references to published works cited, part 1 dates between 1720–1727; nothing indicates dates for the several separate series of part 2.

9. Amsterdam, 1720.

10. Utrecht, 1727. Reflections are uniquely in the form of a letter to an unidentified friend.

11. P. 509. It is unclear whether A.F. considers the "mauvaise imitation" by Mme de Lafayette herself or another writer.

12. Dangeau, *Journal,* 29 septembre 1718. See also H. Thirion, *Madame de Prie* (Paris: Plon, 1905), p. 129.

13. On Antoine Ferrand, see Asse, pp. lxxiii, 261–70.

14. Pascal, pp. 531, 535 (on "raillerie"); Montaigne, p. 516; Plutarch (the only textual citation), p. 532.

15. Less a salon than a circle, A.F.'s has been glimpsed only through the *Mémoires du marquis de Franclieu* (Champion, 1896). See for a reconstruction, G. Syveton, "Une Femme de magistrat sous Louis XIV," *La Grande Revue* 9 (1905): pp. 318–21.

16. Langlois's typology of the *précieuse* on the model of Mme de la Sablière (pp. 497–98) is at best approximate. The points concerning religion are contradicted by the text edited.

17. On the scandal of the "pièces à quatre sols" and Bellinzani's still undetermined part, see Lionel Rothkrug, *Opposition to Louis XIV . . .* (Princeton:

Princeton University Press, 1965), pp. 167, 216, 222. Cf. Inez Murat, *Colbert* (Paris: Fayard, 1980), pp. 364–65.

18. Marie de la Grange Neuville, wife of Jean-Jacques Charron de Menars, brother of Mme Colbert. An extant undated letter of A.F. is addressed at Menars during a stay there (B.N. MS. fon. fr. 24.442, f. 295).

19. P. 596: "... les filles, dont la sagesse et la piété ont été hors de toute atteinte, *et qui a produit des retours dans ceux que la jeunesse et le mauvais exemple avoient écartés.*" If the underscoring is in the MS., Langlois's claim for self-confession seems justified.

20. "Des biens de fortune," 16 (1st ed). Louise Chevreau was the daughter of a notary.

21. *Satyricon*, p. xi. The story was an easily recognizable commonplace of less than hardcore misogynistic writing.

22. A note to B.N. MS. n.a. 4040 identifies the "Pédant" as abbé Miramion; P. Bonnefon argues for abbé Lannion, *L'Amateur d'autographes* n.s. 5 (1905), pp. 157–67.

23. A MS. "vers 1688" is cited after the Claudin catalogue (1858) by Fernand Drujon, *Les Livres à clef . . .* (Paris: E Rouveyre, 1888), I: 468–69. Arsenal MS. 3809 is certainly prior to 1689 and perhaps corrected in A.F.'s hand. B.N. fon. fr. n.a. 4041 is posterior (1691–96?). A fourth MS. is cited after the Pierre Louÿs catalogue (1929) by Y. Guiraud, *Bibliographie du roman épistolier* (Fribourg: Editions Universitaires Fribourg Suisse, 1977), p. 22. Toulouse MS. 848 does not contain the letters.

24. *Le Roman français au XVIIe siècle*, pp. 235–36.

25. See e.g., B. Bray, *Lettres portugaises . . .*, p. 31. Parallels with the 5th and the 4th *Portugaises* cannot conclusively be identified as textual citation.

26. *Phèdre* (v. 89) may be heard here; but the primary reference is Plutarch's life of Theseus (section 24).

27. Elaboration is primarily Langlois's (pp. 499–501). His suggestion of Fontenelle's authorship is discounted by Alain Niderst, *Fontenelle à la recherche de lui-même* (Paris: Nizet, 1972), p. 21. Langlois is followed by R. Godenne, "Présentation," pp. 3–7. Bernard Bray (p. 30) implicitly departs from this tradition.

28. The point has often been made that "Bélise" derives from the French pronunciation of Bellinzani; the Moliéresque association is made but not developed by Langlois. It is supported by the recurrent theme of Bélise's lack of physical beauty.

29. *Lettres portugaises . . .*, pp. 30, 182.

30. I have used B.N. MSS. D'Hozier, P.O. 1127, 1128; D.B. 265; Carrés 254. The principal documents may be found in Asse.

31. See Asse, pp. xlv–viii. The act of separation is given, p. lxv, n.3.

32. Pp. 8, 26, 34. "Correction" to "mon amant" occurs in some instances in the Arsenal MS.

33. See above (note 23). I have considered the order and corrections of this MS. elsewhere. The MS. was not used by Asse.

34. The last published letter is 13th in the MS. (f. 12^v–16). In Asse's conjec-

tural dating it, as well as the two preceding letters, would thus be closer to 1680 than 1684.

35. For the entry into the legal "annals," see P. F. Besdel, "Histoire de Mademoiselle Ferrand," *Abrégé des causes célèbres et intéressants* ... 4th ed. (Rouen: Machuel, 1786), III: 29–30.

36. Interrogatoire du 12 août 1735. See Asse, lxx, n. 2.

37. After Michel Ferrand's death, A.F. sought the return of 156,000 livres from his estate. See Asse, p. xlii, n.3.

* It is a pleasure to thank The College of Humanities of the Ohio State University for the Faculty Professional Leave during which my research on Anne Ferrand was done.

IV
The Lyric

La Fontaine, *Les Vautours et les pigeons* (VII, 8): An Intertextual Reading

Jules Brody

. . . il en est de la lecture comme des auberges espagnoles, et de
l'amour . . . : on n'y trouve que ce qu'on y apporte.

—ANDRÉ MAUROIS[1]

The most striking single feature of so-called French classical literature is
its extraordinary, programmatic commitment to the binary. This is no
doubt why the uninitiated reader often finds this kind of writing so mo-
notonous and difficult to appreciate; this is also why certain individual
passages are so easy to remember, often impossible to forget. It is a matter of evidence that the works of Corneille, Pascal, Racine et al., are lit-
tered with such statements as these, in which antithesis is the central
rhetorical support:

> Je consens, ou plutôt j'aspire à ma ruine.
> [Corneille, *Polyeucte*, IV, 2, 1139]

> S'il se vante je l'abaisse, s'il s'abaisse, je le vante.
> [Pascal, *Pensées*, Lafuma, no. 130]

> La magnanimité méprise tout pour avoir tout.
> [La Rochefoucauld, *Maximes*, no. 248]

> J'ai pour moi la justice et je perds mon procès.
> [Molière, *Misanthrope*, V, 1, 1492]

> Toujours prête à partir, et demeurant toujours.
> [Racine, *Andromaque*, I, 1, 131]

What these texts have in common is a style which asks to be read as the
surface manifestation of a deep semantic structure, and more pointedly

---

This essay had its origins in an MLA panel discussion (Chicago, 1985) orga-
nized by David Lee Rubin under the title "New Approaches to the *Fables* of La
Fontaine"; *Les Vautours et les pigeons* was the text on which Richard Danner,
Marcel Gutwirth and myself were invited to focus our remarks.

still as the rhetorically and syntactically coded expression of a habitual, collective way of thinking about human psychology and behavior: its duplicity, its tensions, its incompatibilities, and its perversity. Turn this style inside out, and it becomes a moral content. Open Corneille or Racine to any page, and you are knee deep in ambiguity, alterity, asperity: the then and the now, the inner and the outer, the lesser and the greater, master and slave, monarch and subject. French classical literature at its most typical surrounds us with nervous, anxious people locked in conflict, often within the claustrophobic space of an alexandrine line.

Open La Fontaine's *Fables* to almost any page and what do you find? Sweetness and light, smoothness, polish, sinuous fluidity—what Leo Spitzer describes, in his magisterial study of the transition in La Fontaine, as an updated version of Horatian *suavitas*.[2] You will look in vain for those charged, tension-ridden antitheses that are endemic to the writing of Racine: "Présente je vous fuis; absente je vous trouve" (*Phèdre*, II, 2, 542); the dominant figure in La Fontaine is the mocking, the witty, the often whimsical *periphrasis:* "Le plus terrible des enfants/Que le Nord jusque-là eût porté dans ses flancs" (*Le Chêne et le roseau*, I, 22, 26–27). In this respect, our access to La Fontaine is oddly skewed and, in the end, severely limited. Or, to put the matter in terms of my earlier characterization of French classical writing: if *antithesis* is a polarizing figure whose function is confrontational, *periphrasis* is a figure of avoidance, whose function is cosmetic, in that its essential role is to interpose aesthetic distance between the reader and the semantic content that it purports to convey. The pages of La Fontaine are filled, to be sure, with concrete, graphic examples of deceit, greed, injustice, and violence. All this evil transpires, however, so decorously and naturally, at times even so pleasantly and appealingly, that the French can still think of the *Fables* as suitable for memorization by their children.[3]

And yet, the memorizable, delightful, elegant La Fontaine is not a figment of the mind either, for it harks back to a perception of the *Fables* that is also firmly grounded in the text; it often seems in fact as if, underneath all that *bonhomie* and *naturel,* there is really nothing much going on. Once begun, the reading progresses with a limpidity and a simplicity that can be highly unsettling, especially to professional, academic readers who labor in the conviction that they should somehow be able to talk about La Fontaine in the same detail and at the same depth as they are accustomed to do with Pascal and Racine. For the serious reader, the problem is always the same: to find some break in the flow of the text, some palpable sign of a hidden complexity, some ungrammaticality to tell us that everything is really *not* alright after all. Where, so we ask, is the catachresis that will lead us to the hypogram? Where in a given fable is La Fontaine's counterpart or equivalent to "La fille de Minos et de Pasiphaé" (*Phèdre,* I, 1, 36)? In the following pages I would like to offer an empirical description of the ways in which one reader has gone about confronting these and related questions as they pertain to a consideration of *Les Vautours et les pigeons.*

My first reaction to this fable was triggered by a personal association to the apparently coincidental collocation in the opening lines of the proper names "Mars" and "Vénus":

Mars autrefois mit tout l'air en émute.
Certain sujet fit naître la dispute
Chez les oiseaux, non ceux que le Printemps
Mène à sa cour, et qui, sous la feuillée
Par leur exemple et leurs sons éclatants,
Font que Vénus est en nous réveillée;
Ni ceux encor que la mère d'Amour
Met à son char; mais le peuple vautour . . .
                    [ll. 1–8]

These same two deities—as I first vaguely recalled, then verified—play a prominent role and, according to the standard authorities, fulfill a seminal allegorical function in Lucretius's prologue to *De rerum natura.* There, in her capacity as *Venus physica,* as what Lucretius will later call "rerum natura creatrix," Venus represents "the creative power of nature," whereas Mars, as god of War, stands by contrast for the countervailing principle of destruction.[4] Taken together, these two antinomial figures recapitulate the complex, conflictual totality of Being, the way Life is, the Nature of Things.

The possibility of a central, structuring Lucretian intertext which, in the absence of any more compelling insight, I chose as my working hypothesis, needed more, however, than my chance personal association for its validation. And upon closer inspection, I was able to bring into play a number of additional elements. I noted first that Venus is not merely referred to in passing, but that her presence in the poem becomes the object of a double overdetermination: 1) the mention of her name in line 6 ("Vénus est en nous réveillée. . . .") is immediately relayed in the next line by the periphrasis "la mère d'amour"; 2) this rather mannered redundancy draws further attention to itself by virtue of the emphasis placed on Ven-

us's connection with birds; first with nightingales as harbingers of Spring
(l. 3: "ceux que le Printemps/Mène à sa cour"), and then with the doves
that draw her chariot (ll. 7–8: "que la mère d'Amour/Met à son char").
This marked feature—the bird-relatedness of Venus—has in turn a dual
reference: 1) to the fable's title, specifically to the word *pigeons,* of which
Venus's doves—snow white, gentle, tender—are a noble variant, and 2)
to the passage in Lucretius's prologue in which Venus is described in
terms of the same two characteristics as La Fontaine was to place in the
foreground: her connection both with the onset of Spring and with birds
of/in love:

> Nam simul ac species patefacta est verna diei
> Et reserata viget genitabilis aura favoni,
> Aeriae primum volucres te, Diva, tuumque
> Significant initum, perclusae corda tua vi.

> When first the day puts on the aspect of spring,
> when in all its force the fertilizing breath of
> Zephyr is unleashed, then, great goddess, the
> birds of air give the first intimation of your
> entry; for yours is the power that has pierced
> them to the heart.
>
> [I, ll. 10–13][5]

I hasten to add that, never having read Lucretius in Latin, I had no personal recollection of these lines, and that I gained knowledge of them
from a note in Régnier's edition of the *Fables* in the *Grands Ecrivains de
la France* collection. It is significant in this regard that Régnier prints the
passage from Lucretius with no gloss or commentary, as if he considered
it so well known and the Latin so accessible that his intended reader of
1884—whether this reader existed in reality or in his own idealization—
would be able to decipher it without difficulty. The baldness of Régnier's
note also suggests that, within the cultural preview of his classically edu-
cated reader, the nature of the kinship between La Fontaine's and Lucretius's juxtaposed descriptions of Venus would be self-evident.

However this may be, I attach considerable importance to the fact that
Régnier, although by another avenue, had been led before me to posit or,
at the very least, to suspect a trace of the Lucretian presence in La Fontaine's poem. On second thought, I should perhaps have said that I found
Régnier's note particularly meaningful not "although," but *because* he
reached Lucretius for other reasons and by a different route from my

own. The fact that he identified La Fontaine's "source" presumably as a result of explicit verbal reminiscence, whereas I hypothesized an intertextual relationship through having read Lucretius thirty years earlier in English translation—the fact that two such different readers, at an interval of a hundred years, coming from two widely separated corners of history, geography, and literary tradition, should have converged in this instance on Lucretius's prologue, points to something basic in the way that *Les Vautours et les pigeons* has been programmed to produce meaning. That is to say, the Lucretian intertext would seem to be so snugly embedded in La Fontaine's poem that, by one means or another, some careful, curious, alert reader had to come along sooner or later and notice it. If both Régnier and I were led back independently to the same passage in Lucretius, does this not suggest that it was *there* all the time waiting to be recovered? In any event, it is certain that some sensitive, perceptive reader was bound to observe, even in complete ignorance of the parallel passage in Lucretius, that Venus and Mars, although not specifically contrasted with each other in La Fontaine, do in fact represent, by the mere presuppositions of their names, such polar qualities as tenderness and violence, creation and destruction, peace and war, or as echoed in the title of the Woody Allen film of some years back, *Love and Death*. In the business of reading, all roads, however circuitous or divergent they may appear to be, eventually lead to Rome.

As an editor working within certain artisanal-formal conventions and within a historically circumscribed notion of literary transmission, Régnier also felt called upon to provide his reader with this note at the proper name Mars: "Le Dieu de la guerre, pour 'la guerre, une guerre.' C'est le ton de l'épopée que La Fontaine sait prendre avec tant d'art quand il veut relever ce qu'il dit." What Régnier did not do—and it is this consideration that distinguishes between the respective dynamics of source criticism and intertextual reading—was to observe or, if he did so observe, to mention, that Mars is also present in the prologue to *De rerum natura*, and at a distance of less than twenty lines from the description of Venus that he himself was to allege at line 6 of *Les Vautours et les pigeons;*

Effice ut interea fera moenera militiai
per maria ac terras omnis sopita quiescant.
Nam tu sola potes tranquilla pace iuuare
mortalis, quoniam belli fera moenera Mauors
armipotens regit, in gremium qui saepe tuum se
reiicit, aeterno deuictus uolnere amoris . . .

Meanwhile, grant that this brutal business of war by sea
and land may everywhere be lulled to rest. For you alone have power to
bestow on mortals the blessing of quiet peace. In your bosom Mars
himself, supreme commander in this brutal business, flings himself down
at times, laid low by the irremediable wound of love.

[I, ll. 29–34]

Once we have, for whatever reason and by whatever process, traced the
names Mars and Venus back to their common locus in *De rerum natura*,
it is no longer possible to prevent the dialectical resonance that inheres in
this conjunction at least from impinging on our reading of the "Mars"/
"Vénus" collocation in La Fontaine. Whereas the indication of a source
or model allows for the assertion of a contact or an "influence," the perception of an intertext, as I am using the term here, invites us to open up
a process of exploration and interrogation. Having been sent out by the
names "Mars" and "Vénus" in *Les Vautours et les pigeons* to the beginning of *De rerum natura*, the reader brings back from it, willy nilly, as
s/he resumes contact with La Fontaine's words, a suggested vision of the
world as it might be, if the antagonism distilled by these two names could
be subdued or dissolved. Lucretius's prologue contains an unexpressed
idea which is actualized and disengaged by the reader when s/he compares Venus's identical effect on the birds in the sky and the God of War:
the former, necessarily, as part of nature, "pierced . . . through the heart"
(*perclusae corda*), succumb to the controlling force of Love; in the same
way, Mars, so it must be earnestly hoped, will similarly be "laid low by
the irremediable wound of love" (*aeterno deuictus uolnere amoris*). This
double seduction by Venus subtends a world view and builds on a cos-
mological theorem that have found lasting, proverbial expression in the
Virgilian maxim: *Omnia vincit amor* (*Eclogues*, X, l. 69).

I readily admit that my interest in wanting to link *Les Vautours et les
pigeons* intertextually with Lucretius's prologue may appear idiosyn-
cratic or arbitrary. I might also concede for the sake of argument that the
convergence of my associations with Régnier's was fortuitous and coincidental. On one point, however, I would stand absolutely firm: the over-
determined status of the name "Vénus," her bird-relatedness, and the
equation *pigeon* = *colombe* are inherent, objective properties of the text.
In the absence of any knowledge of Lucretius or of any earlier literary
treatments of Venus and her doves, the careful, docile reader must nevertheless attend to the emphasis laid on the generic word "oiseaux" (l. 3),
which La Fontaine first pushes into relief through the *enjambement*

Mars autrefois mit tout l'air en émute.
Certain sujet fit naître la dispute
Chez les oiseaux . . .

and then foregrounds further in the polarizing sequence: "*non* ceux . . .
Ni ceux encor . . . *mais* le peuple vautour . . ." (ll. 3–8). Whereas the
vultures are named outright, the other birds that are mentioned in antic-
ipatory contradistinction to them ("*non* ceux . . . *Ni* ceux encor"), are
not identified, but presented to us at one remove from behind the veil of
periphrasis, which it becomes the reader's first order of business to penetrate. To take up this challenge, to defeat La Fontaine's periphrastic evasion, and thus fill the semantic void which it is designed to create, is to
participate in the production of meaning and to collaborate with the poet
in his chosen distribution of emphasis. But, even the lazy, insensitive, or
ignorant reader who declines this invitation will not be let off that easily,
since La Fontaine's editors, as self-appointed or commercially enlisted
guardians of his text, are there in chorus to remind us that our response
to *Les Vautours et les pigeons* will be incomplete and deficient as long as
we do not know that the bird of spring is the nightingale and the bird of
Venus is the dove. Only with this information at our command, so they
insist in behalf of the poet who is no longer there to defend the integrity
of his words, are we equipped to read on intelligently.[6]

Having said this much, however, and having recovered the submerged
content of La Fontaine's circumlocutions, the editors still do not tell the
story in all its intricacy, for La Fontaine's periphrastic overdeterminations
are compounded further by the fact that the nightingale is not only the
harbinger of Spring, but it is also, in the same way as the dove, a bird of
Venus, inasmuch as Spring stands metaphorically for the season of Love.
Thus, at line 8, with the long-heralded, long-awaited mention of the word
vautours, several preliminary generalizations become possible: 1) The sequential set: bird of spring > season of Love > birds of Venus signals a
first amplification of the titular word *pigeons* by way of a proleptic and
gratuitous actualization of the word *colombe*. I say "gratuitous," because
nothing at this point in the text's narrative line requires such specializa-
tion of meaning. La Fontaine is doing here by indirection what he had
done straightforwardly in *La Colombe et la fourmi* (II, 12, 12), where he
describes the bird in the title periphrastically as a "oiseau de Vénus." 2)
We find next, parallelwise, a proleptic and gratuitous mention of Venus,
first as metaphor for love or desire (line 6: "Vénus est en nous réveillée"),
then, periphrastically and tautologically, as mother of cupid (line 7: "la

mère d'Amour"), who, in that capacity, rides in a chariot drawn by doves. The contextual function of this powerfully concatenated network of periphrases, is to attune the reader's response to the idea that the *pigeons* of the title are to be read, retroactively, not as the common, mottled, dirty rooftop or courtyard kind, but as the snow white, sentimentally and poetically refined variety, of noble affect and irenic disposition, perched at the very top of the columbiform paradigm, or in Littré's terse definition, s.v. *Colombe;* "Pigeon, en style élevé." 3) If once we take the word *pigeon* (= dove = bird of Love) as emblematic of the presence of Venus, we may go a step past description to interpretation and attribute proleptic semiotic value to the juxtaposition of "pigeons," the last word in the fable's title, and "Mars," the first word in the fable's text. 4) The first eight lines of *Les Vautours et les pigeons* may now be read as a tautological amplification in Greco-Roman or mythological code of the same polarity that the fable's title expresses in ornithological code:

$$\frac{\text{Vautours}}{\text{Pigeons}} = \frac{\text{War Birds}}{\text{Love Birds}} = \frac{\text{Mars}}{\text{Venus}} = \frac{\text{War}}{\text{Peace}}$$

Moreover, this opposition between "Mars" and "Vénus," as representative of two antiphrastic affective postures and cultures, is exemplified elsewhere in La Fontaine: in *Le Meunier, son fils et l'âne* (II, 1, 81), we read: "Quant à vous, suivez Mars, ou l'Amour ou le Prince . . ."; and in *A Monseigneur, le duc de Bourgogne,* (XII, 1, 9 and 17), "Le métier de Mars" is set contrapuntally against "les Ris et les Amours." There is further evidence of calculated antique resonance both in the mock-epic description "Maint chien périt, maint héros expira" and the ensuing reference to "Prométhée" (ll. 14–15), as well as in La Fontaine's pseudo-Homeric description of the battle scene,

> Tout élément remplit de citoyens
> Le vaste enclos qu'ont les royaumes sombres
> [ll. 23–24]

a clear echo of the invocation to the Muse at the beginning of the *Iliad,* where the wrath of Achilles is described as having "hurled in their multitudes to the house of Hades strong souls of heroes" (Lattimore trans.).

When the reader reaches lines 25–27,

Cette fureur mit la compassion
Dans les esprits d'une autre nation
Au col changeant, au coeur tendre et fidèle . . .

the equation *pigeon* = *colombe* and the polarizing thrust that it portends become, in Riffaterre's aggressive formulation, "obligatorily perceptible." This "autre nation," soon to be identified as "le peuple pigeon" (l. 30), is presented to us by means of a periphrasis ("Au col changeant, au coeur tendre et fidèle") that actualizes the two essential features in the traditional descriptive system of the dove: its loving, faithful nature and its iridescent neckline. The dove's susceptibility to variegated color change is listed in the *Thesaurus linguae latinae* (s.v. *Columba* II) as foremost among its proverbial characteristics (*de proprietatibus columbarum, quae in proverbium venerunt*). Cicero mentions the dove's "plumae versicolores" (*De fin.* 3, 18) among nature's ornaments, along with the beards of men and peacocks' tails; many other writers, among them Lucretius, specify that this distinctive coloration is localized in the region of the neck;

pluma columbarum quo pacto in sole uidetur,
quae sita ceruices circum collumque coronat . . .

Observe the appearance in sunlight of the plumage that
rings the neck of a dove and crowns its nape . . .
[*De rerum natura*, II, ll. 799–802]

Apuleius describes the doves that pull Venus's chariot in terms of the same stereotypic feature, "quattuor candidae columbae . . . picta colla torquentes" ("Four white doves . . . bowed their rainbow-colored necks," *Golden Ass* 6, 6, Aldington-Gaselee trans., Loeb) that La Fontaine was to subsume in the expression "Au col changeant."[7] As for the pigeon or dove as lovebird, not even the casual reader of La Fontaine will fail to summon up at the words "au coeur tendre et fidèle" the corresponding verse that opens one of his best known fables: "Deux pigeons s'aimaient d'amour tendre" (IX, 2, 1). This association, once it has been made, is in itself sufficiently powerful to send us back to the beginning of *Les Vautours et les pigeons,* specifically to the periphrastic description of those birds affected to the service of "la mère d'Amour" (l. 7). At all events, it is now possible to view the words *vautours* and *pigeons,* both in the title and in the body of the fable, as semiotic markers that point attention to the same antagonism which pits Mars against Venus, killers against lov-

ers. This theme or scheme of irreconcilable alterity is instinct and inscribed, moreover, in the very word *colombe,* which, again according to
the *Thesaurus linguae latinae* (s.v. *Columba* II A), is opposed, in a bevy
of examples from across the range of Latin literature, to such "wild and
rapacious birds" (*opponitur avibus ferocibus et rapacibus*) as eagles,
kites, crows, and vultures.[8]

When I originally suspected that the "Mars"/"Vénus" opposition in
Les Vautours et les pigeons might be read as a tautological variant of the
Lucretian message—"That's the nature of things," "That's the way things
are"—I did not know that the binary idea of the prologue to *De rerum
natura* was itself tributary to a larger, even more ancient cosmological/
metaphysical vision. It was in Cyril Bailey's standard English edition and
commentary (II, l. 590), which I consulted out of a mixture of curiosity,
ignorance and obstinacy, that I learned of the tendency in classical scholarship to view Lucretius's conjunction of Mars and Venus as the intertextual excrescence of an *Ur*-text in Empedocles (ca. 493–ca. 433 B.C.), who
had reduced the secrets of the universe and the nature of things to a series
of dialectical encounters between Strife and Love (*Neikos* and *Philotēs*).
My fortuitous access to this bit of information proved useful in several
unpredictable ways. To begin with, the emergence of the word "Strife"—
not the idea, but the mere word—in polar conjunction with the word
"Love," set me to wondering whether the Mars/Venus binary in Lucretius
and La Fontaine were not simply continuous with the venerable *discordia
concors-concordia discors* motif that had become so familiar to me as a
reader of Montaigne.[9] This question was sufficiently tantalizing to send
me on a trip to the *Oxford Latin Dictionary,* where I was quickly and
well rewarded for my pains, since I was able to recover there, under the
entry *Discors* 2, the Horatian "rerum concordia discors," which when
traced to its source reads thus:

> quid velit et possit rerum concordia discors,
> Empedocles an Stertinium deliret acumen?
>
> What is the meaning and effect of nature's jarring concord?
> Is it Empedocles or shrewd Stertinius that's talking nonsense?
> [*Epist.* I, 12, ll. 19–20][10]

Re-enter through another door Empedocles and, fast on his heels, Lucretius! I found some cause for satisfaction in the fact that the *concordia
discors* topic had proven to be the missing link in an intertextual chain

that extended from Empedocles—at first a proper name on which I had stumbled, but eventually a conceptual fountainhead—to Lucretius, Horace, Montaigne, and La Fontaine, while passing on the way through a number of equally noteworthy intermediary stations in Lucan, Manilius, and Ovid.[11] In short, I was encouraged to observe that, whatever its ultimate utility in interpreting *Les Vautours et les pigeons*, the Mars/Venus collocation seemed to be branching out, taking on a life of its own, and, in the course of its peregrinations, generating an expanding nexus of tautological examples. What Régnier had casually noted as a "source" was emerging as a prominent strand in an increasingly intricate intertextual web.

Although I was not prepared to say whether La Fontaine knew anything about Empedocles and pre-Socratic philosophy or, even, for that matter, whether he had any serious first-hand knowledge of Lucretius, I was convinced, as a matter of principle—even as an article of faith—that whatever he did have to say about the idea of cosmic, universal "Strife" would somehow have to crystallize around the French word *discorde* which, as I quickly ascertained through the concordance to his writings, he does in fact use. *La Querelle des chiens et des chats, et celle des chats et des souris* (XII, 8) opens with this series of declarations:

La discorde a toujours régné dans l'univers.
Notre monde en fournit mille exemples divers:
Chez nous cette déesse a plus d'un tributaire.

After this exordium there follows the body of the fable, which illustrates the permanence of Discord in human affairs, and, later on, the moral:

J'en reviens à mon dire. On ne voit sous les cieux
Nul animal, nul être, aucune créature
Qui n'ait son opposé: c'est la loi de nature.
                              [ll. 38–40]

With the recovery of this passage, a third, major superimposition becomes possible: we need only look in isolation at the words "discorde" and "univers" (l. 1), "opposé" and "nature" (l. 40), to witness yet another replication of the message shared by the Lucretian prologue and *Les Vautours et les pigeons*: Mars and Venus, by their mythological history and the accumulated presuppositions of their names, recapitulate a primal, conflictual dispensation, instinct in the Cosmos, which La Fontaine, in the wake of Lucretius and Empedocles, now compresses into the single word "Discorde" as locus of an overarching principle that governs the relations between dogs and cats, cats and mice, vultures and pigeons, Love and War. This is the way of the world and the nature of things. "C'est la loi de nature." [12]

Now this latter formulation, which is exceptionally forthright and outspoken for the habitually understated La Fontaine, happens to figure elsewhere in the *Fables;* as Régnier points out in a note to line 40 of *La Querelle des chiens et des chats,* this very same hemistich appears earlier in the opening line of *L'Ane et le chien* (VIII, 17): "Il se faut entr'aider; c'est la loi de nature . . ." In the context of this fable, La Fontaine's liminal maxim proves to be cruelly ironic in that, in practice, the reverse turns out to be true; it is the case here, with all the rigor of natural law, that no one helps anyone except with stale, platitudinous, indifferent advice. In *Les Vautours et les pigeons,* to which I now revert by way of the word "s'entr'aider"—a verb that aptly describes the doves' treatment of the vultures—altruism is in fact depicted as destructive and suicidal. It is as if it were also written into the scheme of things that the attempt to "s'en-tr'aider," to eliminate conflict and harmonize dissonance—"*accorder* une telle querelle" (l. 29), "*accomoder* un peuple si sauvage" (l. 40)—as if the effort to unravel the *concordia discors,* to reconcile Mars and Venus, were to violate the order of nature and to unleash disaster.

In further illustration of this pattern, I would now like to offer a last example, which, just like all the others, came my way in a completely fortuitous manner. Very late in my reading, just to see whether I might not have overlooked other significant parallels, I checked in the Littré under the word *Colombe,* and this is what I found as the first entry:

Pigeon, en style élevé. Le Saint-Esprit descend sous la figure d'une co-lombe. Notre-Seigneur a dit: "Soyez prudents comme les serpents et simples comme les colombes."

Since the dove/serpent binary was new to me, I naturally wanted to doc-ument it further. More particularly, I was curious to know whether this opposition was current in La Fontaine's day, and soon learned from Fure-tière (s.v. *Colombe*) that it was:

Femelle de pigeon. Le St. Esprit apparut en forme de *colombe* sur la tête du Sauveur, quand il fut baptisé par St. Jean. Il faut avoir la prudence du serpent, et la simplicité de la *colombe*. . .

I was struck here by two things: 1) the dove is identified as female of the species, and credited with spiritual and moral qualities (simplicity and its presuppositions) that are presumably less prominent in the male;[13] 2) the words of Jesus (which originate in Matthew X, 16) are cited by Furetière, without indication of origin, as proverbial.[14]

And when we return this saying to its source in Scripture, another series of intertextual connections and superimpositions begins to come into view:

> Ecce ego mitto vos sicut *oves* in medio *luporum*. Estote ergo *prudentes* sicut *serpentes* et *simplices* sicut *columbae*.

> Voici: je vous envoie comme des *brebis* au milieu des *loups*. Soyez donc *prudents* comme les *serpents,* et *simples* comme les *colombes*. [Segond trans., rev.]

With the emergence of the dove/serpent and lamb/wolf variants of the original pigeon/vulture and Venus/Mars binaries, we can add to our list, now mediated in a familiar biblical code, yet another pair of tautological reductions of a recurrent and constant message. Matthew is telling his readers, as Jesus was telling his disciples, that the world and humanity are split down the middle, in internecine hostility, by a principle of discord and a force of moral disjunction that was built into the original Creation in the person of the serpent, who, we may now recall, was introduced to the reader of Genesis (III, 1)—Matthew's intertext in the present instance—as cunning and clever, *callidior cunctis animantibus*.[15] Doves are to serpents, as saints are to sinners, as angels are to devils, as lambs are to wolves. And, of course, the practised reader of La Fontaine can hardly write these words, or even begin to think these thoughts, without embarking on yet another intertextual journey, without effecting yet another re-entry into the binary universe of the *Fables*, ruled by *La Discorde*, where *Les Loups et les brebis* (III, l. 13) and *Le Loup et l'agneau* (I, 10) had earlier and variously rehearsed the ritual encounter between crafty predator and innocent victim—the very same ritual that was to be duly re-enacted in *Les Vautours et les pigeons*.[16]

The wheel has come full circle and I am back once again at my starting point, where I will indulge in one last observation, which derives and takes its substance, in turn, from La Fontaine's last observation in *Les Vautours et les pigeons,* just prior to his pronouncement of the *moralité*. Here are the words with which his fable proper ends:

La gent maudite aussitôt poursuivit
Tous les pigeons, en fit ample carnage,
En dépeupla les bourgades, les champs.
Peu de *prudence* eurent les pauvres gens
D'accommoder un peuple si sauvage.
[ll. 36–40]

Here, at the word "prudence," *Les Vautours et les pigeons* coincides with
Matthew X, 16, and relays the proverbial wisdom recorded in Furetière;
in so doing, it redeploys the reader's attention back down the intertextual
chain to the fable's beginning and its subsequent reverberations. All roads
lead to Rome.

As for La Fontaine's *moralité* itself, it recapitulates in its fashion, but
in no uncertain terms, the extensive and expansive intertextual message
of the entire fable: division, discord, difference are built into the world
order; any attempt, however well intentioned, to correct or alter this dispensation will go down as an assault on the essential, radical alterity of
life and the human condition. Why so? Because the innocent are not prudent, because the prudent are not innocent. *De deux choses l'une.* One is
wolf *or* lamb, vulture *or* pigeon, Mars *or* Venus. This, after all, is the real
motivation behind the seemingly superficial, frivolous anthropomorph-
ism that informs such routine political and topographical periphrases as
"le *peuple* vautour," "le *peuple* pigeon," "une autre *nation*, and "la *gent
maudite*." The weak and the strong, the lovers and the killers of this
world, are consigned by nature—*c'est la loi de nature*—to irrevocable
difference, to be lived out extraterritorially in perpetual estrangement and
alienation. This is the nature of things. If in the opening to this fable, we
were allowed to entertain ever so briefly the intertextual image of Venus
and Mars lying together in peaceful, exhausted exhilaration in illustration of the implicit maxim *omnia vincit amor,* by the time we reach La
Fontaine's *moralité* this message has been turned upside down:

Tenez toujours divisés les méchants:
La sûreté du reste de la terre
Dépend de là. Semez entre eux la guerre,
Ou vous n'aurez avec eux nulle paix.
Ceci soit dit en passant: je me tais.

The fable that lies in between the original evocation of Venus and Mars
and this negative and cynical conclusion, the space covered by the story

of columbine altruism and its lethal effects, illustrates, if anything, another unstated maxim which, in parody of the Lucretian hope, might be rewritten thus: *omnia vincunt amorem.*

Northrop Frye, writing in another connection, recalls the following remark by the 16th-century Anabaptist Hans Denck: "Whoever leaves an antithesis without resolving it lacks the ground of truth." Frye follows this fascinating quotation with this equally fascinating comment: "Brave words, but they are the words of a theologian who must put all things under his feet." [17] It is not hard to see what position La Fontaine would take on this question. As a *moraliste,* with no melioristic expectation, he has chosen to tread a privileged and perilous piece of ground where the twain never meet, where contradictions elude simplification, where complexity transcends reduction, where unresolved antitheses are multiplied and revisited in infinitely renewable, interchangeable variants. This statement would be true enough as a mere intratextual catalog and description of the *dramatis personae* of the *Fables,* where reed and oak, fox and crow are squared off dialectically against each other, where lamb and wolf, pigeon and vulture are yoked together in exemplary prolegomena to violence.

It has been the purpose of this essay to suggest and, with hope, to demonstrate and persuade how the divisions and tensions that are so obviously present *intratextually* in La Fontaine's *Fables,* have an *intertextual* dimension as well—a dimension that far outstrips in importance the superficial affiliations between La Fontaine, Aesop, Phaedrus, Abstemius, and the other earlier fabulists. Given the inherent slightness of the fable as a vehicle, its lowly place in the generic hierarchy, and the irresistible tendency to think of it in terms of infantile pedagogy or overt didacticism, we are always in danger of reading La Fontaine down from his proper philosophical and intellectual eminence, when we study him within what seems to be his natural milieu. Or to put it in another way: when we view La Fontaine intratextually, we see with utmost clarity how consistent and coherent his ideas are as we move horizontally across his book from fable to fable, and sample the varied riches of their content. It is, however, an indispensable complement to this approach to La Fontaine *tel qu'en lui-même* to measure the status and impact of his message vertically and intertextually, by tracking it diachronically along a continuum that stretches from remote antiquity to the most impressive modern appropriations of classical culture. It is only along this axis that we can begin to appreciate the true sophistication and toughness of La Fontaine's world view, as we watch it overlap and localize under a common grid and in a shared network with Empedocles and Lucretius, Horace and Ovid, Jesus and Montaigne—his true predecessors and his most appropriate intellectual and spiritual partners.

NOTES

1. André Maurois, *Art de vivre* (Paris: Plon, 1939), p. 128.

2. Leo Spitzer, "The Art of Transition in La Fontaine," in his *Essays on Seventeenth-Century French Literature,* ed. and trans. David Bellos. (Cambridge: Cambridge University Press, 1983), pp. 169–71.

3. At the MLA session in question, Richard Danner drew spontaneous and audible laughter when he quoted these lines from *Le Chat, la belette, et le petit lapin* (VII, 15, 44–45):

> Grippeminaud le bon apôtre
> Jetant des deux côtés la griffe en même temps,
> Mit les plaideurs d'accord en croquant l'un et l'autre.

4. Lucretius, *De rerum natura,* ed. Cyril Bailey (Oxford: Clarendon Press, 1947), II, 589. For the several generalities concerning Lucretius that I will have the occasion to advance here, I rely on Bailey's notes and commentary.

5. Lucretius, *On the Nature of the Universe,* trans. R. E. Latham (Harmondsworth, Middlesex: Penguin, 1975).

6. All the standard and current editions (e.g., Régnier, Couton, Collinet) identify the veiled or submerged meaning of these two periphrases; the mannered form of the message, by drawing attention to itself, encourages, even constrains the reader to place a proportionately greater emphasis on the content of each periphrasis once that content has been revealed. For a similar reaction, at the simple level of readerly response and appreciation, compare Chamfort's comment at the words, "non ceux que le Printemps/Mène à sa cour": "Tournure, poétique qui a l'avantage de *mettre en contraste,* dans l'espace de dix vers, les idées charmantes qui réveillent le printemps, les oiseaux de Vénus, etc. . . . et les couleurs opposées dans la description du peuple vautour" (*Eloge de La Fontaine* in his *Oeuvres complètes* [Paris: Chaumerot, 1824], I, 124, my italics).

7. In Marvell's *The Garden,* the dove, a symbol for the liberated, heavenbound human soul, is described in terms of the same inherited topos as waving "in its plumes the various [= changing] light" (l. 56).

8. Cf. Chamfort's comment at line 27, "Au col changeant, au coeur tendre et fidèle": "Description *charmante,* qui a aussi l'avantage de *contraster* avec le ton *grave* que La Fontaine a pris dans les quinze vers précédents" (ibid., my italics). Here again, Chamfort's reaction is triggered by a contextual emphasis, actualized

in this instance by the periphrasis, on the antinomial presuppositions of the words "colombe" and "vautour."

9. See my *Lectures de Montaigne* (Lexington, Ky.: French Forum Monographs, 1982), pp. 63 and 157, n. 8, and my article "Les Oreilles de Montaigne," *Romanic Review* 84 (1983): 129–31.

10. Horace, *Satires and Epistles,* trans. Niall Rudd (Harmondsworth, Middlesex: Penguin, 1979). In the *Apologie* Montaigne quotes these lines and then goes on to mention in a similar connection "la discorde et amitié d'Empedocles" (*Essais,* ed. Villey-Saulnier. [Paris: PUF, 1965], pp. 538–39).

11. Cf. Horace, *Ars poetica,* 374; Ovid, *Metamorphoses,* I, l. 433; Lucan, *Pharsalia,* I, l. 98; and Manilius, *Astronomica,* I, l. 142. In his commentary on Manilius, Theodor Breiter documents in great detail the Empedoclean background to the *discordia concors* motif. For a fuller discussion see Empedocles, *The Extant Fragments,* ed. M. R. Wright (New Haven: Yale University Press, 1981), pp. 30–34.

12. The *concorde/discorde* binary, that inhabits and informs *Les Vautours et les pigeons* at the hypogrammatic level, had been fully actualized by two of La Fontaine's predecessors: Abstemius, no. 96, *De accipitribus inter se inimicis quos columbae pacaverant* and Haudent, part two, no. 153, *Des colombz et des esperviers.* In his moral, Haudent uses *discorde/concorde* as emblematic of the fable's message:

> La fable monstre laisser viure
> Les mauluais en noyse & discorde
> Car quand entre eulx sont en concorde
> Aux bons sont veuz tout mal poursuyure.

La Fontaine in his moral will use *guerre/paix* to effect the same emphasis.

13. The *Dictionnaire de l'Académie Française* (1694) also lists the *colombe* as "femelle de pigeon."

14. This saying was apparently proverbial already in the time of Jesus; see the *Theological Dictionary of the New Testament,* ed. Gerhard Friedrich; trans. and ed. Geoffrey W. Bromiley (Grand Rapids, Mich.: Eerdmans, 1968), s.v. *Dove,* VI, 70. These typologies were apparently secure enough for Boccaccio that he felt free to mix and juggle them in ironic, playful combinations. Cf. *Decameron,* Giornata ottava, novella settima, ed. Enrico Bianchi et al. (Milan: Ricciardi, 1952), I, 575: "quantunque io *aquila* non sia, te non *colomba,* ma *velenosa serpe* conoscendo, come antichissimo nimico, con ogni odio e con tutta la forza di perseguire intendo . . ." I thank Philip Berk for bringing this example to my attention.

15. At Genesis III, 1 the Septuagint gives "phronimōtatos"; the Segond translation has "le plus rusé" and the King James "more subtle."

16. The same verbal/conceptual stereotype is found in Ovid:

> Ut fugiunt *aquilas,* timidissima turba, *columbae,*
> Utque fugit uisos *agna* nouella *lupos,*
> Sic illae timuere viros sine lege ruentes . . .

As doves, most timorous of birds, flee from the
eagles, and the weanling lamb when it spies the wolf,
so feared they the men rushing wildly on them
(*Ars amatoria* I, ll. 117–19; J. H. Mozley trans., Loeb)

... sic *agna lupum,* sic *cerva leonem,*
sic *aquilam* penna fugiunt trepidante *columbae,*
hostes quaeque suos ...

So does the lamb flee from the lion; so do doves
on fluttering wing flee from the eagle; so every
creature flees its foes.
(*Metamorphoses* I, ll. 505–7; F. J. Miller trans., Loeb)

17. *Times Literary Supplement,* January 17, 1986, p. 51.

Generic Modulation in Consolations by Malherbe, Tristan l'Hermite, and Théophile de Viau

Robert T. Corum, Jr.

The concept of genre has been a fundamental means of literary classification for many centuries, yet critics have invariably complained that the study of genre theory is deficient. Northrop Frye, for example, laments that literary criticism lacks precise terminology for many kinds of works and that three general labels of drama, epic, and lyric are inadequate to distinguish among an enormous diversity of poetic types.[1] On the other hand, one may argue that the indiscriminate extension of generic categories is neither feasible nor desirable. In such an enterprise the critic would have to consider a myriad of artistic features before granting a label to a particular text. Which factors to weigh—subject matter, structure, tone, mode of presentation, intended emotional effect, cultural attitudes—as well as relative weighting of each, pose added difficulties to the dogged critic who persists in categorizing literature. That the concept of genre encompasses so many qualities explains the proliferation of labels used in delimiting literary sets and subsets.

Despite taxonomic imprecision, genre provides the reader a ready means of orientation. Indeed, a genre functions as "a code of behavior ... between the author and his reader," who may be drawn into the "proper" mode of experiencing the text.[2] In other words, the genre creates a set of expectations and, consequently, particular responses in the reader. The generic "fix" becomes in this light another means by which the author manipulates his reader and conveys meaning: certain interpretative possibilities may be eliminated or remain unconceived because of generic assumptions made by the reader.[3] Inasmuch as the author may narrow interpretative possibilities by focusing upon a specific genre, the poet, by mixing his generic signals, may disrupt the reader's expectations and thereby create new meanings.[4]

The Soviet structuralists have provided a useful vocabulary for the critic interested in describing the phenomenon of mixed genres. This method is based upon the Russian formalists' notion of hierarchical levels forming an interdependent system which possesses informational content inherent to its structures. A network of oppositions within and between these textual strata creates tension within the reader and tends to disrupt the automatism of his perception. Disruption of automatic responses is proper to the poetic text; nonartistic languages depend upon perceptual automatism.[5]

The Soviet critic Yury Lotman has suggested an important extension of the concept of levels. For Lotman the textual-strata concept extends to the reader insofar as he interprets the poem in the light of his own culturally determined system of knowledge, experience, and expectations. The process gives rise to what Lotman calls the "alien word" in the poetic text. Accompanying the tension in and among various levels and the resultant deautomatization of the reading, the alien word comes into play when the reader's expectations are disrupted by the introduction, in a particular level, of a mode incongruous with the dominant mode of that level.[6] A poem by Saint-Amant may serve to illustrate this device. In his well-known sonnet "L'Hiver des Alpes," the second word, "atômes" ("Ces atômes de feu qui sur la neige brillent"),[7] evokes the scientific-philosophic domain of such ancient thinkers as Democritus, Epicurus, and Lucretius. This circumstance constitutes a clear departure from the dominant topographical-descriptive code of this lyric poem. Although "atômes" is proper to an "alien" code, it integrates into the rest of the piece and actualizes a possible interpretation, namely, that the work provides a playful "scientific" explanation for the absence of thunder during the winter months. The alien word has implications which bear directly on fixed generic categories and their disruption. While generic expectations draw the reader into the "proper" mode of experiencing a text, the alien word forces him to abandon one code and to invoke a new system based upon his cultural and personal resources.

Recent criticism of sixteenth- and seventeenth-century French poetry has revealed a general tendency to redefine inherited systems.[8] This spirit of innovation strove to "deautomatize" the reader's reactions, to create "new" works derived from older schematisms, and, perhaps, to create a new audience capable of assimilating these artistic innovations. Utilizing the basic concepts of deautomatization and alien word, I will examine a genre common in the period, the consolation, in order to test this assumption.

Derived principally from the Senecan model found in the *Epistulae*

Morales, LXIII and XCIX, this poetry of bereavement forms a group of works which share similar themes and generic norms. Close reading of Seneca reveals the major themes of this genre: grief is an indulgence too often abused; one must mourn sparingly; death is part of life; we are all subject to death's rigors; one must resign oneself to its inevitability. In keeping with the somber subject, the standard consolation presents recurring images of destiny and death, often personified, with attendant images of transience and separation. The speaker poses as an affectionate but strong-willed and logical friend whose tone of moral exhortation is intended to jolt the addressee out of his self-pitying malaise. The speaker is careful, however, not to scorn the bereaved or to belittle the dead. Often the speaker alludes explicitly to grief-stricken mythological or historical figures as noble examples or to dead heroes as a means to emphasize death's inevitability.

The best-known consolation in seventeenth-century poetry is Malherbe's "Consolation à Monsieur du Perier, Gentilhomme d'Aix en Provence, sur la mort de sa fille." [9] In this poem Malherbe follows closely the Senecan themes: his emphasis on God's will and design in the poem's conclusion corresponds to the Roman's frequent recourse to destiny and fate. The piece also contains an abundance of mythological and historical allusions, frequent images of death and flux, and personified nature symbolizing death's inevitability. From a generic perspective this poem utilizes a single code. Based upon knowledge of Malherbe's model and upon other contemporary consolations, the reader's generic expectations are not frustrated.

Malherbe remains within the boundaries imposed on the genre in his other consolations. [10] An exception is "Consolation à Caritée, sur la mort de son mary" (*Oeuvres,* I: 155). Adumbrated in the poem's second stanza, ("O *trop* fidelle Caritée:" v. 15, my emphasis), an alien code competing with the standard consolation linguistic system belongs to the popular *carpe diem* mode. [11] This circumstance, however, is not uncommon in consolations addressed to young widows, and would not lead the reader to make an incorrect generic guess in a first reading of the poem. The speaker refers to the grieving lady's "beaux cheveux" (v. 43), her "vive couleur" (v. 52), and that "vous semblez entreprendre / De ruïner vostre beauté" (vv. 41–42). Presented as a means to convince Caritée that the living must turn away from life-consuming grief, the *carpe diem* motifs yield to the sober admonition in the poem's concluding stanza:

Le temps d'un insensible cours
Nous porte à la fin de nos jours:
C'est à nostre sage conduite,
Sans murmurer de ce défaut,
De nous consoler de sa fuite
En le mesnageant comme il faut.

[vv. 73–78]

The speaker's appeal to reason characteristic of Malherbe's other consolation poems reasserts the generic confines of this piece.

The limited intermingling of two generic codes in the 1598 poem
emerges as a systematic interaction in a number of consolations by Tristan l'Hermite written in the 1630s and 40s. In his "Consolation à son
cher amy xxxx," the familiar Senecan commonplaces on the vanity of
grief are underlined by the speaker's trenchant imperatives in the first two
stanzas:

ACASTE, c'est assés pleurer;
Ta douleur est trop obstinée;
Cesse enfin de plus murmurer
　　Contre la Destinée,
Et finissant un si grand dueil,
Laisse les morts dans le cercueil.

Je sçay bien que ton pere avoit
Tant de vertus & tant de charmes,
Que ta pieté luy devoit
　　Un deluge de larmes.
Mais quoy? tes pleurs moüillent ses os.
Et tes crys troublent son repos.[12]

This tone of moral exhortation reminiscent of Malherbe's "Consolation
à M. du Perier"[13] leads to another stock device, explicit comparison between the addressee and a historical or mythological character, in this
case Aeneas on the death of his father Anchises. Just as the mythical hero
conquered his profound sorrow and proceeded to fulfill his noble destiny,
so must the addressee set aside grief. This brief allusion (vv. 13–24) to
Aeneas and his ultimate achievement ("Il chercha l'Empire Latin / Que
luy promettoit le Destin," vv. 23–24), unveils to the cultured reader a
vast literary backdrop. Immediately subsequent to the death of Anchises

in Virgil's epic is the famous Dido episode, in which love serves to mitigate Aeneas's pain over his father's death.[14] The concluding stanza suggests a parallel course:

> Pense donc à te consoler,
> Et venir presenter ton ame
> A cet astre qui sçait brusler
>   D'une divine flamme:
> Et qui promit l'autre jour
> D'estre sensible à ton amour.

A second "Dido" has materialized, offering love and consolation to a young man lost in grief. In this poem Tristan has grafted onto the conventional consolation the well-known *carpe diem* motif. Although the *tempus fugit* topos naturally provides a common ground between the two genres, and indeed is implied in the consolation itself, Tristan's use of allusive comparison based on yet another genre, the epic, assures smooth transition from one mode to the other. The repetition of an adjective basic to the code of love lyrics ("beaux jours de ta vie," v. 28; "Ce que ton âge a de plus beau," v. 30; "Le Sort Tyran des belles choses," v. 32) confirms this generic interpolation. As in Malherbe's "Consolation à Caritée," an "alien" linguistic system disrupts the reader's expectations, forcing a shift in generic orientation. Unlike Malherbe's poem, however, this piece does not revert to the conventional consolation's ultimate call to reason over emotion; the work's last word, "amour," verifies that emotion and desire can assuage the pangs of loss.

Due, perhaps, to the exalted social position of its subject, another consolation taken from *La Lyre* makes abundant use of the amorous code without passing overtly to the *carpe diem* mode. In "Consolation à Madame la Princesse Marie sur le trépas de feu Madame la Duchesse de Longueville sa tante," the opening lines recall themes common to innumerable *carpe diem* love lyrics:[15]

> Le Sort dont la rigueur contraire aux belles choses
>   Ternist si tost les roses:
> Pour les plus beaux Objets a le plus de couroux.
> Et c'est la raison seule, ô charmante MARIE!
>   De cette barbarie
> Que sa jalouse humeur exerce contre Vous.
>
>   [vv. 1–6]

The speaker continues to praise and pity the desolate princess in the three subsequent stanzas and, after a perfunctory panegyric to the dead aunt ("Ce miroir de Vertu qui n'eut point de pareil:" v. 27), he resorts to the standard moral admonishment:

> Apres avoir payé dessus sa sepulture
>   Les droits de la Nature
> A quoy vos sentimens se trouvent obligez:
> Ne croyez pas tousjours en r'ouvrant vos blessures
>   Rejetter les censures
> Que la raison veut faire à vos sens affligez.
>   [vv. 37–42]

The poem's final lines, however, revert to the lyric love code introduced in the opening stanza:

> Et l'on espere encor, que vos beautez divines
>   Franchissant des Espines,
> Meriteront enfin de marcher sur des Fleurs.
>   [vv. 46–48]

Marie's "beautez divines" and her close association with flowers suggest a covert comparison with Venus—in Roman mythology goddess of gardens as well as love. In this work the evocation of a poetic mode alien to the standard poem of bereavement obliquely suggests to the addressee that the pleasures of love may divert grief. Whereas in "Consolation à son cher amy xxxx" the speaker refers explicitly to the potential of love, here the speaker relies on the cultural apparatus of the reader to provide additional meanings.

In these poems the speaker combines disparate genres, yet in each case the poem does not actually acquire all the features of the conventional *carpe diem*. The speaker, for a variety of reasons, does not offer his affections to the grieving addressee. This audacious, indeed irreverent, device diverges widely from the Senecan model, yet it is a logical step, given the nature of the two genres and their modulation observed here. Tristan's best-known consolation, "Consolation à Idalie, sur la mort d'un parent," opens on a familiar note.[16] The deceased, although possessed of wondrous merit, has met the fate reserved for all mortals:

> Puisque votre parent ne s'est pu dispenser
> De servir de victime de la guerre,

C'est, ô belle Idalie, une erreur de penser
Que les plus beaux lauriers soient exempts du tonnerre.

  Si la mort connaissait le prix de la valeur
Ou se laissait surprendre aux plus aimables charmes,
Sans doute qu'Etios, garanti du malheur,
En conservant sa vie eut épargné vos larmes.

                                        [vv. 1–8]

Despite the speaker's guise as moral counselor, the adjective "*belle* Idalie"
immediately delineates the addressee and sets the tack of the poem. The
same adjective applied to the unfortunate Etios ("les plus beaux lauriers") suggests an analogy between Idalie and Etios based on their
shared mortality: she is also subject to death. The speaker affirms the
physical attraction of Idalie in v. 6; her "aimables charmes" are power-
less to stay the hand of fate, just as the "valeur" (v. 5) of Etios had no
effect. The speaker's pose as preceptor continues in the fourth stanza, in
which the deaths of ancient heroes corroborate his teachings:[17]

  Alexandre n'est plus, lui dont Mars fut jaloux,
César est dans la tombe aussi bien qu'un infâme,
Et la noble Camille, aimable comme vous,
Est au fond d'un cercueil ainsi qu'une autre femme.

                                        [vv. 13–16]

Analogy remains the prime device in these lines. Alexandre and Caesar
are to Etios as Camille is to Idalie. The speaker's repetition of the adjective "aimable" and his direct comparison in v. 15 intensify his rhetorical
attack. The addressee should not fail to grasp his designs. The last three
words, "une autre femme," initiate an associative transition to the following stanza, which sets aside considerations of Etios to focus solely on
Idalie. This shift accompanies a distinct generic reorientation; the *carpe
diem* emerges to displace the standard consolation mode:

  Bien que vous méritiez des devoirs si constants,
Et que vous paraissiez si charmante et si sage,
On ne vous verra plus avant qu'il soit cent ans,
Si ce n'est dans mes vers, qui vivront davantage.

                                        [vv. 17–20]

Despite the distressing impermanence of Idalie's earthly existence, the
speaker offers immortality based on the eternal merit of his poetic art.
This device recalls, of course, many sixteenth-century *carpe diem* love

sonnets intended to persuade the reluctant lady to accept the speaker's advances.[18] Her acquiescence rewards the speaker's pains, while he in turn repays the lady by conferring figurative immortality upon her. Having abandoned the conventional consolation at this point in the poem, the speaker returns in the following stanzas to the dreadful fact of death's omnipotence while concomitantly insisting on Idalie's divine perfection:

> Par un ordre éternel qu'on voit en l'univers
> Les plus dignes objets sont frêles comme verre,
> Et le ciel, embelli de tant d'astres divers,
> Dérobe tous les jours des astres à la terre.
>
> [vv. 21–24]

The last stanzas conclude the speaker's argumentation:

> Dès que nous commençons à raisonner un peu,
> En l'avril de nos ans, en l'âge le plus tendre
> Nous rencontrons l'amour qui met nos coeurs en feu
> Puis nous trouvons la mort qui met nos corps en cendre.
>
> Le temps qui, sans repos, va d'un pas si léger,
> Emporte avec lui toutes les belles choses:
> C'est pour nous avertir de le bien ménager,
> Et faire des bouquets en la saison des roses.
>
> [vv. 25–32]

The parallelism in vv. 27–28 telescopes the *carpe diem* themes expressed here. Although the repetition of the key adjective "aimable" in earlier lines signaled the poem's orientation, the crucial word "amour" in v. 27—in a rhythmic position identical to "mort" in v. 28—prescribes unmistakably both a remedy for Idalie's grief and, in a larger sense, a means of softening the harsh truth of death's inevitability. In this light, Tristan's poem remains a kind of "consolation." The speaker's role as wooer, already evoked in vv. 19–20 by the theme of eternal life through art reminiscent of the *carpe diem* mode, becomes more manifest in the last stanza. *Tempus fugit,* imperceptibly, perhaps, but all that is lovely (especially youthful, passionate desire, v. 27), must and will be swept away. While in the preceding stanza the first-person plurals point to humankind, the ambiguous "nous" in v. 31 may be taken as including only the speaker and addressee, typical usage in a standard *carpe diem* piece.[19] The last lines express clearly the speaker's desire to gather rosebuds while he (and Idalie) may. The "bouquets" and "roses" project the reader to a body of poetry whose linguistic system is far removed from that of the traditional consolation. The moral tone of the poem's opening has yielded to an invitation to pluck the roses of youth and love. The sexual connotations of "bouquets" and "roses" in the code of *galant* poetry need hardly be emphasized.[20] By gradually shifting generic codes, Tristan's poem of consolation in bereavement has become a *poème amoureux*. The speaker's subtle proposition to Idalie to enjoy the fruits of desire with him transforms his role from moral preceptor to passionate lover.

The moral stance of the speaker in a traditional Senecan *consolatio* such as Malherbe's "Consolation à M. du Perier" can be subverted by devices other than the gradual infiltration of *carpe diem* motifs. A curious piece by Théophile de Viau, "A Monsieur de L., sur la mort de son père," presents another example of generic modulation.[21] Whereas the title of the poem appears to set the poetic mode, the opening stanza upsets the reader's expectations:

Oste-toy, laisse-moy resver:
Je sens un feu se souslever
Dont mon Ame est toute embrasée,
O beaux prés, beaux rivages verds,
O grand flambeau de l'Univers
Que je trouve ma veine aisée!
Belle Aurore, douce Rosée,
Que vous m'allez donner de vers!

The speaker's brusque imperatives are obvious alien forms, immediately striking a note foreign to the firm yet gentle tone with which a consolation normally begins. Indeed, this first line nullifies the most basic condition of any consolation, namely, intimate communication between consoler and bereaved. Here the addressee must withdraw so that communication of another sort—between speaker and nature—can be initiated. Although nature is not absent in the standard consolation, the speaker's desire for solitude, his observation of and praise for natural beauty as source of inspiration set the reader on another generic tack, that of the typical *solitude*. Imitating a poetic mode transmitted from antiquity, the traditional solitude presents the speaker seeking a balm for the pangs of an unrequited love far from other human beings within a pastoral *locus amoenus*.[22] Contemporary poets created variations of the inherited model; compare for example Saint-Amant's "La Solitude," Tristan's "La Mer" and "Le Promenoir des deux amants," and Théophile's own "La Solitude."

The subsequent two stanzas of this "consolation" bear motifs belonging to the solitude code:

> Le vent qui s'enfuit dans les ormeaux
> Et pressant les fueillus rameaux
> Abat le reste de la nuë,
> Iris a perdu ses couleurs,
> L'air n'a plus d'ombre, ny de pleurs,
> La Bergere aux champs revenuë
> Moüillant sa jambe toute nuë
> Foulle les herbes et les fleurs.

> Ces longues pluyes dont l'hyver
> Empeschoit Tircis d'arriver
> Ne seront plus continuées,
> L'orage ne fait plus de bruit,
> La clarté dissipe la nuit,
> Ses noirceurs sont diminuées,
> Le vent emporte les nuées
> Et voila le Soleil qui luit.
>   [vv. 9–24]

The air of optimism following a violent storm evokes a return to mental equilibrium after a period of profound emotional storm and stress. The winter's "longues pluyes" (v. 17) which had prevented the addressee, Tircis, from "arriving" reinforce this interpretation. The poem thus turns obliquely to the subject of consolation by reference to natural events. The "Soleil qui luit" (v. 24) signals a new beginning, recovery from past grief, and a bright future.[23] The conventional motifs of the solitude—nature's beauty and effervescence, inspiration in solitary meditation, pastoral sensuality (vv. 14–16)—are here utilized to introduce a decidedly unconventional consolation.

The sun's brilliance described at the close of the third stanza leads to an abrupt change of subject in the following stanza, where a dialectical shift initiates an extended meditation on nature's apparent counterpart, death:

> Mon Dieu que le Soleil est beau!
> Que les froides nuicts du tombeau
> Font d'outrages à la nature!

La mort, grosse de desplaisirs,
De tenebres et de souspirs,
D'os, de vers, et de pourriture,
Estouffe dans la sepulture
Et nos forces, et nos desirs.

[vv. 25–32]

Contemporary solitudes often treated the hideousness of death. The intervention of the sinister and the horrific thus maintains the solitude-like aura of the poem while simultaneously focusing on a subject closely linked to the consolation. These lines serve as transition to a series of stanzas which develop death-related themes familiar to standard consolations: death is all-powerful; no one is immune to its rigors; Tircis, too, will meet death; his dead father, unaware of his son's grief, has passed on to inexorable oblivion. Moving from mortal mankind's irrevocable fate ("Les Mores et les Africains," v. 34; "Cesar comme le bucheron," v. 37; "Vostre pere est ensevely," v. 49; "Il est aussi mort qu'Alexandre," v. 55), the speaker magnifies his funereal vision in the last five stanzas to depict the ultimate dissolution of all creation. Although not a feature of the traditional solitude, this grandiose contemplation of Apocalypse recalls another famous solitude, Saint-Amant's "Le Contemplateur," which in turn shares elements with the contemporary devotional lyric.[24] Théophile's poem emerges as a curious hybrid incorporating no less than three well-known lyric genres, the solitude, the religious meditation, and the consolation.

The Pléiade's Aristotelian dictum against mixed genres did not prevent the formation of subgenres derived from pre-existing models, yet the very creation of a genre system produced readers and writers who, in effect, knew what was expected in a given text.[25] Such a system, however, invites subversion by poets desiring to break away from the Tradition. Yury Lotman sees this phenomenon as a means of increasing the text's informational potentialities:

An important means for the informational activization of a structure is *its violation*. An artistic text does not merely represent the implementation of structural norms, but their violation as well. It functions in a dual structural field consisting of the tendency to establish order and to violate it. Although each tendency tries to dominate and destroy the opposing one, the victory of either would prove to be fatal to art. The life of an artistic text depends on their mutual tension.[26]

Lotman also relates the degree of violation to a text's aesthetic value:

> Thus, performing the function of "good poems" in a cultural system is the prerogative of only those texts which are highly informative for that culture. This implies a conflict with the reader's expectation, tension, struggle, and in the final reckoning, forces the reader to accept an artistic system that is more meaningful than his usual one. But in convincing the reader, the writer takes upon himself the obligation to go further. The conquered novelty is converted into cliche and loses its informativeness. Novelty is not always in the invention of the new. Novelty has a meaningful relationship to tradition in being simultaneously the resurrection of its memory and non-coincidental with it.[27]

The quest for innovation in a poetic generation striving to liberate itself from the Pléiade doubtlessly prompted the generic "instability" examined here. We see in these poems the capacity of genres to be tinted by the introduction of extrinsic—alien—modes. Although Malherbe's appeals to reason, Tristan's to love as well as lust, and Théophile's to both reason and emotion appear quite different, the speaker's rhetorical end remains the same: to console the grieving addressee.

Within the limited consolation genre, Malherbe proves to be the most conservative. Tristan and Théophile reveal themselves as artists no less bound to their literary antecedents. They exhibit, nonetheless, a greater willingness for aesthetic experimentation. While it must be said that the reader's knowledge of generic norms is crucial in deciphering a poetic text, the author's expectations must also be considered. Tristan and Théophile viewed their generic inheritance as a long-standing tradition ripe for subversion. The eminently serious—even religious—consolation becomes in their hands a poetic type subject to transformation. These poems are statements of professional conviction made by writers who wished to assert their own places in literary history.

NOTES

1. See, for example, Northrop Frye, *Anatomy of Criticism* (Princeton: Princeton University Press, 1957), pp. 13, 246; Alastair Fowler, *Kinds of Literature, An Introduction to the Theory of Genres and Modes* (Cambridge: Harvard University Press, 1982), pp. 235–55; Paul Hernadi, *Beyond Genre, New Directions in Literary Classification* (Ithaca: Cornell University Press, 1972), pp. 1–9; René

Wellek and Austin Warren, *Theory of Literature,* 3rd. edition (New York: Harcourt, Brace, and World, 1956), pp. 226–37.

2. Heather Dubrow, *Genre,* "The Critical Idiom," 42 (London: Methuen, 1982), p. 2.

3. It is worthwhile to quote Fowler (p. 259) here: "The processes of generic recognition are in fact fundamental to the reading process. Often we may not be aware of this. But whenever we approach a work of unfamiliar genre—new or old—our difficulties return us to fundamentals. No work, however avant-garde, is intelligible without some context of familiar types."

4. See "The Historicity of Genres," in E. D. Hirsch, Jr., *Validity in Interpretation* (New Haven: Yale University Press, 1967), pp. 102–11. On these points Fowler (p. 22) is unequivocal: "Of all the codes of our literary *langue,* I have no hesitation in proposing genre as the most important, not least because it incorporates and organizes many others. Just how many other codes are generically articulated remains uncertain. Probably far more than we are aware of. At any rate there is no doubt that genre primarily has to do with communication. It is an instrument not of classification or prescription, but of meaning."

5. See, for example, Roman Ingarden, *The Literary Work of Art,* trans. George G. Grabowicz (Evanston: Northwestern University Press, 1973), pp. 29ff, for a discussion of textual strata. The concept of deautomatization is fundamental in Russian formalism. For a critique, see P. N. Medvedev and M. M. Bakhtin, *The Formal Method of Literary Scholarship,* trans. A. J. Wehrle (Baltimore: Johns Hopkins University Press, 1978), p. 88–90.

6. Yury Lotman, *Analysis of the Poetic Text,* trans. and ed. D. Barton Johnson (Ann Arbor: Ardis, 1976).

7. *Oeuvres complètes,* ed. Jean Lagny and Jacques Bailbé, 4 vols. (Paris: Didier, 1967), II: 124.

8. See especially Edwin M. Duval, *Poesis and Poetic Tradition in the Early Works of Saint-Amant* (York, South Carolina: French Literature Publications, 1981); John D. Lyons, *The Listening Voice: An Essay on the Rhetoric of Saint-Amant* (Lexington: French Forum, 1982); David Lee Rubin, *The Knot of Artifice: A Poetic of the French Lyric in the Early 17th Century* (Columbus: Ohio State University Press, 1981).

9. Malherbe, *Oeuvres poétiques,* ed. René Fromilhague and Raymond Lebègue, 2 vols. (Paris: Société d'édition "Les Belles Lettres," 1968), I: 158. For recurring "death" themes in the poetry of this period, see Henri Lafay, *La Poésie française du premier XVIIᵉ siècle* (Paris: Nizet, 1975), pp. 98–101.

10. For example, "Consolation à Monsieur le premier Président, sur la mort de Madame sa femme," in which the speaker entreats his addressee to serve the state as a means of assuaging his grief.

11. The expression originates, of course, in Horace, *Odes,* I: 11: "fugerit invida aetas / carpe diem, quam minimum credula postero."

12. Tristan l'Hermite, *La Lyre,* ed. Jean-Pierre Chauveau (Geneva: Droz, 1977), p. 243.

13. In his splendid critical edition, Chauveau also draws a parallel with Malherbe, p. 243.

14. For Aeneas's reaction to Anchises's death, see *Aeneid*, III: 908–17. It is interesting that the consolation motif is doubled in Virgil, for Dido is in deep mourning over the death of her husband Sychaeus when Aeneas arrives in Carthage. Her sister entreats her to abandon her grief and to surrender to her nascent love for Aeneas. See IV: 38–73.

15. *La Lyre*, p. 231.

16. Tristan l'Hermite, *Les Plaintes d'Acante et autres oeuvres*, ed. Jacques Madeleine (Paris: Cornély, 1909), p. 155. The piece has been anthologized in *Anthologie de la poésie française,* ed. Marcel Arland (Paris: Stock, 1960); *Anthologie poétique française, XVIIe siècle, I,* ed. Maurice Allem (Paris: Garnier-Flammarion, 1965); *An Anthology of Seventeenth-Century French Lyric Poetry,* ed. Odette de Mourgues (Oxford: Oxford University Press, 1966); *Textes et contextes: Anthologie de la poésie française du premier dix-septième siècle,* ed. David L. Rubin (Paris: Jean-Michel Place; Tübingen: Gunter Narr, 1986). It is significant that Odette de Mourgues classifies this poem under the rubric "Philosophical Commonplaces and Official Poetry."

17. Cf. Malherbe, "Consolation à M. du Perier," vv. 49–64; "Consolation à Caritée," vv. 1–6; Tristan, "A Monsieur le Comte de Mons, Consolation sur la mort de son frère," vv. 49–54; "Consolation à son cher amy xxxx," vv. 13–24.

18. Ronsard expresses this notion repeatedly. On offering an amaranth ("sempervive") to Hélène:

> Elle vit longuement en sa jeune verdeur:
> Long temps apres la mort je vous feray revivre,
> Tant peut le docte soin d'un gentil serviteur,
>
> Qui veut, en vous servant, toutes vertus ensuivre.
> Vous vivrez (croyez-moy) comme Laure en grandeur,
> Au moins tant que vivront les plumes et le livre.
> [*Sonnets pour Hélène, Second Livre*, II]

19. Indeed, of Tristan's other consolations, three utilize the first-person plural; in "A Madame de Gournay, sur la mort de sa fille":

> Mais si nostre Sauveur prit cette Fleur nouvelle
> Pour en parer les Cieux et la rendre immortelle,
> Quelle raison vous porte à verser tant de pleurs?
>
> C'est mal vous souvenir de ses bontez divines,
> Faut-il avoir regret qu'il emporte nos fleurs,
> Il a bien pris soin de porter nos espines?
> [*La Lyre*, p. 270]

in "A Monseigneur le Chancelier, sur la mort de son gendre":

> Mais bien que la Raison t'ordonne de pleurer,
> Garde que ta santé vienne à s'en altérer,
> Et t'empêche d'agir où l'estat te convie.
>
> Tes prudentes clartez éclairans son Conseil,
> Il ne t'est pas permis d'abreger une vie
> Qui nous est necessaire autant que le soleil.
> [*Les Vers héroïques*, p. 271]

and in "Consolation à son cher amy xxxx," discussed above. In each case the meaning is unequivocal.

20. In his *Dictionnaire universel* Antoine Furetière cites an interesting contemporary meaning of "bouquets": "on dit qu'une femme fait porter le *bouquet* à son mari, quand elle lui est infidelle."

21. *Oeuvres poétiques. Seconde et troisième parties,* ed. Jeanne Streicher (Geneva: Droz, 1958), p. 214. This poem is discussed in an article by Frank J. Warnke, "Some Consolations," in *The Equilibrium of Wit: Essays for Odette de Mourgues,* ed. Peter Bayley and Dorothy Gabe Coleman (Lexington: French Forum, 1982), pp. 109–16.

22. Richard A. Mazzara, "Théophile de Viau, Saint-Amant, and the Spanish *Soledad,*" *Kentucky Romance Quarterly,* 14 (1967): 393–404. See also Edwin Duval, *Poesis and the Poetic Tradition* (1982), pp. 17–21.

23. A similar treatment may be seen in the "La Mer." See my "A Reading of Tristan l'Hermite's 'La Mer,'" *Papers on French Seventeenth Century Literature,* 9 (1978), pp. 11–28.

24. John D. Lyons, *The Listening Voice* (1981), pp. 18–19. See also Terence Cave, *Devotional Poetry in France, c. 1570–1613* (Oxford: Oxford University Press, 1969), pp. 156–64.

25. Rosalie L. Colie, *The Resources of Kind: Genre-Theory in the Renaissance* (Berkeley: University of California Press, 1973), p. 26.

26. Yury Lotman, *The Structure of the Artistic Text,* trans. Ronald Vroon (Ann Arbor: University of Michigan Press, 1972), p. 299.

27. *Analysis of the Poetic Text,* p. 131.

V
The Moralists

Camera Obscura: Image and Imagination in Descartes's *Méditations*

John D. Lyons

For the late Renaissance and early modern period, a major tension exists between what can be seen and what can be said. Seeing and saying are acts that tend to go their own separate ways, as different and scarcely compatible instruments for representing the world. Foucault and others have given us various descriptions of this parting of the ways for a culture that no longer saw the world as a text. But the divorce between seeing and saying was a painful and embarrassed one, all the more so because the art of seeing, refined into artificial perspective, was in some ways the guiding discipline of this revolution in knowledge. Not even René Descartes, master though he was in the art of renunciation and doubt, could sacrifice the concept of vision without a struggle. I would like to explore briefly some of the problems that Descartes encountered when he adopted, as criteria for truthfulness, terms that belong chiefly to the visual arts. Although Descartes did find ways to move from seeing to saying—or, in other words, from visual to verbal models of truth—he had to travel a path marked with images of monsters and ghosts.

When Descartes tells the story of his discovery of the principles of his method during a stay in Germany, he places an unaccustomed emphasis on the physical surroundings of his cogitations. There, he tells us, "n'ayant d'ailleurs, par bonheur, aucuns soins ni passions qui me troublassent, je demeurais tout le jour enfermé seul dans un poêle . . . "[1]. This retreat from distraction and external stimulus is representative of the Cartesian project of discovering knowledge within the mind alone. Descartes's heated room can be a useful landmark for students of the rhetoric and history of philosophy.

In the *Discours de la méthode,* Descartes tells us his room was warm. In the *Méditations* he tells us that it was dark and quiet, filling completely his needs for the exclusion of all that was not himself. A dark room is a particularly apt place for Descartes to set the scene for his investigation into first philosophy because it is against this darkness that qualities of truth can shine forth in the figurative terms that Descartes uses. For him, true ideas are clear and distinct ideas. By proclaiming the qualities of clarity and distinctness as the criteria of truthfulness, Descartes took for philosophical reflection terms more often associated with the description of images, in particular of painted images. This move incorporated into the procedures of his research in first philosophy a problematic trope borrowed from a field which was also the object of his scientific research. In the history of optics, Descartes enjoys a place of importance along with his contemporaries Snell, Fermat, and Grimaldi. His mathematical statement of refraction furthered the study of light that was later advanced by Newton and Huygens. But Descartes's study of natural light (light from the outside, material world) is less central to his work in general than the antithetical concept of *lumière naturelle,* the light of reason, or inner light.[2]

This appropriation of optical terms in their figurative sense reveals a number of very fragile constructions in the Cartesian system, which can be thought of globally as one in which the subject flees external stimuli in a radical attempt not only to doubt, but also to exclude, all that is not the "I" of the subject.[3] Philosophy is described metaphorically in the *Principia* as superior to sight: "le plaisir de voir toutes les choses que notre vue découvre n'est point comparable à la satisfaction que donne la connaissance de celles qu'on trouve par la philosophie" (p. 558). The philosopher's eyes seem to be opened to a different sight, one which has nothing to do with *notre vue* in the usual sense. Sense perception is deprecated, and with it sight. Philosophy becomes the discipline of sight in the sense of the disciplining, that is, the repression, of sight. Yet the repression of literal sight permits the formulation of the metaphoric sight which is opened within. We are all familiar with the Cartesian gesture of retreat into an isolated and enclosed space. Yet in that space (for example, the heated room of the *Discours de la méthode*) the outside world appears as image, posing the further challenge of mentally judging the clarity and distinctness of all ideas that are presented as images to the faculty of judgment.

In this attempt to reduce stimuli, distractions, and uncertainty, while maintaining clarity and distinctness as the marks of truth, Descartes seems to install within the mind a replica of the external, doubtful world. The *cause* of that replica becomes a question of ever greater significance, for outside the immediate apprehension of the *cogito,* the genesis of ideas is paramount. Which ideas are illusions and which are not? What is the role of the mind (*esprit*) in the production of ideas? If an idea appears clearly and distinctly must not the cause of that idea be an existing thing outside the mind? Because clarity and distinctness are terms used in the study of optics and in the application of such optical devices as the *camera obscura* to drawing and painting, it is not surprising to see that Descartes turns to the description of painted images to help recognize and circumscribe sources of error and distortion.[4] The purpose of the *camera obscura*, which Descartes describes in *La Dioptrique* (e.g., V: 214–15), is to project inside a chamber an inverted image of something that is outside. The distinctness of the internal image, as Descartes notes, is increased by decreasing the size of the hole in the side of the chamber. The *camera obscura* is useful because of its combination of receptiveness and restriction. Distinctness is proportional to the restriction of light from the outside. On the other hand, the movement outward from the sure foundation of metaphysical knowledge in the discovery of the essential and purely spiritual subject, the *ego* or "I," conflicts with an optically based model requiring the movement inward of light from outside the subject.

The faculty governing this inward replica is the imagination. To understand the role of imagination, a faculty which Descartes alternately invests with a decisive importance and even describes as necessary for judgment or *entendement* to occur and, on the other hand, castigates as a major source of error, we must recognize that for Descartes everything that can be known, including everything that can be known about the self, must pass through the test of representation. By the test of representation, I refer to that process by which the idea to be judged is brought to mind or perceived. Perception includes imagination and conception (*Principes*, §32, p. 585). Imagination is the act of representing something to the mind in a way that resembles the stimuli of the senses, most often the sense of sight. The act of conceiving consists of perceiving (that is, representing to the understanding) what cannot be represented in any form resembling sensory data. Unlike seeing (that is, *voir*, in the ordinary sense), imagining produces images that are without a detectable source outside the mind of the subject.[5] Some things can be imagined but not seen, other things can be seen but not imagined. Descartes's example of something that can be seen but not imagined is the geometrical figure of the chiliogon, a figure with a thousand sides. Although such a figure can be seen, the mind cannot, according to Descartes, produce a specific picture of it. When the imagination fails in this way, conception is the faculty by which the mind represents a thing:

> [Je] remarque premièrement la différence qui est entre l'imagination et la pure intellection ou conception. Par exemple, lorsque j'imagine un triangle, je ne le conçois pas seulement comme une figure composée et comprise de trois lignes, mais outre cela je considère ces trois lignes comme présentes par la force et l'application intérieure de mon esprit; et c'est proprement ce que j'appelle imaginer. Que si je veux penser à un chiliogone, je conçois bien à la vérité que c'est une figure composée de mille côtés, aussi facilement que je conçois qu'un triangle est une figure composée de trois côtés seulement; mais je ne puis pas imaginer les mille côtés d'un chiliogone, comme je fais les trois d'un triangle, ni, pour ainsi dire, les regarder comme présents avec les yeux de mon esprit. Et quoique, suivant la coutume que j'ai de me servir toujours de mon imagination, lorsque je pense aux choses corporelles, il arrive qu'en concevant un chiliogone je me représente confusément quelque figure, toutefois il est très évident que cette figure n'est point un chiliogone, puisqu'elle ne diffère nullement de celle que je me représenterais, si je pensais à un myriogone, ou à quelque autre figure de beaucoup de côtés . . . [*Méditations*, VI: 318]

The mind cannot easily make pictures of all things, and Descartes tests the boundaries of what can be pictured and what cannot be pictured. Like a somewhat malevolent drawing teacher, Descartes gives the mind tests of what it can trace. It is important to emphasize that this test applies to the picturing, not to what is pictured. Triangles and pentagons can be imagined, whereas chiliogons and myriogons can only be conceived. This distinction does not indicate a defect in the chiliogon, some inherent escape from the laws of optics, but rather a limitation of the mind in its visualizing capacity.

All visual perception seems to be a distancing from the essence of the mind. If conception as pure intellection *cannot* produce images, while imagination, which is not part of the essence of the mind, *can* do so, then the distinctness of image increases as the subject's attention moves away from itself or from its essence (cf., p. 321). Yet at the same time the subject is testing its capacity to produce such images, and the boundaries of sense, imagination and conception are located by *failure* of distinctness. The more confused the image, the closer the mind to an activity that passes into the pure realm of conception. The mind (*esprit*) seems to be a failed maker of images, dependent on some other faculty or source, a source outside the dark chamber of the mind.

It is repeatedly asserted in the *Méditations* and the *Principes* that prior to exercising judgment the mind must perceive the idea to be judged. The role of the subject in the genesis of these perceptions is debated. Sylvie Romanowski argues that the production of evidence by the thinker, and in particular through the imagination, is a dangerous procedure. Truth, she argues, should be "*trouvée, non pas faite par moi, non pas l'objet de quelque travail imaginatif, mais être découverte, toute faite, prête à être cueillie par ma pensée.*"[6] This opposition between activity and passivity is a useful delimitation of one source of error perceived by Descartes, but it is perhaps not forceful enough to account for the twists and turns of the Cartesian description of the production and judgment of images. Ideas (actively imagined or conceived) can be erroneous or true, though the active production of ideas is only a stage in obtaining knowledge. Descartes's use of the verbs *imaginer* and *concevoir* seem to indicate an active presentation of perceptions to the judgment, a presentation in which these faculties replace the doubtful perceptions of the senses. Produced perceptions or perceptions which are treated as ideas of things rather than as the things themselves are what we would call representations. We have already seen that Descartes traces the boundaries between imagination and conception, the two principal faculties of representation, by locating cases in which these faculties fail to represent. The imagination fails to represent a chiliogon; the conception fails to represent a mountain without a valley (*Méditations,* V: 313). Because a mountain cannot be represented without a valley, a mountain cannot exist without a valley. This is an example of the way representation becomes interesting to Descartes primarily in cases of failure, for successful representation does not guarantee existence: "comme il ne tient qu'à moi d'imaginer un cheval ailé, encore qu'il n'y en ait aucun qui ait des ailes, ainsi je pourrais peut-être attribuer l'existence à Dieu, encore qu'il n'y eût aucun Dieu qui existât" (p. 313). One might conceive or imagine a God, and yet that God might not exist, but one cannot, Descartes argues, represent God without representing at the same time His existence. This failure to represent a nonexistent God is a convincing argument in Descartes's text whereas the successful representation of God is not convincing.

When we possess an image and know that we could not ourselves make that image, we know that the image is true, that it comes from outside the *camera obscura* of our mind. So the "image d'une vraie et immuable nature" can be certified as a *true* image, since it surpasses the powers of the imagination itself, but the winged horse is a mere image, entirely within the power of the subject. The image itself is not called into question but rather the subject's ability to fabricate or feign images. Hence it seems appropriate to accept failed activity rather than simple passivity as the model of the Cartesian perception of the image.

The image of a true and immutable nature which is the image of God passes this "failure-test" of imagination. Such an image is present to the "eyes of the mind" yet is apparently beyond the ability of the subject to create. "Reality" (or truth) in perception seems to coincide with the failure of conception and imagination combined (e.g., "il ne m'est pas possible de concevoir deux ou plusieurs Dieux de même façon . . . " p. 314).

The gradual escape of the image from the will of the thinker guarantees the autonomous and self-sustaining quality of the image because the mind is revealed as failing to invent, or be able to remove, these aspects of the image.[7] This discovery, moreover, unfolds in time. Something changes between the first moment I imagine the triangle and later when I am forced to perceive certain properties of the image. This temporality of knowledge emphasizes a difference between the subject (or the mind) and something which is in the mind. Descartes supposes that the triangle is unchanging. Each time I imagine it, it is the same. But my knowledge of the triangle does change. The mind is cast in the role of describer of an image. The image remains the same, but the mind makes ever more complete descriptions.

There seems to be something curiously satisfying to Descartes in the initial failure to perceive the entirety of the image of the triangle. The contrast between the changelessness of the image across time and the changing description/perception of the image confers on it a status of "immutability," one of the properties of certain truths, while this contrast also consigns the subject's understanding to the realm of change. By producing an immutable and richly describable image, imagination permits judgment to operate as a mutable, descriptive faculty. As a consequence of this, we can say that the "clarity" of an image does not preclude the subject's failure to grasp or recognize its implications. Because the mind recognizes more and more clearly the properties of a triangle, while the image in the imagination does not change, clarity of recognition cannot in itself be taken as proof of truth, for this clarity of recognition changes while the truth pertaining to the triangle does not. The truth of the triangle does not increase as the mind increases its knowledge of the triangle. The image produced by the imagination is therefore the pretext for a temporally characterized translation of the image into words—the words of a description in which the atemporal qualities of the image are rendered more accessible to the "eyes of the mind."

What appears to the eyes of the mind exists in the mind. The question is, does such a representation, and in particular such an image, come from the outside or the inside of the mind? What is there about these gradually described still images that can reveal their source? Do they enter the *camera obscura* from the outside? Or are they productions from within the chamber? In the *Discours de la méthode* appears one of the major examples of deceptive images, the chimera. Descartes returns again and again to the dream image as a major threat to his system, a threat made possible by his grounding of truth in clear and distinct perception, for the images in dreams are often quite distinct. How can we distinguish them from waking images?

Paradoxically, imagination, which is associated with the doubtful perception of a doubtful object (material nature), is associated with the perception of that which has never been in material nature. In criticizing the proponents of the maxim that nothing is in the mind which has not first been in the senses, Descartes says that such people "n'élèvent jamais leur esprit au-delà des choses sensibles, et qu'ils sont tellement accoutumés à ne rien considérer qu'en l'imaginant, qui est une façon de penser particulière pour les choses matérielles, que tout ce qui n'est pas imaginable leur semble n'être point intelligible" (p. 151). In assigning to imagination the function of thinking about material things, Descartes seems to prejudge the existence of material nature. But the dream image poses the additional and converse problem that it is *not sufficiently* associated with the supposed material world. Although the dream image and the waking image proceed from the same faculty, the waking image is tainted by being excessively associated with the external world, while the dream image is defective because it is insufficiently associated with the external world. Yet this defect of the dream image is hidden by its excessive vividness and distinctness, so that the dream image is in some ways the apogee of distinct imagery in Descartes, the triumph of the image.

The conclusion of the fourth part of the *Discours de la méthode* addresses this problem and attempts to exorcise the image. Descartes first supposes that while sleeping, a geometer invents a new demonstration, then asserts that sleep alone (or the fact that the demonstration appears in a dream) does not prevent the demonstration from being true. But the argument slides back and forth—its purpose somewhat dubious. The paragraph begins by arguing for the validity of our waking thoughts. These thoughts are somehow threatened by dreams: yet "les rêveries que nous imaginons étant endormis ne doivent aucunement nous faire douter de la vérité des pensées que nous avons étant éveillés" (p. 152). Oddly, Descartes chooses to combat this threat from the images of dreams by defending the validity of one such hypothetical dream. The most ordinary error of dreams is, in a next step, described as being the similarity between dreams and sense perception. Descartes does not, however, use the similarity to defend the accuracy of dreams. Instead, he uses this parallel to attack the senses. Although the seventeenth century was a period of increased emphasis on making pictures correspond to actual sight, Descartes finds the correspondence between mental image and sensorial image a defect, not a positive quality. For Descartes such correspondence becomes a source of condemnation of visual perception in general:

> Et pour l'erreur la plus ordinaire de nos songes, qui consiste en ce qu'ils nous représentent divers objets en même façon que font nos sens extérieurs, n'importe pas qu'elle nous donne occasion de nous défier de la vérité de telles idées, à cause qu'elles peuvent aussi nous tromper assez souvent sans que nous dormions; comme lorsque ceux qui ont la jaunisse voient tout de couleur jaune . . . [p. 152]

This argument contains the basis for a defense of the dream image as no less accurate than the senses, but Descartes uses it to subvert the senses, displaying them as no more accurate than the dream image.

At this point Descartes invokes the strangest and most ambivalent example, the image of the chimera:

> [Et] nous pouvons bien imaginer distinctement une tête de lion entée sur le corps d'une chèvre, sans qu'il faille conclure pour cela qu'il y ait au monde une Chimère; car la raison ne nous dicte point que ce que nous voyons ou imaginons soit véritable, mais elle nous dicte bien que toutes nos idées ou notions doivent avoir quelque fondement de vérité . . .

Descartes goes from listing failures of seeing "external" things (failures caused by jaundice and distance) to describing the case of a distinct image of something never seen. Having begun with the example of a geometer discovering a *correct* (or true) demonstration in his sleep, Descartes moves to an image which is false despite its distinctness. But the two forms of validity are quite different. The demonstration is true without reference to material actualization. If one imagines a triangle or other geometrical figure, it has a certain truth even if it is never formed in the physical world. But the chimera is called false simply because it is not formed in the outside world but is *only* an image. Descartes realized that this line of argument has contradicted the self-contained validity of the geometrical demonstration by introducing a figure (or image) which can be judged false only by reference to an ontological judgment about the outside world. The geometrical demonstration does not have to refer to the world outside the dream to be true; the chimera is being judged on the basis of such a reference.

Once more, Descartes sees the implications of this contrast—the paragraph contains the basis for the "truth" of a chimera, even if no chimera can be located in the material (or waking) world. Reason does not tell us that what we see or imagine—that is, what we possess as images—is true. Reason does tell us, however, that *all ideas* (including images) must have some basis (*fondement*) in truth. Therefore the chimera cannot be rejected as entirely false. Descartes is caught in the grip of the ideology of his *camera obscura*.

Let us look at this chimera, a monster designed to alert us to some disturbance produced by imagination. The chimera is false; it is a form of incarnate or imaged fallacy. Moreover the image of the chimera is composite, the head of a lion on the body of a she-goat. This composite nature is for Descartes the mark of imperfection (p. 150), and the way the chimera is composed expresses the particular kind of imperfection that concerns Descartes—I should note that I find this passage in Descartes irresistibly inviting a parallel reading with Montaigne's "De l'oisiveté" (I: 8). The chimera's head is that of a lion (masculine in grammatical and perhaps physical gender)—here the superiority of reason or *esprit* is emblematized—and its body that of a she-goat (female) with all that that conventionally implies of sexuality, carnality, proliferation of matter.[8] This is a clue to the major disruptive force of images in general in the Cartesian system. They are combinations and hence confusions—things joined together. It is difficult to isolate and purify these things, or to "defuse" the power of the image. Jaundice infuses everything with a yellow color. How can that color be removed from the image which it permeates and vitiates? Yet some images that come to us in dreams are distinct. The chimera is such a distinct product of the imagination. Its composition is clear and yet it may not exist in the world. The chimera is therefore, on one hand, disconcertingly like the theoretical constructions of geometry—it fails only by not being outside the mind. It is not *sufficiently* composite; it exists only in the mind and not in the body. Yet on the other hand the chimera is vastly inferior to a geometrical figure because it is based on images from outside the mind. The chimera thus blocks the distinction of inside and out. The falseness of the chimera can only be determined by reference outside the mind; hence the invocation of this image forces the mind to turn outside if it is to avoid the monster. On the other hand, if the mind wishes to remain within the realm of reason it must admit the "truth" of the chimera, and with the chimera, the status of the imagination as a faculty productive of truth.[9]

In a more general and deeper sense the chimera points to Descartes's problem of relating mind and body and to the particular role of sight. "Seeing" and "imagining," here placed in a position of equivalence as untrustworthy guides to truth, are also described as untrustworthy guides to fallacy, since both sight and image-production have some basis in truth. They are placed, after all, in the mind by God ("car il ne serait pas possible que Dieu, qui est tout parfait et tout véritable, les eût mises en nous sans cela," p. 153).

The image in general, of which the chimera is an example, is a graft (*ente*) of truth and fallacy, and of two natures. The divine, all-perfect and all-true part of the image is united to the human imperfection, which prevents our thoughts from being all-true. The composite and impure image of the chimera thus figures the nature of all human thought. Yet Descartes's frantic and somewhat clumsy effort to escape the chimera and its possible truth places waking sensory perception, especially sight, and dreaming or imagining in direct conflict—miming the chimera itself, with its conflicting pieces. The chimera can only be said to be untrue to the extent that a diligent search for the chimera is fruitless. Our senses do not offer any confirmation of the existence of the chimera represented in our mind. Yet our senses are not to be trusted. The dream image can only be disproven by the waking image, yet both are deceptive.

In the first *Méditation,* Descartes again addresses the problem of dreams and the clarity and distinctness of the impressions dreams make. Attempting to locate a difference between dreams and waking, Descartes turns to painted images for an analogy. His principal aim is to argue that the elements of dream images are derived from existing things, and that they are thus externally caused:

> Toutefois il faut au moins avouer que les choses qui nous sont représentées dans le sommeil, sont comme des tableaux et des peintures, qui ne peuvent être formées qu'à la ressemblance de quelque chose de réel et de véritable; et qu'ainsi, pour le moins, ces choses générales, à savoir, des yeux, une tête, des mains, et tout le reste du corps, ne sont pas choses imaginaires, mais vraies et existantes. Car de vrai les peintres, lors même qu'ils s'étudient avec le plus d'artifice à représenter des sirènes et des satyres par des formes bizarres et extraordinaires, ne leur peuvent pas toutefois attribuer des formes et des natures entièrement nouvelles, mais font seulement un certain mélange et composition des membres de divers animaux; ou bien, si peut-être leur imagination est assez extravagante pour inventer quelque chose de si nouveau, que jamais nous n'ayons rien vu de semblable, et qu'ainsi leur ouvrage nous représente une chose purement feinte et absolument fausse, certes à tout le moins les couleurs dont ils le composent doivent-elles être véritables. [*Méditations*, I: 269]

Even a painter attempting to represent sirens and satyrs takes as models the parts of existing animals. Images have a certain syntax, we might say, in which the paradigmatic selections are combined in a new and artificial way. The paradigms are true, but the combination is false. Truth and fallacy in painting can be measured by the correspondence of the image to something that exists outside the painting. Hence paintings are themselves only manifestations of the absence of something—e.g. of eyes or a head—that really *exists* somewhere else. A painter proceeds by combining absences, or the signs of absences, into something that is either overtly deceptive, like the recognizably fantastic siren or satyr, or covertly deceptive, that is, a believable picture. This whole image structure is considered by Descartes as doubtful and uncertain because of the syntactic operation of combination or composition.

This devaluation of the composite—explicit in the first *Méditation*—actually overlays something more fundamental in the simile of painting for dream, namely, the criterion of absence. The painting, and hence the dream, are only syntactically flawed; the paradigmatic basis for paintings is true: painters, even in their most artificial fancies are constrained by the repertory of imagery that exists in nature. Yet this constraint, which makes the fragments of the image true, reveals the paradox of true image.

If the image truly represents something, that thing is elsewhere and hence absent. Conversely, if the image in a painting is not a vehicle of absence, a marker of something that is not entirely *there* in the painting, the painting is false. Should a painter, says Descartes, be so "extravagant" (i.e., mad) as to invent "quelque chose de si nouveau, que jamais nous n'ayons rien vu de semblable, et qu'ainsi leur ouvrage nous représente une chose purement feinte et absolument fausse" (p. 269) at least the colors would have to be true, that is, would have to exist elsewhere in nature. Yet at the same time one can argue, following the inventive genius of the extravagant painter, that should he create something entirely new, its complete being would be in the painting—it would be entirely present, hence false, because nonexistent in the world outside the painting.

The excessive presence of the paradigmatically false painting is related to the temporal characteristics of painting in general. Falseness is measured by reference to the past experience of the subject. Artists in general do not use "formes bizarres et entièrement nouvelles," but reuse old forms. The extravagant painter, on the other hand, invents something "si nouveau, que jamais nous n'ayons rien vu de semblable . . . " (p. 269). The excessive presence of the false image is connected to its attachment to the present time. The false image, even in its selective components, has no past, whereas paintings in general are new only in respect to their composition, not with regard to the elements that form their paradigmatic source. To the extent that the painter is limited to composition, the painting can claim a basis in truth. The more inventive the painter is with respect to the elements of selection, the more *feinte* and false the painting is. Hence the truth of the painting depends on limitations in the acitivity, or at least, the inventiveness, of the painter.

In the first *Méditation* Descartes admitted that he could not distinguish conclusively between dream and waking. At the end of the *Méditations,* he pursues the attempt to eliminate the dangerous equivalency between the images that occur to the mind in these (perhaps) different states. In *Méditation* VI, Descartes identifies the recognition of the dream image as the decisive step in terminating what he calls the hyperbolic and ridiculous doubt, "particulièrement cette incertitude si générale touchant le sommeil, que je ne pouvais distinguer de la veille . . . " (p. 334). The difference between dream images and waking images is based on the continuity of waking vision or of the supposed continuity of the world into which the waking vision is inserted:

Car à présent j'y rencontre une très notable différence, en ce que notre mémoire ne peut jamais lier et joindre nos songes les uns aux autres et avec toute la suite de notre vie, ainsi qu'elle a de coutume de joindre les choses qui nous arrivent étant éveillés. Et, en effet, si quelqu'un, lorsque je veille, m'apparaissait tout soudain et disparaissait de même, comme font les images que je vois en dormant, en sorte que je ne pusse remarquer ni d'où il viendrait, ni où il irait, ce ne serait pas sans raison que je l'estimerais un spectre ou un fantôme formé dans mon cerveau, et semblable à ceux qui s'y forment quand je dors, plutôt qu'un vrai homme. Mais lorsque j'aperçois des choses dont je connais distinctement et le lieu d'où elles viennent, et celui où elles sont, et le temps auquel elles m'apparaissent, et que, sans aucune interruption, je puis lier le sentiment que j'en ai, avec la suite du reste de ma vie, je suis entièrement assuré que je les aperçois en veillant, et non point dans le sommeil. [*Méditations*, VI: 334]

Units of vision in the waking state do not appear *suddenly* and can be explained as coming from and going to someplace. At the end of the *Méditations* the image once more is distinguished from other ideas, which are judged on the basis of clarity and distinctness, and is evaluated in terms of the absences with which the image is surrounded. In the earlier passage the absence concerns the elements out of which a painting is composed. In the closing paragraphs of the *Méditations* the image as a whole, in its composite state, is considered in terms of the absences which precede and follow it. A new criterion is adduced to distinguish true and false images, a criterion based on the invisible continuity of the seen. Dream images are not contested as less clear and distinct but precisely as *too* distinct (in the sense of permitting conception of them as *separate* from something else). In order to be acceptable an image is itself disregarded in favor of an off-stage or off-screen continuity (not unlike cinematographic continuity in the *hors-scène*).

By emphasizing knowledge of what precedes and follows an image rather than its appearance in the present, Descartes moves from optical qualities towards narrative ones. The thinker expects to be able to say what happened before and what happens after the things appeared in his visual field. The before and after of a verbal account become more important than the presence of the image and the present tense of a description of the figure in the image. While the figure in a dream is just as clear and apparently present as the images we perceive while awake, figures from the two types of image differ in their resistance to questions about their past and future. The temporal qualities of the image—or at least the temporal qualities of the figure *in* the image—are thus given priority. Presence and "the present" are identified as descriptive terms and in the same gesture devaluated as ontologically probative terms.

A picture presents special difficulties of interpretation. While it may seem to represent an existing thing, a picture does not make an unequivocal statement about being and time. An image, unlike a sentence, does not declare that what it portrays "is" or "might be," "was" or "will be." Unlike most languages, images *per se* have neither tenses nor modal indications. Various systems have been constructed to overcome these limitations of the single, isolated image by forming image-clusters or strips that are read in a certain order to decode temporal sequence. Descartes, however, usually speaks of images as isolated and disconnected (e.g., a chimera, a siren, a triangle), not as part of sequences, much less as a perpetually changing but never broken visual continuum. Such images are therefore frozen moments in time, or rather without any time except a generalized present.

I have already mentioned the contrast between the posited immutability of the image and the ever-changing apprehension and description of the image that is made by the thinker. At the end of the *Méditations,* Descartes gives a new and different account of the discovery of the image in time, an account designed specifically for the image of things that are supposed to exist materially. In the case of the image of the triangle, the thinker returns repeatedly to the same, unchanging and solitary image to discover in more detail the contents of that image. The image exists apparently outside time, while the discovery and description of the image occur in time. The image described at the end of the *Méditations* has a temporal quality that derives from its integration into a series of images, each of which has a firm and specific assignment in time. In this concluding passage of the book, the isolated image, which, in earlier sections, served to support geometrical demonstration, is abandoned as a paradigm of internal vision in favor of the sequence of images made out of (presumed) sensory data and recapitulated by memory. With this gesture, Descartes has reversed the temporal situation of the viewer and the image that obtained in the description of triangles. A changing, learning thinker confronted an unchanging geometrical image. Now, at the end of the *Méditations,* an apparently unchanging thinker studies a changing scene. Waking images, though still thought of individually, are supposed to be part of a temporal series guaranteeing their truth. On the other side—that is, in the thinker—is a transcendant faculty called memory which has no significant history of its own, but is only concerned with the history of the images which it stores and knits together.

Such a shift in Descartes's description and evaluation of images is possible only because of a shift in the amount of certain knowledge available to the thinker at the end of the *Méditations*. It is not mere coincidence that the single, clear, and distinct image and the *cogito* are associated in an earlier phase of the *Méditations*. The *cogito* is a statement in the present tense about a fact that is certain only in the present moment. As Descartes writes in *Méditations* II: "*Je suis, j'existe:* cela est certain; mais combien de temps? A savoir autant de temps que je pense . . . " (p. 277). By the end of the *Méditations* the knowledge of God has permitted the thinker to advance to a reasonable certainty of the past ("pouvant user de ma mémoire pour lier et joindre les connaissances présentes aux passées . . . " p. 333). Therefore, in practice, clarity and distinctness in the present are no longer as uniquely important as they were at an earlier stage of the discovery process. In a way—speaking rather freely but without departing too much from Descartes—we can say that the Cartesian God is more on the side of the writer than of the painter, or, at least, that He favors the narrative painter. The act of connecting times and cumulating experiences modifies what is available to the judgment, thanks to continuity supplied by a truthful God. With this switch from an isolated present to a series of separate perceptions that are compared, the scale of Descartes's description of images is modified.

In describing the chimera, the siren, and the satyr, Descartes indicated that composition, rather than the paradigms of anatomical elements, was the source of their novelty, and thus of their falsehood. Composition is also invoked in the discussion of the specter or phantom in the conclusion of the *Méditations,* but the level or scale of composition has changed. The whole of the individual image itself is now the paradigmatic element, not the details or fragments of the individual image. Descartes is not concerned with the way this specter looks, in fact it seems that the specter looks like anyone else, *quelqu'un.* In other words, the specter is not itself a grotesque composite image made out of recognizably disparate pieces but is a whole, an entirety, apparently received from the world outside the mind. The truth ascribable to paradigmatic elements derived from the material world now seems to inhabit the entire image and to render that image (even in its combination of elements, its composition) true or at least indistinguishable from true, waking life. If paradigmatic qualities were earlier the source of truth and compositional qualities the source of falsehood then the dream image seems to reduce the instruments of image description to a state of paralysis, to deprive us of weapons against the chimeras and the specters. *But,* by a reversal of the previous approach, Descartes now permits the compositional or syntagmatic qualities of the image to serve as the determinants of truth. The individual image is the invariant element which, however false, can be exposed by combining it with appropriate images of before and after along a chronological sequence.

Playing *fort/da* with the specter, Descartes supposes that the viewer of a waking image has a secondary repertory of images with which to account for the unseen part of the visualizable sequence. Being able to imagine where someone came from and where that person went upon leaving the visual field means, in effect, not only maintaining a smooth series of primary images that are composed in time, but also being able to sequence hypothetical unseen images, that is, to suppose that the person does not cease to exist upon becoming invisible. This is the inverse of the specter, for the specter is visible but does not exist, whereas persons may be invisible and yet exist. The exactness of representation which is possible in an image, even a dream image, is less important at this point than the plausible fabulation which permits the movement of figures into and out of the image. The restriction of vision which is the basis for forming a distinct image in a *camera obscura* yields to a wider, less precise but highly comforting knowledge that the figures which disappear into the dark do not cease to exist, for we can make up stories about where they went.

NOTES

1. *Le Discours de la méthode,* in *Oeuvres et lettres,* ed. André Bridoux (Paris: Gallimard, "Bibliothèque de la Pléiade," 1953), p. 132. The French texts of all subsequent quotations from Descartes are from the Pléiade edition. I have used the Latin text of the *Meditationes de Prima Philosophia* in vol. 7 of the edition of the *Oeuvres de Descartes* by Adam and Tannery (Paris: Léopold Cerf, 1904).

2. John Morris, "Descartes' Natural Light," *Journal of the History of Philosophy* 11, no. 2 (April 1973): pp. 169–87.

3.   On the figurative use of visual terms see also Pierre Zoberman, "Voir, savoir, parler: La rhétorique et la vision au XVIIe et au début du XVIIIe siècles," *XVIIe Siècle* 133 (Oct./Dec. 1981): pp. 409–28, and also the issue of the same journal (136, July/September 1982) devoted to "Matière et lumière au XVIIe siècle."

4.   Arthur K. Wheelock, in *Perspective, Optics, and Delft Artists around 1650* (New York: Garland Publications, 1977), p. 138, cites the work of Barbaro for the use of *distintamente* and *chiaro* in Renaissance terminology. See also Michael Baxandall, *Patterns of Intention: On the Historical Explanation of Pictures* (New Haven: Yale University Press), pp. 80–104.

5.   John Morris has shown that the term *lumen naturale* is generally associated in Descartes's works with the power of understanding, or more particularly, with what Morris describes as the passive form of understanding, and *not* with the active or quasi-active faculty of conceiving. Hence imagining, or making images, lies at the opposite pole of mental activities from the "natural light."

6.   Sylvie Romanowski, *L'illusion chez Descartes* (Paris: Klincksieck, 1974), p. 165.

7.   "Je trouve en moi une infinité d'idées de certaines choses, qui ne peuvent pas être estimées un pur néant, quoique peut-être elles n'aient aucune existence hors de ma pensée, et qui ne sont pas feintes par moi . . . Comme par exemple, lorsque j'imagine un triangle, encore qu'il n'y ait peut-être en aucun lieu du monde hors de ma pensée une telle figure, et qu'il n'y en ait jamais eu, il ne laisse pas néanmoins d'y avoir une certaine nature, ou forme, ou essence déterminée. . ." (*Méditations*, V: 311).

8.   Cf. Montaigne, "De l'oisiveté" (I: 8).

9.   In some ways we have detected Descartes reversing the movement described by Reiss in the "concevoir motif," for while Descartes does use conception as a means to argue the material existence of that which is only proven ideally, through conception and judgment, the imagination motif shows Descartes struggling to undo (selectively) consequences of admitting into the mind the image of something of which he is not willing to grant the existence outside. See Timothy Reiss, "The 'concevoir' Motif in Descartes," in *La Cohérence intérieure*, ed. J. Van Baelen and D. L. Rubin (Paris: Jean-Michel Place, 1976), pp. 203–222.

A Reading of the First *Liasse*

Peter Bayley

Readers of Pascal's *Pensées* tend to skip the first *liasse*. This is not, of course, to say that a great deal of scholarly attention has not been paid to it in the decades since the Lafuma edition of the *Copie* became the normal classroom text;[1] but it is not scholars whom I primarily have in mind. The first-time general reader, confronted with "Les psaumes chantés par toute la terre" as the first paragraph, will as likely as not think to himself that the title "Ordre" means something technical which he can learn about later, or that it relates only to the controversies concerning the fragmentation and conjectural reconstructions of the text which he may have read about in a preface. He rapidly passes on to something more solid and more recognizable as prose—say the long fragment (44) on Imagination—and settles down to enjoy the vertiginous generalizations he has been led by a long tradition of selective quotation to expect from a French moralist like Pascal.

Had my untutored reader paused a little longer over the first paragraph of *Ordre,* pondering it in the light of what is still not too far from being general knowledge in Western culture, he would have learned that to read and enjoy the text as a series of discontinuous generalizations might not be the most appropriate response or, at least, the one to which he is invited. For "les psaumes chantés par toute la terre" has a fairly specific focus. It is a reminder of that cliché of religious apologetic which locates the first evidence for the existence of God in man's experience of the visible world, a cliché summed up, in the Judaeo-Christian tradition, by Psalm 19: "The heavens declare the glory of God, and the firmament sheweth his handywork. Day unto day uttereth speech, and night unto night showeth knowlege. There is no speech or language where their voice is not heard. Their line is gone out *through all the earth,* and their words to the end of the world."[2] It is a tenacious doctrine: the twentieth-century television viewer is hardly less likely to have come across it than the seventeenth-century Frenchman; it is the foundation of vague enlightened Deism and the inspiration of much amateur science. It knows no sectarian boundaries: a Huguenot of Pascal's time would recall its appearance as the cornerstone of Calvin's *Institutes*[3] just as his Catholic counterpart would identify it as the substance of endless hours of meditation and preaching.[4] As a representative and randomly selected collection of sermons reprinted throughout the period when Pascal was growing up puts it: "Bref, ce monde en toutes ses parties n'est autre chose qu'un livre qui propose, un tableau qui exprime, une voix qui presche, une trompette qui annonce, un heraut qui publie la Majesté, la grandeur, et les perfections de la Divinité." [5]

Here, then, is an initial paragraph which, in its echo of this vast and familiar tradition, provides the reader with some purchase on the text he has just opened. It is going to be about religious apologetic. There is no clue yet as to what direction it may take—for all he knows, it may turn into a treatise on optics or Rosicrucianism. What will his reaction be? It may be complacency, if he is a believer who has never doubted the proposition, or it may be a degree of rejection: this is the sort of stereotype which he thinks needs at the very least some sort of critical scrutiny. He will have to wait another five lines before he can make out how the text is likely to treat readers in his position; but meanwhile it is precisely that notion of critical scrutiny which is now introduced.

> Qui rend témoignage de Mahomet? lui-même. J. -C. veut que son témoignage ne soit rien.
> La qualité de témoins fait qu'il faut qu'ils soient toujours, et partout, et misérables. Il est seul.

The first part of these remarks confirms, if nothing more, the opening impression: this is indeed a work of religious apologetic and it is going to take into account more than one religion, although its stance toward Islam (no doubt a seventeenth-century Frenchman would have said "toward the Turks") is from the first a combative one. The second part is more intriguing, not least because it is difficult to construe. Does it mean that it is the nature of witnesses to be everywhere in time and space as well as evidently not standing to gain from their testimony? Or does the "toujours" merely mean that this rule applies universally? One thing is clear: critical scrutiny can be applied to this subject in exactly the same way as it is to a lawsuit. The witnesses can be questioned and their suitability weighed; we can already begin to think about the sort of evidence that will be necessary. It is this idea of evidence that binds the three parts of the first *pensée* together. We may for a moment suppose that the notion of bringing to bear on a familiar cliché the methods one is familiar with from the law might be particularly attractive to a sceptical *robin;* but we hardly need that sort of historical information to make some sense of the fragment.

Pensée 2 confronts the untutored reader with a rather different "order" of approach to such questions: it exploits the very fact that questions are running through his mind—"Que dois-je faire?"—and gives expression to the objection which may already be his response to the opening sentence: "Je ne vois partout qu'obscurités." The very invention of such a voice may quicken his interest in the book he has opened: it is not going to be a treatise, it may even be like a drama. For here we have appearing, not as an object of derision but as a participant in a dialogue which (for all we yet know) may occupy the remainder of the book, a voice with which he may identify.[6] "Je ne vois partout qu'obscurités" may indeed be his reaction to the notion that creation sings psalms; it may, for that matter, be his reaction to the text he is reading (for it would not be the only occasion on which Pascal draws attention to the struggle a reader has in understanding a text).[7] The use of "je" directs his gaze upon himself. And two possible consequences of self-contemplation are then spelled out, with that brevity and almost mathematical leap across the trivial steps of an argument to its logical conclusions which our reader may by now be coming to relish as the characteristic tone of his text: "Croirai-je que je ne suis rien? Croirai-je que je suis dieu?" He may guess, if he has any commonsense, that the answer is going to lie between these two extremes, but also that they will be boldly faced. He will probably also note that behind these two positions there lie ancient philosophical systems and debates that a Christian apologist is obliged to engage with no less than the existence of other religions.

The exciting sense that the text is going to turn into a dialogue grows as we meet the third fragment, as does the play with the commonplaces of religious apology. The sonorous and alliterative statement that "toutes choses changent et se succèdent" may be a grandiose expression of the sceptical reader's approach to religions that claim to trade in absolutes; the devout reader may confidently expect a denial of it; the seventeenth-century French reader would find himself confronted again by one of the tired but apparently inescapable topoi of preaching, meditation and religious poetry. They are all catered for and then confounded by Pascal's three *points de suspension:* "Vous vous trompez, il y a . . . " And the dialogue then becomes quite heated, at least on what seems to be the skeptic side: "Et quoi ne dites-vous pas vous-même que le ciel et les oiseaux prouvent Dieu?" We are back where we began, with the heavens declaring the glory of God, a notion here evidently mocked by the skeptic as he trivializes creation in terms of the sky and the birds, and accuses his interlocutor of having said this very thing (as it might be, in the first fragment). We have virtually a miniature preview here of the libertine's response to Sganarelle's elaborate demonstrations of the great chain of being, the French *locus classicus* of foolish theologizing on this theme, in Act V, Scene 3 of Molière's *Dom Juan:* "O le beau raisonnement!" The calm "non" of the reply comes as a shock, provoking what may be either a more serious question or a final scoff to show that the skeptic knows better: "Et votre religion ne le dit-elle pas?" The "non" here may disconcert more than just the skeptic; and the qualification that follows serves to reassure the devout, at the same time as it quite definitely and abruptly sides with those "qui ne voient partout qu'obscurités":

> Car encore que cela est vrai en un sens pour quelques âmes à qui Dieu donna cette lumière, néanmoins cela est faux à l'égard de la plupart.

This is spoken with the voice of authority, such as one might expect to meet if one picked up an apology for the Christian religion; but what the voice says scythes through the tired dogmas and replaces certainty with doubt. It speaks confidently of God, it explains how belief in the clear evidences of his existence comes to be (for the believing soul is repeatedly reminded that he is "très légitimement persuadé"),[8] but at that very moment it makes an act of faith in the sincerity of the skeptic. This exciting, dramatic text is not going to be one in which (save at a much later stage) the dice are loaded. Whether the "untutored reader" lives in the seventeenth or the twentieth century, the originality, freshness, and directness of this approach to him makes it very unlike the common run of religious pamphleteering.

As indeed does the next notion to hit him: something like a plan for a novel (or perhaps an allegorical play) which again starts not from an easy assurance that God exists but that he will have to be sought. It takes us back to fragment 2, the systems of thought which make of man a nothing or a god, and it promises a hard passage: "Lettre pour porter à rechercher Dieu. Et puis le faire chercher chez les philosophes, pyrrhoniens et dogmatistes qui travailleront celui qui le recherche." The skeptic is, once again, going to be met on his own ground.

As the idea of this possible scenario of a letter is more fully sketched out, that skeptic now becomes a friend. When we deal with any friend, we consult his wishes, we try to understand his motives; that is what our authorial voice now once again shows himself willing to do, in another fragment of dialogue which ends with a tantalizingly mysterious phrase:

> Une lettre d'exhortation à un ami pour le porter à chercher. Et il répondra: mais à quoi me servira de chercher, rien ne paraît. Et lui répondre: ne désespérez pas. Et il répondrait qu'il serait heureux de trouver quelque lumière. Mais que selon cette religion même quand il croirait ainsi cela ne lui servirait de rien. Et qu'ainsi il aime autant ne point chercher. Et à cela lui répondre: La Machine.

There has been a shift of position here: the reader is taken into the confidence of one participant in the dialogue, he is made to see how the friend can be persuaded. Equally well, should he feel himself to be in the role of the skeptic, he is flattered by it being made clear that his knowledge of religion is not negligible (faith has to be absolute, he thinks, and his simply cannot be). Again his good will is taken for granted—"il serait heureux de trouver quelque lumière"—and his guess that, for him, the exercise will prove to be pointless is answered by a "ne désespérez pas" which may console and certainly excites the curiosity: where will this search, this story of the letter, end? For the moment it seems to involve a gnomic utterance which again incites to further inquiry: "La Machine."

At this point, like Pol Ernst,[9] let us mark a pause. Our untutored reader has been bombarded with dialogues, letters, a meditation on the nature of evidence, a sweeping away of the traditions of apologetic. If he is a Christian, he has been given hints that his position is reserved (for he may be one of those "quelques âmes à qui Dieu donna cette lumière"); more importantly, if he is a skeptic he has found himself faced not with condemnation but with sympathy. His sincerity has been accepted right from the beginning: it is going to become one of the cornerstones of the text, whether because his honest difficulties in finding evidence of God in Nature will lead to a rethinking of the mode of God's revelation and even of God's character, or because his curiosity and desire for the chase—awakened here—will form the basis for a whole depiction of human personality in general. This start to an apology, however, is highly original only in terms of what we normally expect of that genre; in terms of the art of persuasion it is merely an application of the old rule that you must begin by getting the audience on your side, the *captatio benevolentiae* which is the function of any classical exordium. As Pascal puts it elsewhere, in *De l'art de persuader*, "quoi que ce soit qu'on veuille persuader, il faut avoir égard à la personne à qui on en veut, dont il faut connaître l'esprit et le coeur, quels principes il accorde, quelles choses il aime; et ensuite remarquer, dans la chose dont il s'agit, quels rapports elle a avec les principes avoués, ou avec les objets délicieux par les charmes qu'on lui donne." [10] It may be stated the other way round: to persuade, you have to know your audience and appeal directly to them; in a work of persuasive apologetic, this means beginning not with God but with Man, perceived as a creature of doubt but also honesty, and above all as receptive to modes of discourse (dialogue, drama, narrative, allusion, sententiousness) which stir his interest. To paraphrase a remark of Hugh Davidson's, one might say that Pascal begins with man and his suppositions.[11] One might even say that here rhetoric has determined theology.

With the mention of "La Machine," we come to a reference which is impenetrable to the "untutored reader." He will find it again in fragment 11, but it is not until the famous *Pari* that this doctrine of man's psychological automatism, able at one and the same time to encompass and confound the view of man as either *ange* or *bête,* will be fleshed out. This is the moment, I think, when the first *liasse* changes direction and begins to set out to its reader a number of plans, or to expand some of the ideas contained in its first part. Thus we find the notion of other religions, the germ of *liasse* XVI, again alluded to in fragment 8, and no fewer than three further mentions of a letter (in 7, 9, and 11). But there is no need to abandon our sequential reading and adopt the quite different strategy implied by a genetic approach. In the classical account of rhetorical *dispositio*, the exordium with its generalities and *captatio benevolentiae* is followed by section called *propositio* or *partitio*. It is the occasion for the author/orator to reveal to his audience the way he intends to divide up his material, and is not infrequently accompanied by enumeration for mnemonic purposes. Fragment 6 follows this pattern precisely:

    (1.) Partie. Misère de l' homme sans Dieu.
    (2.) Partie. Félicité de l' homme avec Dieu.
                autrement
    (1.) Partie. Que la nature est corrompue, par la nature même.
    (2.) Partie. Qu'il y a un réparateur, par l' Écriture.

Now, a *propositio* is not necessarily exhaustive; it acts as a guideline
through the narratives, arguments, "confirmations" which constitute the
section of the discourse primarily concerned with proof. And proof, as it
happens, is the subject of the very next fragment, with its suggestion that
proof is itself part of the wider art of persuasion ("Par la Machine"), and
that proof and faith are different. Theoretically, at any rate, this brief
reference perhaps provides an answer to the apparent disparity I noted
earlier between Pascal's simultaneous acceptance and rejection of rhetorical strategies in *De l'art de persuader:* while "les vérités divines . . . sont
infiniment au-dessus de la nature," that is no reason why men may not be
guided towards them by means of those same pointers and witnesses we
read of in the first fragment, *fides ex auditu.* And the quotations here
from Romans may make us reflect on Paul's elaborate outline in chapter
1 of that Epistle of the evidences of God in Nature. Paul is there anxious
to show that the ungodly are rightly condemned, "for the invisible things
of him from the creation of the world are clearly seen, being understood
by the things that are made, even his eternal power and Godhead; so that
they are without excuse" (Rom. I. 20). It is perhaps at this point that our
reader, recalling the rejection of that idea in the earlier part of the *liasse,*
understands the novelty of what he is reading—a recasting of the tradition of apologetic exemplified by Paul into terms that are acceptable to
the "modern" skeptic. He is reading a text the basis of which is to be his
own rejection of that tradition and his own radical doubt about the
clichés he associates with religion.

One of these will be justice, or at least the abstract idea of it. And is
not the radicalism of thought already noted in fragment 2 now brought
to bear on exactly that question in fragment 9?

> Dans la lettre de l' injustice peut venir.
>   La plaisanterie des aînés qui ont tout. Mon ami vous êtes né de ce côté
> de la montagne, il est donc juste que votre aîné ait tout.
>   Pourquoi me tuez-vous?

It is obvious that this will need to be filled in, as it is for example by
fragment 51,[12] in the same way as the elliptical "ils ont pris le divertissement" of the next *pensée* will be rounded out by the whole of the eighth
liasse. But those will be merely examples—albeit magnificent and mem-
orable ones—of the rhetorical device of amplification, and in essence the
idea of what Richard Parish calls an "anthropological" apology[13] is al-

ready sketched out in this rapid survey of the fragility of human institutions, of man's persistent attempts to avert his gaze from the abyss, indeed of man's own psychological automatism.

That appeal to man through a study of man, reinforced by the references to "La Machine" in fragment 11, is now reformulated in the very different register of the twelfth and final fragment:

> Les hommes ont mépris pour la religion. Ils en ont haine et peur qu'elle soit vraie. Pour guérir cela il faut commencer par montrer que la religion n'est point contraire à la raison. Vénérable, en donner respect. La rendre ensuite aimable, faire souhaiter aux bons qu'elle fût vraie et puis montrer qu'elle est vraie. Vénérable parce qu'elle a bien connu l'homme. Aimable parce qu'elle promet le vrai bien.

Again, this is programmatic, but its tone is one of exhortation rather than exposition. It carries the reader forward by its persuasive rhythms, by repetition, asyndeton, antithesis, isocolon: what may be technically identified as the schemes appropriate to the "sublime style" of a peroration, in fact, just as the personification of "la religion" is the appropriate trope of prosopopoeia. The text speaks of two levels of persuasion— "montrer" and "faire souhaiter"—and at the same time operates on those two levels. The intellectual and the emotional are not separated but fused into a single, though complex, appeal.

Throughout the *Pensées* that appeal will be based firmly and in the best rhetorical traditions on an analysis of those to whom it is made. The *dogmatistes* will be confounded by the *pyrrhoniens,* and vice-versa; the Jews will be confronted with their own venerated prophecies of a Messiah; the gambling man will be offered a wager; the lawyer concerned with title will be handed a bulky brief of *preuves.* Each group, however, will be approached by a *captatio benevolentiae,* their cherished beliefs or particular emphases will be adopted, nor will they be refuted. Since all types of *libertin* are men, how could it be otherwise in a religion which is "vénérable parce qu'elle a bien connu l'homme"? Like its phrasing, the method will be antithetical, and breathtaking in its use of the figure of *concessio:*

> Tous leurs principes sont vrais, des pyrrhoniens, des stoïques, des athées, etc. . . . mais leurs conclusions sont fausses, parce que les principes opposés sont vrais aussi. [619]

In a sense this extends the question of voices in the *Pensées* beyond those who actually speak in it, for Pascal peoples the text with what John Cruickshank has called the "ideas and sentiments which he expressed not to represent his own outlook but that of the *libertins* to whom his apology was addressed." [14] To return to our untutored reader, the play of mirrors which confronted him when he opened the first *liasse* continues far beyond it: his own possible opinions are reflected or refracted back to him, though constantly modified by his growing sense of a controlling authorial presence. I spoke earlier of the vertiginous generalizations he might have opened the book to seek. When he finally comes to the most anthologized remark of all—"Le silence éternel de ces espaces infinis m'effraie" (fr. 201)—will he not recognize in it not some autobiographical Angst on the part of his author but his own inability (now subtly tinged with terror) to discern those evidences of God in Nature with which the *liasse* began?

This cardinal aspect of free thought has, then, been seized upon as a starting-point, and by the end of the *liasse* has been conjoined with many and various others. What links them is not merely the demonstrable rhetorical *dispositio* of the piece, important though it is if we are to grasp the coherence of the moves from general to particular points and back again to a general one, nor even the traces of a systematic *elocutio* which can modulate from the striking question and the sonorous allusion to the "division en points" and then to the *oratio numerosa* of fragment 12. This apparent disorder in fact shows the unity of the *liasse* and its author's attentiveness to the precept that "l'éloquence continue ennuie"; its fragmented nature exemplifies in some detail the profoundly writerly perception that "la nature agit par progrès, *itus et reditus*. Elle passe et revient, puis va plus loin, puis deux fois moins, puis plus que jamais, etc." [15] The formal rhetorical organization of this brief text is however but one manifestation of the larger meditation which it contains: a meditation which includes in its sweep the traditions of apologetic that constrain St. Paul as well as Pascal's more immediate predecessors, the traditions of radical free thought which encompass Montaigne as well as Lucretius, and yet which remains firmly based upon a precept (of rhetorical theory rather than form) which will guide the inquiry to its end—the principle that one's audience is to be treated as if sincere. The implications for a Christian apologetic addressed primarily to those who do not believe (as opposed to a ratification for the faithful) are immense. Since it is commonplace to exploit the "mere jottings" of the first *liasse* as a gloss on "later" longer *pensées,* I hope it will be permitted to conclude by citing one of the *papiers non classés,* or *pensées mêlées* (n° 781) as a gloss which unfolds those implications, more particularly those of its very first sentences, and prefers Matthew and Isaiah to Paul:

> Préface de la seconde partie.
> Parler de ceux qui ont traité de cette matière.
> J'admire avec quelle hardiesse ces personnes entreprennent de parler de Dieu.
> En adressant leurs discours aux impies leur premier chapitre est de prouver la divinité par les ouvrages de la nature. Je ne m'étonnerais pas de leur entreprise s'ils adressaient leurs discours aux fidèles, car il est certain que ceux qui ont la foi vive dedans le coeur voient incontinent que tout ce qui est n'est autre chose que l'ouvrage du Dieu qu'ils adorent, mais pour ceux en qui cette lumière est éteinte et dans lesquels on a dessein de la faire revivre, ces personnes destituées de foi et de grâce, qui recherchant de toute leur lumière tout ce qu'ils voient dans la nature qui les peut mener à cette connaissance ne trouvent qu'obscurité et ténèbres, dire à ceux-là qu'ils n'ont qu'à voir la moindre des choses qui les environnent et qu'ils y verront Dieu à découvert et leur donner pour toute preuve de ce grand et important sujet le cours de la lune et des planètes et prétendre avoir a- chevé sa preuve avec un tel discours, c'est leur donner sujet de croire que les preuves de notre religion sont bien faibles et je vois par raison et par expérience que rien n'est plus propre à leur en faire naître le mépris. Ce n'est pas de cette sorte que l'Écriture qui connaît mieux les choses qui sont de Dieu en parle. Elle dit au contraire que Dieu est un Dieu caché et que depuis la corruption de la nature il les a laissés dans un aveuglement dont ils ne peuvent sortir que par J.-C., hors duquel toute communication avec Dieu est ôtée. *Nemo novit patrem nisi filius et cui filius voluit revelare.*
> C'est ce que l'Écriture nous marque quand elle dit en tant d'endroits que ceux qui cherchent Dieu le trouvent. Ce n'est point de cette lumière qu'on parle comme le jour en plein midi. Ou ne ditpoint que ceux qui cherchent le jour en plein midi ou de l'eau dans la mer en trouveront et ainsi il faut bien que l'évidence de Dieu ne soit pas telle dans la nature. Aussi elle nous dit ailleurs: *vere tu es deus absconditus.*

NOTES

1. Most recently by A. R. Pugh (*The Composition of Pascal's Apologia,* Toronto: U. of Toronto P, 1984, pp. 29–45), who notes that "one naturally assumes

[this bundle] to have been the basis of an opening chapter," calls it "puzzling," and then goes on somewhat confusingly to attack Pol Ernst's treatment of it as "by definition a first chapter." My sympathies go to Pol Ernst's attempts, in Pugh's words, to build "a hypothetical introduction out of these twelve fragments alone" (Pugh, p. 29); indeed, what I am attempting is a restatement of Ernst, *Approches pascaliennes* (Paris: Gembloux, Duculot, 1970, pp. 17–47). The difference is that I am pretending, for the moment, that there is no need to try to reconstruct Pascal's "project" but merely to try to understand his "notes." The question I explicitly ignore here has been neatly put by Jean Massard: "Faut-il voir dans cette liasse un simple dossier de travail, sorte d'échafaudage qui aurait disparu de l'oeuvre achevée? Ou bien Pascal avait-il l'intention de s'expliquer devant ses lecteurs de l'ordre suivi? (*Les Pensées de Pascal,* Paris: Sedes, 1976, p. 179). If this were a sermon, my text would be Hugh Davidson's remark that "Pascal seems intent on introducing not systematically but succinctly all the terminology necessary for his apologetic argument" (*The Origins of Certainty: Means and Meaning in Pascal's "Pensées,"* Chicago and London: 1979, p. 75). Quotations are from Pascal's *Oeuvres complètes,* ed. Louis Lafuma (Paris: 1963).

2. The King James Bible version, vv. 1–4 (my emphasis); the psalm is n° 18 in the Vulgate. In view of Pascal's echo of the last sentence, Sellier's (unsubstantiated) gloss on this text seems to me excessively narrow: "Le peuple juif," he says, "dispersé dans tout le monde connu, chante, sans en comprendre la portée réelle, les Psaumes où le Messie est annoncé. Hostiles aux chrétiens, les Juifs sont à leur insu les meilleurs témoins de la vérité du christianisme" (*Pensées*, ed. Philippe Sellier, Paris: 1976, p. 40, n. 1). This interpretation connects the sentence neatly to the non-Christian religion mentioned in the next, and I should certainly not want to exclude it; but it offers none of the cross-references to fragments 2 and 3 which I hope to demonstrate. Ernst's reading (*Approches pascaliennes,* pp. 35–37) is much wider.

3. For example, *Institution de la religion chrestienne,* I: 5, i: "non seulement il a engravé ceste semence de religion que nous avons dite en l'esprit des hommes, mais aussi il s'est tellement manifesté à eux en ce bastiment tant beau et exquis du ciel et de la terre . . . " (ed. J.-D. Benoît, Paris: 1957–63, I: 68).

4. See my *French Pulpit Oratory* (Cambridge: Cambridge UP, 1980), chap. 7 ("Nature, that universal and publick Manuscript").

5. Etienne Molinier, *Le Mystère de la Croix* (Toulouse; 1635), p. 63. First published in 1628, this collection was reprinted in 1635 and 1643.

6. The most recent and fascinating discussion of these potentially very vexed questions of dialogue and identification is by Richard Parish: "«Mais qui parle?» Voice and Persona in the *Pensées,*" *Seventeenth-Century French Studies* (VIII: 1986), pp. 23–40.

7. See n° 257.

8. N° 110; cf. n° 382.

9. See his graphic plan (*Approches pascaliennes,* p. 40) where he marks a break here between the "préliminaires à l'Apologie" and the outline or "dessein de l'Apologie elle–même" which follows it.

10. *Oeuvres complètes,* 356. This contrasts with Pascal's apparent disavowal of the principle earlier in the same text: "tout ce qu'il y a d'hommes sont presque toujours emportés à croire non pas par la preuve, mais par l'agrément. Cette voie est basse, indigne et étrangère: aussi tout le monde le désavoue [. . .] Je ne parle pas ici des vérités divines, que je n'aurais garde de faire tomber sous l'art de persuader, car elles sont infiniment au-dessus de la nature . . ." (*Ibid.,* 355).

11. *The Origins of Certainty,* pp. 4–5: "Pascal appears to see proof as implied in a play of *suppositions* and what may be advanced as suitable *presuppositions.* Since he is not discovering the truth but defending it, he starts logically with suppositions and moves backward to what they presuppose [. . .] Pascal characteristically begins with Nature and Scripture, with man and God; the proofs we find relate to these two."

12. And, of course, its simple meaning will have to be explored. Ernst (*Approches pascaliennes,* p. 34) reads: "Dans la Lettre «De l'Injustice» peut venir la plaisanterie . . . "; this enables him to speculate at some length about the difference between this and other *Lettres.* Pugh follows him (*The Composition of Pascal's Apologia,* p. 32). Sellier places a comma after "venir," yet somewhat perversely makes the words that follow it into a separate paragraph. One might construe "de l'injustice" in the Lafuma text as a partitive.

13. "Voice and Persona," 23.

14. *Pascal: Pensées* (London: 1983), p. 35.

15. Here I have preferred Sellier's punctuation (*ed. cit.,* 319, n° 635). The fragment is n° 771 in Lafuma.

Toward a Semiotics of Blaise Pascal's *Pensées*: A Model for Geometrical and Rhetorical Persuasions

Roland A. Champagne

> Tout auteur a un sens auquel tous les passages contraires s'accordent ou il n'a point de sens du tout.
>
> BLAISE PASCAL, Pensées[1]

> L'important n'est donc pas le temps ou l'espace mais, comme l'écrit Khlebnikov, "la mesure, l'ordre et l'harmonie." Son but premier est de dénoncer le "soi-disant hasard," de montrer qu'il n'y a rien de fortuit, que l'arbitraire n'est rien d'autre qu'une relation encore ignorée. L'harmonie universelle règne; l'homme doit l'honorer par un calcul généralisé, qui en révélera les règles.
>
> TZVETAN TODOROV, Poétique de la prose[2]

The *Pensées* of Blaise Pascal constitute a rich document for the application of computer technology to the semiotics of epistemology. "Semiotics" is understood here to mean the rhetorical communication used by Pascal, and epistemology is the progress toward certitude he was demonstrating to his Interlocutor. The content of the *Pensées* was concerned with the attainment of certain knowledge by the Interlocutor, and yet its fragmentary and incomplete form apparently vitiates the coherence of the presentation. This form, however, is also an ideal testing ground for the assimilating and organizational potential of the computer to confirm the deceptiveness of appearances and the bedrock of underlying unity in Pascal's presentation of the struggle for knowledge.

As a mathematician and "moraliste," Pascal certainly had the inclination in the *Pensées* to examine the ties between his mathematical and his rhetorical concerns. Prior to this work, he had published an essay on the geometrical properties of cones (1640) and also a proposal for an "arithmetic machine" called a "pascalien" (1642). These mathematical concerns give us some of the keys to unlock his *Pensées* from the apparent confusion of its fragmented appearance. We may thereby gain access to the unity of this rhetorical piece and to Pascal's insights into the mathematical precision of human understanding. In seeking this unity, the computer, as exemplified by the Davidson-Dubé Concordance to the *Pensées*,[3] has indeed already revealed subtle components and patterns among Pascal's reflections. In this essay, I will concentrate on Pascal's presentation of the problems with time because Pascalian time contains the vital properties of knowledge in that he used his spatial or geometrical sensitivity to reveal the existential bond between time and being.

In his earlier work, Pascal observed that "la géometrie . . . a expliqué l'art de découvrir les vérités inconnues; et ce qu'elle appelle analyse."[4] But even prior to analysis, the information in question must be gathered and organized in a certain manner so that the perspectives of geometry can be applied and studied in discovering "les vérités inconnues." A case in point is Pascal's own *Pensées* whereby he sought to convince an unsympathetic Interlocutor of the need for religious faith. Prior to this work, Pascal had learned from geometry what he called "l'art de persuader."[5] He later distinguished geometrical proofs from syllogistic and dialectical ones. In his concerns with the nature of time in the *Pensées*, Pascal linked all three types of proof in order to isolate the quantitative and qualitative certainties about time, a phenomenon which appeared to be relative to the observer. Quantitatively, time engaged the Interlocutor thus: "Combien de temps faut-il? Un temps proportionné à notre durée vaine et chétive" (31). Likewise, a qualitative perception of time appears arbitrary. For example, Pascal noted that "toute histoire qui n'est pas contemporaine est suspecte" (436).

However, Pascal set out to engage the Interlocutor in a discussion that would lead toward certainty. The geometrical, syllogistic, and dialectical modes of reasoning about time were especially appropriate. Professor Davidson, in his *Origins of Certainty*, gave us one of his now classic "schémas," used in this case as a graphic means to "promote the intelligibility" of Pascal's nuances in the procession toward certainty:

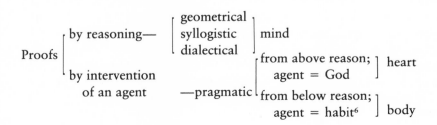

Within this "schéma," we isolate the model of geometrical proof laying the basis for a procedure whereby the human mind could proceed in an architectural fashion, building a pyramidal scaffold (figure 1) pointing toward KNOWLEDGE at the apex of the structure. The pyramid is based (figure 2) on axioms, demonstrations, and definitions. Each of its three sides (figures 3, 4, and 5) has a method to attain KNOWLEDGE. Epistemology, rhetoric, and argumentation are all modes in the procession toward certainty. For epistemology, intuition provides the resolution for the conflict between reason and sense-perception. For rhetoric, thesis and antithesis can be attenuated through analogy. For argumentation, in this case about the problem of time, the contrary views of time as present moment and movement can be absorbed within the larger framework of time as duration. This pyramidal form exemplifies Pascal's ternary logic in the *Pensées* and enables us to understand his insights into time and being therein.

The use of definitions, axioms, and demonstrations as a model of ternary logic has survived Pascal's own geometrical sensibility to be a sign of modern times also. Anthony Wilden for example discusses this ternary logic as the heart of the analog and digital language of computer technology.[7] Hence, the "pascalien," which may have seemed impractical to seventeenth-century society, may be lurking in the structure of the rhetoric in the *Pensées*. For example, there is a scientific model for Pascal's dialogical presentation of time. Louis Marin noted in his semiological studies of Pascal that "the *Pensées* constitute a sort of text-laboratory that permits the production of a text to be tested against its form which is the fragment, against its discursive mode which is interruption, and against its own logic which is digression."[8] The test for us here is to discover how Pascal's rhetoric, with its triangular structure (figure 3), is viable as persuasion within such a context.

In his essay on the "art of persuasion," Pascal observed that disagreement is a common human problem because of the inconstancy of human whims.[9] However, his *Pensées* also point out that the multiplicity of opinions is necessary: "La multitude qui ne se réduit pas à l'unité est confusion; l'unité qui ne dépend pas de la multitude est tyrannie" (604). The computer respects this tension by providing us with a concordance that allows us to see the unity of the text without disavowing its components. Appropriately, Pascal recalled Zeno of Elea's Paradox in explaining apparent spatial contradictions in geometry through temporal infinity (part

Pascal's Ternary Logic

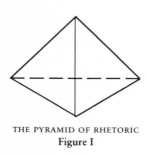

THE PYRAMID OF RHETORIC
Figure I

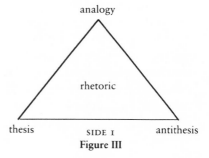

demonstrations

explicit
& univocal   BASE   self-
definitions   **Figure II**   evident
axioms

analogy

rhetoric

thesis   SIDE I   antithesis
Figure III

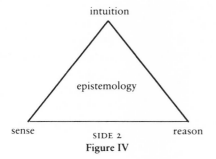

intuition

epistemology

sense   SIDE 2   reason
Figure IV

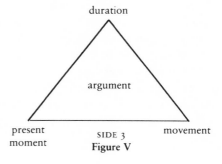

duration

argument

present   SIDE 3   movement
moment   **Figure V**

of Parmenides' argument for essential being rather than the plurality of change).

In order to allow his Interlocutor to see the unity of argument in the *Pensées*, Pascal utilized the scientific method of geometrical certitude. His discursive grasp of "time" exemplified the rigor of this method and unified his discourse. The notion of time was crucial for Pascal because by it the interlocutor could use the three faculties of knowing—sense-perception, reason, and intuition (figure 4)—in order to measure and observe the proportions and disproportions of the universe.

The Davidson-Dubé Concordance to the *Pensées* is especially helpful in orienting the reading of time in Pascal's work. This concordance gives us the principal allusions to time both by frequency lists of the predominant temporal themes and by their location in certain sections of Pascal's discussions. With this information, the reader can return to the *Pensées* and be more apprehensive about the pivotal references to time and to the contexts of their occurrences. The ternary logic of geometry then surfaces as Pascal views the paradoxical nature of human time.

On the one hand, the human faculty of sense perception (figures 4 and 5) influences humanity to prefer the isolated present moment when reflecting upon time. Georges Poulet, in his presentation of Pascal's sense of time, identified such a human feeling thus: "la tragique et l'absurde de la condition humaine, c'est que l'homme apparaisse comme incapable de renoncer à son présent et d'opter pour le futur." [10] Hence, time is defined as the present moment. The Concordance isolates significant recurrences of such words as "durer" (35 times) and "présent" (26 times). Pascal observed in one of his reflections (199) that humanity needs time to endure. The Interlocutor's own life could well be measured in this manner. Yet Pascal was not content with such a definition because he was aware that "le présent d'ordinaire nous blesse" (47). The word "temps" occurs on 144 occasions within the *Pensées*. However, the contexts of that word indicate Pascal's need for precision. The most frequent words associated with time—"même" (16 times), "à" (19 times), and "qui" (16 times)—indicate Pascal's concern with specifying the word further. He observed that ". . . nous errons dans des temps qui ne sont point nôtres . . ." (47). So the present moment is an illusion about what time appears to be to our sense perceptions.

On the other hand, the human faculty of reason, the second means of epistemological apprehension (figure 4), provides proofs that time is a dialectical problem of moment *and* movement. Haunted by his rhetorical

need for "le renversement continuel du pour et du contre,'[11] Pascal realized that rational proofs can be given for "l'écoulement du temps" (131)
from the past (human memory as proof, 47), to the present (which can't
be sustained despite the human predilection for an eternal present, 489),
and on to the future (the moment about which we have no assurance
of attainment, only a faint glimmer of a dream). Humanity is caught
in a vortex of infinite time, within which human time dialogically contains man. The *Dasein* or Awareness of Being, so well-conceived
by Martin Heidegger in his *Being and Time*,[12] was already understood
by Pascal in his rhetorical sense of engaging the Interlocutor with the
authenticity of living ("ex-istence" and "ec-stasy" literally point to
stepping outside of infinite time while still being involved in human
time).

Humanity is so haunted by "l'écoulement du temps" that distractions
must be sought. Ironically, "ils croient chercher sincèrement le repos et
ne cherchent en effet que l'agitation" (136). Time does not appear to
console in the long run: "Le temps guérit les douleurs et les querelles
parce qu'on change; on n'est plus la même personne; ni l'offensant, ni
l'offensé ne sont plus eux-mêmes" (802). However, the human aging process is measured against time also. Time as history-in-the-making allows
us to measure our human shortcomings and weaknesses. Pascal referred
to Biblical history for ample evidence of predictions which, when fulfilled, prove the rational contradiction of time as moment and movement.
The word "prédit" recurs on 63 occasions throughout the *Pensées* to
reinforce the importance of prophecies as testimonies to the dialectic of
time. The Scriptures thus depict "le mouvement infini, le point qui remplit tout, le moment de repos" (682). The Interlocutor is called upon to
respect the prophetic fulfillment of "Jésus Christ prédit et prédisant"
(462). While Pascal observes that "tous les hommes passeront et seront
consommés par le temps" (483), he points to the example of Christ as
"un homme qui prédit clairement des choses qui arrivent et qui déclarent
son dessein . . ." (344). Although reason allows us to read and to learn
from the Bible, that human faculty does not take us beyond the contradiction which is human time. It is within human time where the uncertainties of life are encountered by Pascal, portraying that condition in this
way:

Voilà notre état véritable. C'est ce qui nous rend incapables de savoir
certainement et d'ignorer absolument. Nous voguons sur un milieu vaste,

toujours incertains et flottants, poussés d'un bout vers l'autre; quelque terme où nous pensions nous attacher et nous affermir, il branle, et nous quitte, et si nous le suivons il échappe à nos prises, nous glisse et fuit d'une fuite éternelle; rien ne s'arrête pour nous. [199]

Hence, Pascal must look elsewhere because, as Professor Davidson has noted: "Pascal cannot start with religious beliefs, but he must locate something equally firm; and we know that he eventually finds it in the instabilities and contradictions of human nature, in the everlasting conflict between what man wants and thinks he is entitled to—truth and happiness—and what he can actually have." [13]

It is the third order of human learning, that of intuition (also called the order of will, 933), which allows Pascal to take the Interlocutor beyond the contradictions of finite time. Having established the axioms of time as moment and as contradictory events (figure 5), Pascal moves to the third side of his geometrical base—that of demonstration (figure 2). Not being able to resolve the contradiction about time by the powers of sense-perception or reason, he moves into an analogical discussion (figure 3) whereby the apparent contradiction is understood within the larger context of nonhuman, that is, divine, duration.

The proportions of human time become upset when presented in a larger framework as Pascal noted "la petite durée de ma vie absorbée dans l'éternité précédente et suivante" (68). Gradually, we begin to realize that "tout cet écoulement de temps, de la vie, et ces divers corps que nous sentons, ces différentes pensées qui nous y agitent n'étant peut-être que des illusions pareilles à l'écoulement du temps et aux vains fantômes de nos songes" (131). In this section on the "Disproportion of Humanity," Pascal also discussed the two infinities of massive and minute size. The introduction of the two infinities into the discussion takes the Interlocutor into another epistemological order wherein intuition plays a key role. Time is relevant to the infinities because perpetuity is posited as the context of human time just as infinity is the context for finite human proportions. Before this "secret impénétrable" (199) of the most minute part of a second on the one hand and the most expansive epoch on the other hand, Pascal invited the Interlocutor to observe the security of Christian Law (149) and Religion (281) which endured because of divine presence among men. Such a context created by divine time transforms the apparent contradiction previously identified in human time. The duration of eternity encompasses human time such that "rien ne peut fixer le fini entre les deux infinis qui l'enferment et le fuient" (199). Instead of the contradiction observed by reason, there is a unity within the universe. That unity is the intuitive order of eternity which leads Pascal the apologist to his wager. The cohesive structure of that eternity ("Je ne vois que des infinités de toutes parts, qui m'enferment comme un atome et comme une ombre qui ne dure qu'un instant sans retour," 427) is thus demonstrated by the ternary logic of geometrical definitions, axioms, and demonstrations (see figure 5) as well as the three-dimensional pyramidal form rather than a simple triangular argument on a single plane.

Similar to the multiplicity of fragments and the twenty-seven structured chapters of the *Pensées* linked by the geometrical rhetoric of Pascal, the problem of human time is likewise governed by a unity which subtly leads the Interlocutor toward certainty. Thus, Pascal's celebrated "esprit de géométrie" gave a formal identity to the more obvious stylistic procedure of the "esprit de finesse." Pascal himself observed that "la multitude qui ne se réduit pas à l'unité est confusion" (604). Yet his conscious design for the *Pensées* was not concerned with imposing that unity as he remarked: "J'écrirai ici mes pensées sans ordre et non pas peut-être dans une confusion sans dessein. C'est le véritable ordre et qui marquera toujours mon objet par le désordre même" (532). Nevertheless, there is a geometrical strain that unites the rhetoric of the *Pensées* despite Pascal's conscious aims. It was Pascal himself who pointed out that "tout auteur a un sens auquel tous les passages contraires s'accordent ou il n'a point de sens du tout" (257). His own example suggests that we can learn much about the proportion and order of discourse from mathematics. There is more that needs to be discovered so that we can establish, with the aid of a computer, a calculus of the rules of rhetoric. Jacques Derrida, in his *De la grammatologie*, announced the hopes of such studies for those of us interested in semiotics: "Mais au-delà des mathématiques théoriques, le développement des *pratiques* de l'information étend largement les possibilités du 'message,' jusqu'au point où celui-ci n'est plus la traduction écrite d'un langage, le transport d'un signifié qui pourrait rester parlé dans son intégrité." [14] Pascal's *Pensées* exemplify this extended understanding of the "message" in a written document. As we discover the subtle principles of rhetorical organization in the structure of this document, we begin to appreciate Pascal's sensitivity to how our being interacts with time by exemplifying how his Interlocutor interacts with learning.

NOTES

1. Blaise Pascal, *Pensées,* ed. Louis Lafuma (Paris: Le Seuil, 1962), p. 257.

2. Tzvetan Todorov, "Le Nombre, la lettre, le mot," in *Poétique de la prose* (Paris: Le Seuil, 1971), p. 200.

3. Hugh M. Davidson and Pierre H. Dubé, *A Concordance to Pascal's Pensées* (Ithaca & London: Cornell University Press, 1975). The frequency lists and the isolated references to time in this study were derived from their presentation.

4. Blaise Pascal, "De l'art de persuader," in his *Oeuvres complètes,* ed. Jacques Chevalier (Paris: Pléiade, 1954), p. 576. The numbers after the selections from the *Pensées* refer to the Lafuma edition.

5. Pascal, *Oeuvres complètes,* p. 575.

6. Hugh M. Davidson, *The Origins of Certainty* (Chicago: University of Chicago Press, 1979), p. 146, n. 2.

7. Anthony Wilden, *System and Structure* (London: Tavistock, 1972), pp. 510 ff.

8. Louis Marin, "'Pascal': text, author, discourse . . . ," trans. Daniel and Maria Brewer, *Yale French Studies* 52 (1975): p. 133.

9. Pascal, *Oeuvres complètes,* p. 596.

10. Georges Poulet, *Etudes sur le temps humain* (Paris: Plon, 1949), p. 74.

11. Pascal, *Oeuvres complètes,* p. 93.

12. Martin Heidegger, *Being and Time,* trans. John Macquarrie and Edward Robinson (New York: Harper & Row, 1962).

13. Hugh M. Davidson, *Audience Words and Art* (Columbus: Ohio State University Press, 1965), p. 135.

14. Jacques Derrida, *De la grammatologie* (Paris: Minuit, 1967), p. 20.

Resisting the Pull:
Pierre Nicole on the Inclination to Sin

Bruce H. Davis

A major concern of Pierre Nicole's in his *Essais de morale* is the soul's preference for the world and its objects, as opposed to God, a problem that he poses in terms of man's insensitivity to the Creator:

> Il est d'autant plus important, que l'âme s'applique à considérer les causes de son insensibilité pour Dieu. . . . Car c'est ce qui nous donne entrée dans l'âme, aux impressions des objets des sens, qui seraient peu capables de la toucher, si elle l'était autant qu'elle le devrait être des choses de l'autre vie. . . . [C]'est cette insensibilité pour Dieu, qui la rend sensible pour les créatures, parce qu'elle ne saurait être sans quelque pente, et qu'il faut toujours qu'elle s'attache à quelque objet. Ainsi un de ses principaux devoirs, c'est de tâcher d'en reconnaître les causes, et d'y apporter tous les remèdes qui lui sont possibles.[1]

The indifference for God that Nicole talks about here and the soul's vulnerability to sense impressions are constant reflexes of his thought. Man's indifference to the Creator, however, does not necessarily explain the soul's preference for the world and its objects, a preference that distinguishes fallen nature, according to Nicole. This "insensibilité," as one might expect, is merely symptomatic of a more profound disorder, a disorder that is not limited to heathens. Indeed, the susceptibility of Christians to the objects of the world, "quelque innocents qu'ils puissent être" ("De la Vigilance chrétienne," IV: 296; hereafter cited as "VC"), seems equally widespread; even the men "que Dieu a éclairés par de si pures lumières" remain subject to the "bagatelles du monde" ("De la Faiblesse de l'homme," I: 62; hereafter cited as "FH"). Furthermore, we know that innocent Adam was subject to these same sense impressions without preferring the world to God. What is different about the soul of *post-peccatum* man?

In analyzing this problem the theologian or moralist inspired by St. Augustine reveals few hesitations. According to Augustine, the perfect rectitude of the soul of innocent Adam has been replaced in fallen man by a disorder in which a sick and evil will (and/or heart) dominates. Sin has become, as it were, instinctive in fallen man, and the natural inclination to sin reveals itself whenever a man chooses the world and its objects over God. This preference or, more precisely, this desire for the world is what Augustinians call concupiscence. From an Augustinian perspective, of course, God is the only proper object of man's desire—all other objects, if they are desired and loved for themselves, are necessarily evil. Augustine thus distinguishes, in the familiar passage from the *City of God,* two categories of objects and two types of love: "Two loves have thus built two cities: the love of self to the point of despising God has built the earthly City; the love of God to the point of despising oneself has built the heavenly City."[2] Since men desire and love those objects that please them the most, the law of delectation,[3] and since the man without grace necessarily finds temporal objects more pleasing than spiritual objects (because of the evil will/heart), it follows that in every instance and at every moment fallen man will reject God in favor of the world, unless the will is healed by grace.

Given the eclectic nature of his thought and the unsystematic arrangement of the *Essais,* it is not always clear to what extent Pierre Nicole subscribes to Augustine's analysis of the springs governing human choice, which is to say, the factors that determine the human appetite. While on the one hand endorsing the Augustinian law of delectation, which makes choice more or less synonymous with the pleasure that one finds in an object, Nicole on the other hand often appears to have been influenced by the Thomist model according to which the will follows, or at least should follow, the recommendations of the reason.[4] Despite this hesitation or confusion, there is little doubt that Nicole's conception of the sensitive appetite is inspired by Augustinian and biblical psychology. He gives expression to the dynamic nature of this psychology in numerous passages in the *Essais de morale:*

> . . . il ne s'y faut pas tromper. Il faut que Dieu, ou le diable, règne en nous. Il n'y a point de milieu. Quiconque ne travaille point à établir en soi le règne de Dieu, travaille à y établir le règne du diable. Dieu y règne quand son Esprit y règne, quand c'est par son Esprit que nous agissons. . . . Le diable y règne quand nous nous laissons conduire à nos passions . . . , en un mot quand ce n'est que la cupidité qui agit en nous. ["Des Quatre Dernières Fins de l'homme," IV: 78; hereafter cited as "QDF"][5]

... il [l'homme] est obligé ... de reconnaître qu'il a dans le fond du coeur une pente contraire à cet amour [la charité], qui le porte à aimer les créatures, à s'y attacher, et à en jouir. Cette pente est un effet de la corruption originelle, qui domine dans ceux qui ne sont pas encore justifiés, et qui reste, quoiqu'elle ne domine pas dans ceux qui le sont. C'est cette pente qu'on appelle la concupiscence, qui sollicite au mal les plus justes, qui excite en eux de mauvais désirs, qu'ils sont continuellement obligés de réprimer. ["L'Emploi d'une maîtresse des novices," V: 217–218]

Nicole poses in the starkest of terms here the choice confronting man— God or Satan, the Creator or the creation—and the expression is an un-mistakable echo of Augustine's (and Port Royal's)[6] "either/or" perspec-tive on the human condition. The antithesis that Nicole expresses so powerfully in these passages is at the very center of the Augustinian dia-lectic. Indeed, one might argue convincingly that Augustine's thought, reduced to its essential components, is only about this choice confronting all men. From another point of view, however, it might be asserted that although Augustine's thought is about a choice—God or the world— words like "choice" and "choose" really have no place in his lexicon. Men of course do make choices and do perform free acts; but, for the Augustinian, all choices ultimately fall into one of two categories: those inspired by a love of God or those inspired by a love of the world. Because of a choice made by the first man, all men born into this world, unless aided by divine grace, infallibly—although freely[7]—choose objects that are temporal in nature and therefore inappropriate to their end. Given this unhappy situation, words like "orientation" and "inclination" seem to represent the Augustinian psychological framework more accurately than a word like "choice." According to this view, which synthesizes Au-gustine's psychology and theology, men are oriented in one of two direc-tions—toward the Creator or toward the creation—and inclined to love one or the other. For a moralist like Nicole, however, the apparent inevi-tability of the choice—and here we are close to the whole question of determinism in the thought of Augustine—does not release men from choosing and from striving to choose correctly: "La vie présente par la-quelle on doit passer, ne lui [à l'homme] est donnée que pour choix de l'un ou de l'autre de ces deux états [l'Enfer ou le Paradis]; et ce choix doit être l'unique emploi et l'unique exercice de sa vie" ("QDF," IV: 180).

In the two passages quoted above, Nicole reproduces with absolute accuracy all the elements of the Augustinian view of nature: original sin, concupiscence, the theory of the two loves—everything is present. This pessimistic view of things is of course explained by the doctrine of the Fall, a doctrine that informs and colors all Nicole's thinking on the relation between nature and supernature. Central to this doctrine is the notion that all men share in Adam's sin—even the most righteous (-appearing) among them. The somewhat puzzling phenomenon of the inclination to sin found in justified Christians, alluded to earlier, as well as their apparent nonchalance in the face of eternal damnation,[8] surprises less when we learn that such a tendency persists in all of Adam's heirs and "stimulates evil desires" whenever it is not opposed by the contrary orientation of charity.

Although it might seem that one could easily identify the two orientations or "pentes" (Nicole's preferred word) that "determine" our behavior, by analyzing and classifying the acts proceeding from them, such is not always the case. In theory, we would assume that those men whose acts are virtuous, as the world commonly understands that word, are turned in the direction of God, while the opposite would be true of men whose actions are vicious. For an Augustinian like Nicole, such an analysis is simply naive. While it is true that those acts that men recognize as vicious are performed by individuals estranged from the Creator, it is by no means certain that "good" acts are performed by men of virtue and are thus meritorious. The key to sorting this out lies in the distinction between exterior and interior acts, between what we "feel" in our heart and what we do; a man who gives alms in order to gain the admiration of his fellow men, with no thought to helping the poor, is, many of us would agree, performing a "good" work, but his intention is vicious, because his end is himself ("De l'Humilité dans les oeuvres de charité," VI: 59).[9] Thus, there is seldom, as Nicole recognizes, a direct correlation between a man's exterior and interior actions, between what the world sees and what lies in a man's heart:

> Il y a cette différence entre les actions extérieures et les intérieures, que l'on connaît beaucoup mieux si les actions extérieures sont conformes ou contraires à loi [sic] de Dieu, que l'on ne le sait des intérieures, qui sont couvertes souvent par les nuages, que la concupiscence y répand; en sorte que nous ne saurions assurer si nous avons le fond du coeur dans l'état où Dieu veut que nous l'ayons. ["De la Soumission à la volonté de Dieu," I: 89; hereafter cited as "SVD"]

> . . . cette innocence extérieure, qui ne consiste que dans l'observation des devoirs extérieurs de la Religion Chrétienne est un signe fort équivoque

de la grâce, et de l'innocence intérieure, puisque ce peut être un pur effet de la coutume, de l'habitude, de la vue des créatures, et d'une crainte purement humaine. ["CD," I: 163–64]

This discrepancy between what others see and what lies in our heart is often paralleled by the language that we use. We say one thing, but mean another, and thereby risk falling into that category of men about whom God says, " 'Ce peuple m'honore des lèvres, et son coeur est fort éloigné de moi' " (Isa.xxix.13; quoted in "CD," I: 164). This is a serious and frightening charge, but a charge that is completely justified by the content of a man's heart. We give alms, but for the wrong reason. On the other hand, however, the desire to deceive God conceals itself with such finesse that men are often unaware of its existence; thus, the man who denies that there is a contradiction between what he says (or feels) and does is, paradoxically, both lying and telling the truth. Hearts have reasons of their own, as Pascal knew and as we shall see.

The attempt to learn more about the discrepancy between what men feel and do requires a descent to the level of the inner person. According to Nicole's topography of the soul, the heart is located in the most profound depths of the individual. Here, Nicole makes an unsettling discovery concerning the ancient philosophic rule that urges men to know themselves.[10] While the moralist certainly agrees that this principle is the foundation of virtue—he quotes St. Bernard and St. Augustine to this effect ("CSM," III: 39)—he also reveals more than a little pessimism regarding the successful outcome of the endeavor: "Il ne faut pas . . . prétendre, quelque progrès qu'on fasse, de pouvoir jamais arriver à se connaître parfaitement; il y a toujours dans le coeur de l'homme, tant qu'il est en cette vie, des abîmes impénétrables à toutes ces recherches" ("CSM," III: 116–17).[11] Even given these natural limitations (natural only since the Fall), men could know more about themselves than they normally do, asserts Nicole. If men do not know themselves better, it is often because they reject such knowledge: ". . . ce qui fait qu'on ne se connaît pas, c'est qu'on ne le désire pas pleinement; et qu'on nourrit dans le fond de son coeur un éloignement secret de la vérité" ("CSM," III: 54). Regarding this aversion for the truth, Nicole recalls Paul's appeal to the Colossians:

. . . il [Paul] nous apprend . . . que lorsqu'on demande à Dieu de connaître sa volonté, il faut avoir un désir sincère de la connaître toute entière, et qu'il ne faut pas avoir dans le coeur des réserves volontaires, par lesquelles nous souhaitions de ne la pas connaître en quelque point, de peur de nous

croire obligés de l'accomplir. . . . Nous avons presque tous de certains
défauts auxquels nous ne voulons pas toucher, et que nous cachons . . . à
Dieu et à nous-mêmes. Et c'est pourquoi saint Paul ne souhaite pas seulement aux Colossiens, qu'ils connaissent la volonté de Dieu; mais il leur
souhaite encore qu'ils soient remplis de cette connaissance . . . c'est-à-dire,
qu'il n'y ait point de replis secrets dans leur esprit, et dans leur coeur, où
cette divine lumière ne pénètre, et qu'ils n'aient point d'attaches volontaires qui empêchent que Dieu ne les remplisse de sa lumière et de sa grâce.
["SVD," I: 82–83]

We see in this passage, with its depiction of wills in conflict (divine will
vs. human will), what some of the heart's reasons might be. First Nicole
tells us that self-knowledge depends on the extent to which the heart
recognizes and renounces its "volontary attachments"—something it is
loathe to do—and welcomes the divine light that illumines its interior in
such a way that hiding places for favorite vices become impossible. The
metaphor of the heart as a vessel is not only traditional, but is also effective in showing how knowledge of God's will must fill the heart (we recall
that either God or Satan must reign there). We also see here that self-
knowledge (awareness of what lies in our heart) and knowledge of God's
will (what God wants) are merely different aspects of the same endeavor,
which is to know the truth. One implies the other; when we know God's
will, we know ourselves, and, consequently, when we reject knowledge
of the one, we reject the other. There are among Christians, Nicole believes, men who show some signs of desiring to know the truth, that is,
who wish to abandon the world in order to know God more perfectly.
However, because the resistance to truth inspired by concupiscence is too
powerful, there coexists with the desire to know and love God an equal
or greater desire to hold on to the world at all costs. Now, while this
attachment for the world is certainly inappropriate, it is also, in Nicole's
view, understandable. Men are weak, and this is true of Christians as well
as of heathens. As Nicole often observes in the *Essais,* echoing Pascal,
they are seeking an "assiette," [12] which will give them a feeling of stability
in an unstable world. As I understand Nicole's use of this word, the *assiette* depends for its steadiness on the world of familiar objects that surrounds men. [13] To abandon the *attaches volontaires* (in the passage quoted
above), which confer a sense of security in an alien universe, requires a
stronger desire to love God and a steadier faith than most men have.
For—and this is essential—the commitment to God must be or become
total; otherwise, the heart will remain "partagé" ("CSM," III: 55): "On

cherche Dieu et le monde ensemble; le coeur est bien-aise de plaire à l'un et à l'autre . . ." ("De la Charité et de l'amour-propre," III: 168–69; hereafter cited as "CAP"). Thus, while there are some men, observes Nicole, who are praying to God to receive the divine illumination that will penetrate the soul's deepest recesses, shining light into shadowy places and replacing blindness with sight and insight, all too often these prayers emanate from a divided heart, which resists abandoning those vices and objects that comfort:

> Ils exposent à Dieu tout le reste de leur coeur; mais pour ce repli où ils ont mis ces imperfections qu'ils chérissent, ils se donnent bien de garde de le découvrir. . . . Ils récitent tous les jours ce Psaume qui ne contient que cette unique prière [de connaître la volonté de Dieu], et il leur semble qu'ils le font de tout leur coeur. Mais c'est qu'outre ce coeur qui prononce ces prières, ils en ont encore un autre qui les désavoue. Ils en ont un pour Dieu, et un pour eux-mêmes. Ils en ont un qui désire d'obéir à Dieu dans quelques actions qui ne leur sont pas fort pénibles; et ils en ont un autre, qui voulant demeurer attaché à certaines choses, ne veut pas connaître qu'elles soient mauvaises. ["SVD," I: 84]

The antithetical tendency of Nicole's way of looking at human nature is nowhere more evident than in this analysis of the ways in which man's heart deceives him and tries to deceive God. Just as there are two opposing cities and two contrary loves, we now learn that there are also two hearts, one for the world and one for God. There is, however, another antithesis at work here, this one within the larger context of Nicole's *morale*. Although the author of the *Essais* condemns the *coeur double* described above (he quotes Ecclesiastes ii.14 at the end of the cited passage: " 'Malheur à ceux qui ont le coeur double.' "), confirming once again his Augustinianism, it does seem that his account of two loves and two hearts coexisting within the soul—this coexistence is, granted, problematic—indicates an important shift in perspective.[14] The law of the two loves, with its implicit notion of their mutual incompatibility, has been somewhat moderated. Man loves God or the world becomes man loves (or is trying to love) God and the world. However, while this transcendence of the Augustinian law is an important movement in Nicole's dialectic, it is only temporary. For Nicole recognizes that a heart divided between a love of the world and a love of God is not going to carry a man very far on the road to the Creator; indeed—and on this point Nicole is not in the least equivocal—the tendency of our love for God must be in the direction of exclusiveness: "Dieu ne demande proprement des hommes que leur amour: mais aussi il le demande tout entier, et il n'y veut point de partage . . ." ("De la Comédie," III: 229). Nicole must be firm about this because, as he goes on to say, man's end is God and God alone. It does seem, however, that the divided heart could be a necessary point of departure for the rehabilitation that must take place. In any case, Nicole's analysis of what is happening on the level of the inner man seems inspired by acquaintance with real men living in a dangerous world of difficult moral choices. And when they examine their heart, these men find, Nicole suggests, an uneasy balance where the desire to know and love the world is accompanied by a desire to know and love God.

At the beginning of this discussion we saw that concupiscence is that love of the world and its objects that competes in the soul of fallen man with the love of God. The man who undertakes the self-examination urged by Nicole soon discovers, however, that concupiscence is more than a simple love of the world. It is first of all a love of self whose tendencies are so singular and whose hold on fallen man is so tyrannical that Nicole has no doubt that this unfortunate legacy of the first man is the principle of all human crimes "depuis les plus légers jusqu'aux plus détestables," ("CAP," III: 124). "Adam," Nicole reminds us, "ne s'est perdu dans son innocence qu'en oubliant Dieu, et en s'attachant dans cet oubli à la contemplation de la beauté des créatures et de soi-même. Combien l'homme pécheur est-il plus capable de se corrompre par la même voie?" ("Dangers des entretiens des hommes," II: 56; hereafter cited as "DEH"). Thus, sin after the Fall continues to be an imitation of the sin of the first man. Although one might be tempted to compare *amour-propre* to the principle of self-preservation,[15] thereby demonstrating that love of self is a completely natural and necessary law of the human condition, there is, however, at least one radical difference here. If it is true that *amour-propre* is a law of nature, it is also true that it is a law of a fallen and corrupt nature whose desires and love became focused on the self only when Adam turned away from God. It is the loss of original happiness, and the resulting void, that explains man's attraction to the world and love of self.[16]

Given the horror that the concept of self-love exercises on the Augustinian imagination, we should not be too surprised by the violence of the images chosen by Nicole to convey concupiscence's despotic nature:

Voilà le monstre que nous renfermons dans notre sein, il vit et règne absolument en nous, à moins que Dieu n'ait détruit son empire, en versant un autre amour dans notre coeur; il est le principe de toutes les actions qui n'en ont point d'autre que la nature corrompue; et bien loin qu'il nous fasse de l'horreur, nous n'aimons et ne haïssons toutes les choses qui sont hors de nous, que selon qu'elles sont conformes ou contraires à ses inclinations. ["CAP," III: 124]

Despite the familiarity of the theme here, Nicole's expression is stirring and fresh, with the power of his description deriving from the aptness of the metaphor. The comparison to a monster is apt because concupiscence, like a monster, is an all-powerful, even overpowering, force and, more importantly, is a force for evil. The energy of the image is reinforced by the words, "empire," "vit," and "règne." The two verbs are especially disturbing. For Nicole, *amour-propre* is a living and, we assume, growing thing; it reigns "absolutely" in the heart in such a way that a man is, for the most part, impotent to control its movements.

While the notion of concupiscence as a dynamic and uncontrollable force—pulling man away from God in the direction of the world—is in itself unsettling, *amour-propre* frightens Nicole and should frighten his reader for another, more basic reason. We know of course that this fundamental orientation, which inclines men to find delight in themselves and in the world, is changed only by the unmeritable gift of divine grace. The Augustinian moralist, never forgetting the seriousness of Adam's sin, has an additional reason for his pessimism. Not only is man corrupt from head to toe ("CSM," III: 63), but this corruption, this *insensibilité* for God, is, quite simply, an irremediable defect of fallen nature:

On a déjà fait voir que cette malheureuse inclination était devenue naturelle à l'homme depuis le péché; et il faut ajouter ici, que la grâce ne la détruit jamais entièrement; et que quelque désir qu'elle nous inspire de ne nous pas aveugler nous-mêmes, il reste toujours . . . dans le fond du vieil homme une pente vers cet aveuglement volontaire. . . . ["CSM," III: 54]

We see in this passage, and elsewhere in the *Essais,* one of the fundamental principles of Nicole's view of man after the Fall; Adam's sin caused a profound mutation in human nature. Consequently, the roots of corruption plunge themselves to such depths within the heart and resist efforts to destroy them so successfully that they are always producing, Nicole maintains, "quelque goût pour les biens de la terre, et quelque dégoût pour les biens du Ciel" ("QDF," IV: 185). In reading these passages, which faithfully echo Augustine,[17] we begin to understand that for every movement of concupiscence (the passions) that a man may succeed in repressing, a new one is born to take its place. Nicole finds this reality utterly demoralizing; to know that the fundamental principle of sin in man can never be completely vanquished in this life is perhaps the most tragic aspect of the Augustinian vision:

> Quelle misère de n'être maître ni de son esprit ni de son coeur, et de voir l'un occupé de mille pensées ridicules et déréglées, et l'autre agité d'une infinité de mauvais désirs et de sentiments corrompus, sans pouvoir arrêter cette malheureuse fécondité! d'être obligé de vivre avec cette foule d'ennemis intérieurs, d'être toujours aux mains avec eux, sans pouvoir jamais les exterminer! ["QDF," IV: 210–11]

Nicole's tour of the heart's secret places makes it clear that Adam's heirs have been burdened with a legacy whose implications are tragic for the pilgrim concerned to stay on the road to the Creator: "Nous naissons tous dans l'ignorance de Dieu et de nous-mêmes, des vrais biens et des vrais maux. Nous apportons de plus en naissant une volonté toute plongée dans l'amour de nous-mêmes, et incapable de rien aimer que par rapport à nous" ("DEH," II: 45). This "natural" corruption which we bring with us into the world makes the pursuit of virtue a difficult and unlikely enterprise, impelling man as it does to find pleasure in himself and directing him away from his true end.

Despite this bleak picture of the consequences of the Fall, however, Nicole's analysis does not stop at mere description of the corruption that fills the heart of man. The author of the *Essais,* in a powerfully drawn image, refuses to conclude that nothing can be done to resist the gravity-like pull of concupiscence:

> Il est difficile d'arrêter un poids qui se précipite par un lieu penchant, lorsqu'il est dans le milieu ou dans la fin de son mouvement, et qu'il a déjà acquis beaucoup d'impétuosité et de violence. Mais souvent il n'y avait rien de si aisé que de l'arrêter au commencement, et la moindre force qui l'eût poussé de l'autre côté, aurait été capable de le retirer. Il en est de même des passions qui produisent les plus grands renversements dans les âmes. Elles sont d'ordinaire assez faibles dans leur naissance. Ce sont des étincelles qu'il aurait été aisé d'éteindre avec un peu d'eau. . . . [M]ais quand on laisse enflammer ces étincelles, elles causent ensuite de terribles embrasements que Dieu impute souvent à la négligence de ceux qui n'y ont pas remédié quand ils le pouvaient. ["Des Supérieures," V: 166–67]

The comparison here between the operations of the passions and the law of gravity is striking. It is especially interesting to note that the same vocabulary describes both phenomena; we have, in fact, seen the words (or their synonyms) here depicting the motion of an object in space applied to the activities of concupiscence: "mouvement," "impétuosité," "violence." While the first comparison (to a weight responding to gravity's pull) may be a more natural one for an Augustinian (we recall Augustine's dictum: "Amor meus pondus meum."), the second analogy (fire), though trite, may be more apt in representing the implications of uncontrolled passions.

It is clear, I think, that we are touching on a fundamental aspect of Nicole's *morale* here.[18] In contrast to the pessimistic view detailed earlier, we now learn, in another example of Nicole's habit of envisaging the human soul as existing in a state of tension between conflicting forces, that control of the passions, in theory at least, can be a relatively simple affair. Just as the motion of a falling weight can be arrested at the beginning of its descent by the slightest push in the opposite direction and sparks of fire can be extinguished by the tiniest amount of water, the movements inspired by concupiscence can be controlled with minimal effort, if such control is begun soon enough.

While Nicole's remedy is by no means original, the Senecan echo, coming from so loyal an Augustinian, is somewhat unexpected.[19] The author of the *Essais* is suggesting that the orientation that we can call concupiscence, the seemingly irresistible inclination in man to act according to what pleases him, may be no more than just that: a "tendency" to act in ways that are certainly predictable, but not necessarily inevitable. And while Nicole does not deny that it is much easier to act in accordance with a natural bent, than to resist, he seems to be telling us that resistance is possible. It is true that as Adam's heirs we come into this world instinctively finding pleasure in its objects and in ourselves. But the impulses of fallen nature can be controlled.[20]

However, what appears simple in theory, control and repression of the passions, seems less so when viewed in terms of men engaged in the distracting and tempting activities of the world. Nicole's analysis has shown us that the heart, as the seat of concupiscence, is a region of tremendous energy manifesting itself as spontaneous movements which tend to pull us away from our true end with all the force of gravity:

> Les effets extraordinaires des passions . . . dépendent de mouvements qui ne sont pas entièrement volontaires. Nous ne pouvons pas exciter en nous

quand nous voulons ces émotions violentes; elles dépendent des objets, et
même de certaines dispositions du corps qui ne sont pas en notre pouvoir.
["Réflexions sur la traité de Sénèque: De la Brièveté de la vie," II: 332–
33]

While it may be true that the coming into being of the emotions is a
spontaneous phenomenon, these movements within the soul are not exempt from all control. If such were the case, the possibility of moral
behavior would vanish.[21] Although a man may be unable on the one hand
to will anger, for example, thus demonstrating that emotions are not volontary, he can at least choose to avoid those objects and situations that
provoke this emotion.[22] Even when this is not possible, a man can condemn and contain within himself the movements of these disruptive
forces:

> Mais si nous ne pouvons pas nous empêcher de les [mauvais désirs, mau-
> vaises pensées] sentir, nous pouvons au moins les condamner et les dés-
> avouer sitôt que nous les sentons, et retenir ce tumulte au-dedans de nous,
> sans qu'il en éclate rien au-dehors. ["VC," IV: 343]

Nicole's censorship of the passions derives not, I think, from their inherent evil, but from what they indicate about the status of a man's soul—
love of self and desire for the objects of the world—and from the interference that they pose for the soul's uninterrupted movement toward the
Creator. This latter consideration has special importance for the moralist.
Although the operations of divine grace remain inscrutable, Nicole, like
Pascal, never doubts that when God speaks to us, it is through the heart:
". . . veiller selon l'esprit, c'est aussi avoir les oreilles du coeur attentives
à la voix de Dieu" ("VC," IV: 293); thus, a soul and a heart whose emotions are constantly aroused will be deaf to His voice. The goal that Nicole has in mind for men is a "solid and unshakable peace" ("Des
Moyens de Conserver la paix," I: 297) where the soul, no longer dis-
tracted by the objects of the world (it may still prefer them—this is an
important point), can give its full attention to its only proper object. Nicole reminds us of God's command to avoid "human movements like
anger" in order to enter a state of calm and tranquility ("De la Prépara-
tion à la mort," V: 308).[23] The means to this end is the acquisition of
moral dispositions, which is to say, habits of right doing.[24] The role of
these habits is to function as regulators, repressing unruly passions. As

Nicole tells us repeatedly, it is only in a state of calm that a man can make the difficult choices the virtuous life requires.

We must not be deceived, however, by the apparent simplicity of Nicole's remedy. The good life remains a fragile enterprise. We are, after all, fallen creatures, a reality that Nicole never allows us to forget. Thus, even when the desire to know God is present and even when the emotions have been quieted for the moment, the movements of concupiscence are always latent. Repressed and quieted passions are always capable of being awakened. While they sometimes appear to be "healed" (Nicole compares them to "wounds"), their cure is no more than an illusion:

> Mais il ne faut pas s'y [à la guérison] fier absolument: car jamais elles [les plaies] ne se referment si bien qu'elles ne puissent s'envenimer de nouveau. Quelque éloignement que nous ayons de certains vices, il reste pourtant toujours en nous assez de penchant pour nous y faire tomber. . . . ["CSM," III: 65]

The cruelest epithet that Nicole can find to label human behavior that fails to conform to the divine will is "animal-like"/"manière toute animale" ("VC," IV: 361). By this, as we have seen, the moralist means the natural inclination of fallen man to act without reflection, in accordance with the movements and impulses of his lower appetite.

Although the Nicolean *morale* is predicated to an important degree on the view that men do those things that give them greatest pleasure, a careful reading of the *Essais de morale* reveals that man is (or can be) more than an appetite seeking the satisfaction of its desires. We may say, then, that if the point of departure of this *morale* is the Augustinian law of delectation, with its profoundly pessimistic view of nature, its point of arrival is a certain optimism in the intellect's capacity to monitor the movements of the sensitive appetite (the moral dispositions discussed above depend on this vigilance). For, despite the similarity in their behavior, men and animals are different. Alone of all creatures, man has been endowed with a reason that allows him to act with consideration. Although it is obvious that men can and do sin with premeditation, Nicole believes that sin is often merely a question of inattention to what God wants:

> . . . ceux qui ont un véritable désir d'être à Dieu parfaitement, ne sont d'ordinaire détournés de la pratique des vertus, que parce qu'ils n'y pensent pas. . . . ["VC," IV: 385]

Of course—and here we return to the point where we began this discussion[25]—the burden of original sin acts as a powerful deterrent to the reflective way of conducting one's life recommended by Nicole. Men prefer to act without thinking: "On ne peut nier que . . . le penchant de l'âme fût d'agir sans tant de réflexions, en se donnant entièrement à ce qui lui plaît . . ." ("VC," IV: 362–63). So the tension remains and will continue to remain. Given the disproportion between God and His creatures, between the eternal and temporal orders, man's desire to know the Creator and to conform his behavior to the divine will is never sufficient in this life to overcome in an absolute way (there are few absolutes in Nicole's moral universe) the pull of concupiscence. Restoring reason's *ante peccatum* hegemony over the passions is a process and the work of a lifetime, for, as Nicole asserts in another gravity image, we are always on the brink:

> Dieu ne l'emporte souvent que de bien peu sur les objets de concupiscence. Nous ne laissons pas d'estimer encore les avantages du monde infiniment plus qu'ils ne méritent d'être estimés. Nous sommes encore près de l'équilibre, et en changeant un peu la balance, c'est-à-dire en augmentant un peu l'impression des choses du monde sur notre esprit, elles reprendraient facilement leur empire, et l'emporteraient sur Dieu. ["DEH," II: 54]

NOTES

1. All references to the *Essais de morale* are to the 1730 edition published in Paris by Deprez. The first four volumes of this work appeared between 1671 and 1678; volumes V and VI appeared posthumously, in 1700 and 1714–15, respectively. References to the text will be given as follows: treatise or discourse title, volume in the 1730 edition, and page number; here, for example: "De la Crainte de Dieu," I: 142–43; hereafter cited as "CD." I have modernized Nicole's spelling in quoting from his works. All further references to the *Essais* will appear in the text.

2. Quotations from Augustine's works are from the *Bibliothèque augustinienne: Oeuvres de saint Augustin,* 85 vols. (projected), (Paris: Desclée de Brouwer, 1945–). This edition gives the Latin text and a French translation; I shall give my own English translation. References will be given as follows: treatise title in Latin, book or chapter, subchapter, volume in the *BA,* page. Here, for example: *De Civitate Dei,* XIV: 28, *BA* XXXV: 464.

3. "Quod enim amplius nos delectat secundum id operemur, necesse est." This fundamental law of human behavior, cited repeatedly in the literature on Augustine, appears in the *Expositio Epistolae ad Galatas.* The key word is, of

course, "delectare." According to the Augustinian analysis, the will is moved to act because of the delight it takes in a thing. As J. Carreyre observes in his summary of the *Augustinus* in the *Dictionnaire de théologie catholique*, "Qu'on demande à quelqu'un pourquoi il a fait et voulu tel acte; à travers des détours, il arrivera à répondre: parce que cela m'a plu, me faisait plaisir." "Jansénisme," *DTC* (1930–50), VIII, 1ère partie, col. 419.

4. "Les hommes ne seraient pas hommes, s'ils ne suivaient quelque sorte de lumière, fausse ou véritable. Leur nature est tellement formée, que la volonté n'embrasse rien qui ne lui soit présenté par l'esprit sous l'apparence de quelque bien. Ils sont donc obligés en quelque sorte de suivre la conduite de la raison." "Discours sur la nécessité de ne pas se conduire au hasard, et par des règles de fantaisie," II: 6. Cf. St. Thomas: "Since the object of the will is the good, or at least the apparent good, the will is never attracted by evil unless it appears to have an aspect of good about it, so that the will never chooses evil except by reason of ignorance or error." *Summa Theologiae* (New York and London: Blackfriars, 1969), 1a, 2ae, 77, 2, XXV, 165. Here, at least, Nicole seems firmly anchored in Thomist/Scholastic philosophical psychology.

5. Cf. E. D. James's treatment of this essential passage: *Pierre Nicole, Jansenist and Humanist: A Study of His Thought* (The Hague: Martinus Nijhoff, 1972), pp. 113–14. I am indebted to James's excellent study for showing me some of the possible ways of looking at Nicole's thought.

6. Although I agree with those who hold the view that French Jansenism was not "monolithic" (there were many Jansenisms and many Jansenists), I shall use the terms "Jansenist" and "Port-Royal" to refer, nevertheless, to a view of the relation between nature and supernature common to many of the figures associated with Port-Royal.

7. Although fallen man retains use of the *libre arbitre,* it is effective only in choosing evil, for he no longer finds delight (*delectatio*) in good as he did when the will was healthy. In other words, man after the Fall is free, but less so than Adam, since his freedom exists only for evil. For penetrating discussions of the complex problem of freedom vs. determinism in the thought of St. Augustine, see F.-J Thonnard, "La Vraie Liberté selon saint Augustin," *BA,* XXIII: 753–762; and John Rist, "Augustine on Free Will and Predestination," in *Augustine: A Collection of Critical Essays,* ed. R. A. Markus (Garden City: Doubleday, 1972).

8. Il [le Chrétien] jouit tranquillement des plaisirs qu'il sait être la cause de son malheur. Ces connaissances que la foi lui donne malgré lui, demeurent sans action et sans effet. Elles ne le troublent point. Il agit, il parle comme un homme qui n'a rien à faire qu'à se divertir en cette vie, et qui n'aurait rien à craindre en l'autre." "CD," I: 149–50.

9. Cf. James, p. 125 and Bernard Chédozeau: "L'action humaine naturelle est entièrement intéressée, même si elle ne le paraît pas au-dehors. . . ." "Religion et morale chez Pierre Nicole (1650–1680)," Diss. University of Paris (Sorbonne), 1975, p. 299.

10. "Le précepte le plus common de la philosophie, tant païenne que Chrétienne, est celui *de se connaître soi-même.* . . ." "De la Connaissance de soi-

même," III, 1; hereafter cited as "CSM." In his treatment of this fundamental theme in the *Essais,* E. D. James emphasizes Nicole's notion that "it is through the observation of others that we can best come to know ourselves" p. 130. Bernard Chédozeau also devotes careful attention to "les limites de cette connaissance de soi" (p. 437) and shows that Nicole, in his discussion of the soul's "replis intérieurs," was pointing to modern theories of the unconscious: "Les 'replis intérieurs,' le rappel permanent de l'impossibilité d'une parfaite connaissance de soi, sont autant de formulations de l'inconscient psychologique" p. 437.

11. Cf. La Rochefoucauld: "Quelque découverte que l'on ait faite dans le pays de l'amour-propre, il y reste encore bien des terres inconnues." *Maximes,* ed. Jacques Truchet (Paris: Editions Garnier Frères, 1967), p. 7.

12. " . . . c'est une chose commune à tous les hommes, d'avoir en quelque temps de leur vie une assiette tranquille. Mais cette assiette est si peu ferme, qu'il ne faut presque rien pour la troubler." "FH," I: 49. Cf. Pascal: "Nous brûlons du désir de trouver une assiette ferme. . . ." *Oeuvres complètes,* ed. L. Lafuma (Paris: Seuil, 1963), Fr. 199 (Br. 72), p. 527.

13. Although Nicole normally condemned any manifestation of *amour-propre,* he was not, however, insensitive to its utility for those who are extremely vulnerable to the attractions of the world. In a Pascalian-like reversal, Nicole recognizes that the human condition is such that some men cannot do without the "satisfaction of self-love" and recommends a "nourishing" of this love which will maintain a certain state of equilibrium in the soul. "Pensées diverses," 7, VI: 178–79. Cf. James's examination of this same passage, pp. 108–9 and p. 113.

14. B. Chédozeau, in a similar discussion, talks about Nicole's "correctif" to the Augustinian law. See pp. 401–3.

15. According to James, Voltaire, as well as other eighteenth-century thinkers, gave in to this temptation, thereby confusing self-love with self-preservation, p. 169.

16. "L'amour de nous-mêmes . . . nous donne une inclination violente pour les plaisirs . . . afin de remplir par là le vide effroyable que la perte de notre bonheur véritable a causé dans notre coeur." *Essais,* "CSM," III: 64.

17. ". . . concupiscence of the flesh is forgiven at baptism, not in such a way that it does not exist anymore, but in such a way that it is no longer imputed as sin. But, although its guilt is removed, this concupiscence remains nevertheless, until our sickness is completely cured. This will take place when, the rehabilitation of the inner man progressing from day to day, the external man has put on incorruptibility. For, concupiscence does not remain in the manner of a substance, like a body or spirit, but is a kind of evil disposition which affects us like a languor." *De Nuptiis et Concupiscentia,* XXV: 28; *BA* XXIII: 116–19.

18. Although the passage quoted above is addressed to those responsible for the moral behavior of inferiors, it seems possible and appropriate to extend the rule described here to personal self-control as well.

19. B. Chédozeau suggests that we should not be too surprised by the affinities between the thought of thinkers like Nicole and certain elements of Stoicism: "Tout le XVIIe siècle a été fasciné par le regard de vigilance que le sage stoïcien

porte sur lui-même, et saint François de Sales, Nicole et Malebranche, par exemple, ont fondé leur morale sur cette exigence première," p. 416.

20. My analysis depends on the distinction between moral and infused virtues. This Scholastic distinction, though never explicitly articulated by Nicole, is, I think, a fundamental principle of his moral theology.

21. "Un acte est moral, ou proprement humain, en tant qu'il est volontaire; or les passions, prises en elles-mêmes, ne sont pas volontaires, et la preuve en est que les animaux ont des passions mais n'ont pas de morale. . . . " Etienne Gilson, *Saint Thomas: Moraliste,* 2nd ed. (Paris: Librairie Philosophique J. Vrin, 1974), pp. 121–22.

22. A knowledge of which objects and situations provoke our emotions is one of the most important fruits of the self-examination recommended by Nicole.

23. Cf. Chédozeau, pp. 416–17.

24. Cf. Aristotle: "Moral goodness . . . is the result of habit. . . . This fact makes it obvious that none of the moral virtues is engendered in us by nature, since nothing that is what it is by nature can be made to behave differently by habituation. For instance, a stone, which has a natural tendency downwards, cannot be habituated to rise, however often you try to train it by throwing it into the air. . . . The moral virtues, then, are engendered in us neither *by* nor *contrary* to nature; we are constituted by nature to receive them, but their full development in us is due to habit.

[. . . .]

Men will become good builders as a result of building well, and bad ones as a result of building badly. Otherwise there would be no need of anyone to teach them: they would all be *born* either good or bad. Now this holds good also of the virtues. . . . In a word . . . like activities produce like dispositions. Hence we must give our activities a certain quality, because it is their characteristics that determine the resulting dispositions. So it is a matter of no little importance what sort of habits we form from the earliest age—it makes a vast difference, or rather all the difference in the world." *The Nicomachean Ethics,* trans. J. A. K. Thomson, ed. Hugh Tredennick (New York: Penguin Classics, 1976), pp. 91–92. Although there is no evidence that Aristotle shaped Nicole's thinking on the role of habit in moral behavior, Nicole's comments in the *Essais,* especially in the treatise "De l'Education d'un prince," are certainly reminiscent of the Aristotelian (and Thomist) notion of moral dispositions. In the "De l'Education d'un prince," (analyzed by James and Chédozeau), Nicole shows how the body has the capacity to acquire through repetition certain *postures* which allow men to act in a consistent manner.

25. The "renversement du pour au contre. . . ." is as characteristic of Nicole's analysis as it is of Pascal's.

Contributors

Peter Bayley is Drapers' Professor of French at Cambridge University, author of *French Pulpit Oratory (1598–1650),* and editor of *Selected Sermons of the French Baroque.*

Jules Brody, former Professor of Romance Languages at Harvard University, has written *Boileau and Longinus, Du Style à la pensée,* and *Lectures de Montaigne.*

Terence Cave is fellow and tutor, St. John's College, Oxford, and is well known for *Devotional Poetry in France, The Cornucopian Text,* and *Recognitions.*

Roland A. Champagne is Professor of French at Trinity University. He has written *Literary History in the Wake of Roland Barthes* and *Claude Lévi-Strauss.*

Robert T. Corum, Jr., is Associate Professor of French, Kansas State University, author of *Other Worlds and Other Seas,* and editor of César de Nostredame's *Les Perles.*

Bruce H. Davis is Assistant Professor of French at Knox College.

Robert Garapon, Professor of French Literature at the Sorbonne, has written *La Fantaisie verbale, Le Premier Corneille, Le Dernier Molière,* and *La Bruyère au Travail.*

H. Gaston Hall, Senior Lecturer in French at the University of Warwick, is the author of *Comedy in Context,* and editor of the Seventeenth-Century Supplement to the *Critical Bibliography of French Literature.*

Judd D. Hubert, Professor Emeritus of French, University of California

235

(Irvine), has written *Essai d'exégèse racinienne* and *Molière or the Comedy of the Intellect.*

John D. Lyons is Professor of French at the University of Virginia and author of *A Theater of Disguise* as well as *The Listening Voice.*

Mary B. McKinley, Associate Professor of French, University of Virginia, is the author of *Words in a Corner: Studies in Montaigne's Latin Quotations* and coeditor of *The Columbia Montaigne Conference Papers.*

Jean Mesnard, Professor of French Literature at the Sorbonne, has written many books on Pascal and is now editing the standard edition of that author's *Oeuvres complètes.*

Odette de Mourgues, late Professor Emerita of French Literature, Cambridge University, was the author of *Metaphysical, Baroque, and Précieux Poetry, O Muse, fuyante proie, Autonomie de Racine,* and *Two French Moralists.*

David Lee Rubin, Professor of French, University of Virginia, and editor of *Continuum,* has written *The Knot of Artifice* and compiled *La Poésie française du premier 17ᵉ siècle.*

Marie-Odile Sweetser is Professor of French at the University of Illinois (Chicago) and has written *La théorie dramatique de Corneille, La dramaturgie de Corneille,* and *La Fontaine.*

Charles G. S. Williams is Associate Professor of French, Ohio State University, and author of *Mme de Sévigné,* as well as editor of *Literature and History in the Age of Ideas.*

Index

Abstemius, 157
l'Académie Française, 45, 53
Adam, Antoine, 51, 52, 114
Aesop, 157
Aesthetics. *See* l'Esthétique
l'Agrément: et Corneille, 85; et Méré, 23, 25, 26; et Pascal, 17, 18
Albanese, Ralph, 117
Ambiguity, 144
Anagnorisis. *See* Recognition
Anciens, les. *See* Quarrel of the Ancients and Moderns
Antithesis: in the comic, 66–67; in La Fontaine, 144, 157; in Molière, 118; in Nicole, 219, 223; in Pascal, 203
Anxiety, 82–98, 144; Pascal and angst, 204
Apologetic, religious: Pascal and, 197, 198, 200–204
Apuleius: *Golden Ass,* 151
Argumentation: in Pascal, 211
Ariosto, Ludovico: Desmarets and, 50–51, 52
Aristotle, 14, 29; Corneille and, 84, 85, 89; Desmarets and, 46, 48, 50; Méré and, 25, 28; Nicole and, 10; and Oedipus, 94, 97, 98; Pléiade and, 171; *Poetics,* 54, 83, 84; and poetics, 82, 83. *See also* Recognition
l'Art: et Desmarets, 48; et Méré, 24, 25, 27, 28; et la nature, 9; et Nicole, 11, 12
Audience: and Corneille's *Cinna,* 105, 106; Pascal and, 201
d'Aumont, la duchesse, 127

Bailey, Cyril, 152
Barante, Brugière de, 10
Barnwell, H. T., 96
Baro, 45
Baumgarten: *Aesthetica,* 3

Bayle, 51
le Beau: Boileau et, 40; la théorie du beau, 3, 21, 22
Bellay, Joachim du, 41
Bellinzani, François, 127, 130, 133, 134
Bellinzani, Mme Louise (née Chevreau), 127–28, 135, 136
Bénichou: and Racine, 94
Bible (Old and New Testaments), 50
Bibliothèque de l'Arsenal, Paris, 45
Boileau: 3, 7, 29, 79; *L'Art poétique,* 34, 35, 39–40, 74–75, 76, 77, 83; and Desmarets, 51; Epistre IV, 73; Epistre XI, 76; et le merveilleux, 47; et la raison, 34, 35, 39–40; Satire II, 73; Satire IX, 74, 75–76, 77; Satire X, 71–72, 113; as satirist, 71–77
Boisrobert: *La Belle Plaideuse,* 113; *Les Nouvelles Muses,* 45
Bosse, Abraham, 49–50
Bossuet, 111
Boyer, Claude: *Le Fils supposé,* 83
Bray, Bernard, 133
Breteuil, Louis-Nicolas Le Tonnelier de, 123, 134, 135
Brody, Jules, 73, 92
Brunschvicg, 21
Burlesque, le: poem by Desmarets, 35, 55

Cairncross, John, 117
Calvin, 197
Catharsis: Corneille and, 84
Caton, 6
Cellamare conspiracy, the, 125
Chabot, Henri, 43
Chapelain, 45
Chappuzeau: *La Dame d'intrigue,* 113
Chauveau, François, 50
Choisy, l'abbé de, 125
Cicero, 12, 16, 151

Cinq-Mars conspiracy, the, 46
Civility. *See* l'Honnêteté
Classicism, French, 65, 67, 69, 75, 77, 79,
    144
Classiques, les, 67; et la raison, 41; et la
    sensibilité, 35
Clérambault, le maréchal de, 23
Cochin, 136
Coeur, le. *See* Heart
Colbert, 117, 125, 127
Combalet, Mme de, 4
Comédie Française, la, 111
Comedy: la tradition comique, 113, 115,
    118
Conrart: his copyist, 50
Corneille, Pierre, 9, 10, 131, 144; *Le Cid*,
    4, 6, 84; *Cinna*, 38, 47, 96, 101–9;
    Clitandre, 4; *Discourse*, 82, 84; *Don
    Sanche*, 86; *Examens*, 82, 84–85; *La
    Galerie du Palais*, 6–8; *Héraclius*, 86,
    90; *Horace*, 42; *L'Imitation de Jésus-
    Christ*, 6; *Medea*, 86; *Oedipe*, 82, 85,
    86, 87–92, 93, 95, 96, 97; *Oresteia*, 86;
    Pascal and, 18; *Polyeucte*, 47, 143; and
    Racine, 93, 94–97; and reversal, 102–3,
    104, 105; *Rodogune*, 84, 86–87, 96
Corneille, Thomas: *Timocrate*, 83
Correspondances, les: Pascal et, 17, 18
Cotin, 74
Counter-Reformation, the: and Desmarets,
    51, 55
Cousin, Victor, 3
Couton, Georges, 118
Crousaz, 29
Cruickshank, John, 204

Dacier: and Corneille, 83, 89–90
Dacier, Mme Anne Lefèvre, 124–25, 126,
    134, 135
D'Aubignac, 92; *Dissertation* on *Oedipe*,
    85–86, 87; *La Pratique du théâtre*, 83
Davidson, Hugh, 3, 110, 117, 201, 214;
    Origins of Certainty, 209
Davidson-Dubè Concordance: to Pascal's
    Pensées, 209, 212
Deism: Pascal and, 196–97
Democritus, 162
Denck, Hans, 157
Derrida, Jacques: *De la grammatologie*,
    215

Desargues, G., 49
Descartes, 5, 9, 10, 11, 19; and chimera,
    185–88, *cogito*, 180, 193; *Compendium
    musicae*, 14; *La Dioptrique*, 181; *Dis-
    cours de la méthode*, 4–5, 8, 10, 180,
    185–86; *Les Méditations*, 179–194; la
    méthode cartésienne, 10, 28; Pascal and,
    17, 20; et la raison, 36; and representa-
    tion, 183, 185; *Traité des passions*, 4,
    13; and truth, 180, 184–85, 189–90
Des Grieux, 133
Desmarets: *Ariane*, 50, 54; "L'Art de la
    poésie," 54, 55, 56, 58–62; *Aspasie*, 53,
    54; *Ballet de la félicité*, 54; *Clovis*, 45,
    47, 50, 54; *La Comparaison*, 55; *Les
    Délices de l'esprit*, 48, 53, 54; *Discours
    de la méthode*, 179; "Discours de la poé-
    sie," 45, 47, 53; *Erigone*, 47; *Europe*,
    46; *L'Imitation de Jésus-Christ*, 6, 48;
    Lettres spirituelles, 50; *Méditations*,
    179; *Mirame*, 54; and Nicole, 51, 54,
    55; *Oeuvres poétiques*, 45, 47; *Office de
    la Vierge*, 51; *Les Promenades de Riche-
    lieu*, 48, 51; *Psaumes de Davide para-
    phrasés*, 47, 50; *Rosane*, 46, 47; *Les
    Visionnaires*, 53, 54
Diction: Molière's, 67–69
Diderot: Boileau et, 35
Discours, le: Nicole et, 11, 12, 13
Dryhurst, James, 45
Du Bose, Jacques: *L'Honnête Femme*, 6
Dullin, Charles, 114

Ehrmann, Jacques, 101
l'Eloquence: et Méré, 24, 25, 28; et Nicole,
    11, 12; et Pascal, 19, 20
Empedocles: and La Fontaine, 152, 153,
    154, 158
Epicurus, 162
Epigrams, 9–10; Pascal and, 15
Epistemology: in Pascal, 211
Ernst, Pol, 200
l'Esprit: et Descartes, 181; et Méré, 27, 28;
    et Pascal, 19, 20, 21; Pascal's "esprit de
    géometrie," 208–15
l'Esthétique, 3; cornélien, 7; de Méré, 23,
    27; de Nicole, 11–14, 21; oeuvres de,
    10; de Pascal, 15, 21, 22; of poetry, 72–
    73
Euripides: and Oedipus, 92, 97

Faret, Nicolas: *L'Honnête Homme,* 5–6
Fermat, 180
Ferrand, Antoine, 126
Ferrand, Michel, 123, 134, 136
Fiction, la: et Corneille, 47; et Desmarets, 46; et Nicole, 12
Fontenelle, 132
Foucault, 179
Fouquet: and Corneille, 85
Freud, 82, 89
Frye, Northrop, 114, 157, 161
Furetière: *Dictionnaire,* 36, 154–55

Genre, 161–72
Géometrie, la: Descartes et, 184–85; Méré et, 28; le modèle géometrique, 11; Pascal et, 20, 22, 208–15
Gleizes, Albert, 49
Godeau, 45
Gouhier, Henri, 48
Goût, le: La Bruyère et, 40; Méré et, 26, 27, 28; Nicole et, 7, 17; Pascal et, 17–20
Grimaldi, 180

Habert, 45
Hamartia: Corneille and, 84, 90
l'Harmonie: de la nature, 22; Nicole et, 12–14; Pascal et, 16–17
Heart: Nicole and, 220–27; Pascal and, 35
Heidegger, Martin: *Being and Time,* 213
Heroic poetry: Desmarets and, 46, 47, 50
Homer: and La Fontaine, 150, 151; and Méré, 25
l'Honnête homme, 5, 8, 29; Descartes et, 14; Méré et, 23, 24, 25, 28; Molière et, 112; Nicole et, 10, 13, 14; Pascal et, 17, 19
l'Honnêteté, 5, 19, 112; Pascal et, 19
Horace, 76, 144; Desmarets and, 49, 50; and La Fontaine, 152–53, 158
Howarth, W. D., 37
Huygens, 180
l'Hyperbole: Desmarets et, 53, 54; Nicole et, 12

l'Imagination, 5, 35; Pascal et, 41
l'Imitation: et Desmarets, 48, 49, 53; et Nicole, 12
Intertextuality: in Ferrand, 124; in La Fontaine, 145–58

Intratextuality: in La Fontaine, 157
Irony: in Corneille, 90; in Ferrand, 132; in La Fontaine, 154

Jansenism, 22
Jésuites, les, 9, 105
Journée des dupes, la, 46
le Jugement, 5, 6; Descartes et, 181, 183–84; esthétique, 10; Méré et, 28; Pascal et, 19, 20, 21
Juste milieu, le: Méré et, 26; Molière et, 112; Nicole et, 11, 13, 14

La Bruyère: Boileau et, 40, 75, 96; *Caractères,* 34, 40; Ferrand et, 126–27, 132; *Des Ouvrages de l'esprit,* 40; et la raison, 34, 40
La Faille, Toulousain Germain de, 10
Lafayette, Mme de. 125
La Fontaine, 26, 80, 104; *L'Ane et le chien,* 154; *Le Chêne et le roseau,* 144; *La Colombe et la fourmi,* 149–50; *Fables,* 144–45; *Le Loup et l'agneau,* 155–56; *Les Loups et les brebis,* 155–56; and Lucretius, 146–49, 154; *Le Meunier, son fils et l'âne,* 150; and Molière, 111; *A Monseigneur, le duc de Bourgogne,* 150; *La Querelle des chiens et des chats,* 153, 154
La Rochefoucauld, 29; *Maximes,* 9, 143
Le Clerc, Jean, 29
Le Gras, 45
L'Estoile, 45
Lever, Maurice, 131, 135
Littré, 150, 154
Longueville, le duc de, 4
Lotman, Yury, 162, 171–72
Louis XIII, 47, 52, 54
Louis XIV, 46, 52, 54
Lucan, 153
Lucretius, 162, 204; *De rerum natura* and La Fontaine, 145–49, 151, 152, 153, 154, 157, 158

Mack, Maynard, 74
Maintenon, Mme de, 123
Malherbe, 172; Boileau and, 75–76; "Consolation à Caritée," 163–64, 165; "Consolation à Monsieur du Perier," 163, 164, 169; and Desmarets, 51, 55

Malleville, 45
Manilius, 153
Marays, 47
Marin, Louis, 211
Martial, 9
Maurois, André, 143
Mauron, Charles, 116
Maynard, 45
Mazarin, 48
Menard, Mme de, 127
Méré, le chevalier de: et les agréments, 25–
    26; *Discours de la justesse*, 23, 24;
    l'esthétique de, 27; et Pascal, 23, 24, 27,
    28
Merveilleux, le: Desmarets et, 46, 47, 53,
    54
Mesnard, Jean, 35
Métaphore, le: Desmarets et, 53; Nicole et
    l'expression métaphorique, 13
Mimesis: Desmarets and, 48
Mock-epic, the: in La Fontaine, 150
Modèle, le: géometrique, 11; de Méré, 28;
    de la musique, 14, 16; de la nature, 8; de
    Pascal, 17, 18, 28
Modernes, les. *See* Quarrel of the Ancients
    and Moderns
Molière, 6, 29, 54, 74, 79; *Amphitryon*,
    110; *L'Avare*, 110–18; *Le Bourgeois
    Gentilhomme*, 69; *Dom Juan*, 110, 111,
    199; *L'Ecole des femmes*, 110, 111; *Les
    Femmes savantes*, 39, 66–69, 132;
    George Dandin, 111, 114; *La Jalousie
    du Barbouillé*, 111; *Le Misanthrope*,
    38–39, 110, 111, 143; et la raison, 40;
    Tartuffe, 5, 37–38, 69–72, 110, 111
Montaigne, Michel de, 25, 152, 153, 158,
    187, 204
Montherlant, 132
Morale, la: in La Fontaine, 144, 155, 156,
    157; Méré et, 23; de Nicole, 223, 225,
    227–29; Pascal et, 19, 20
Morel, Jacques, 111, 114
Musique, la: Descartes et, 14, 16

Nadal, l'abbé, 23, 85
Nature, la: et Corneille, 8; et Desmarets,
    48; et Méré, 27; et Nicole, 220; et Pas-
    cal, 200, 202, 204; et Théophile de
    Viau, 169

Nature humaine, la: Nicole et, 10–14, 17;
    Pascal et, 16, 18, 20, 21, 22, 23
Naturel, le: Descartes et la lumière natu-
    relle, 180; La Bruyère et, 40; dans La
    Fontaine, 144
Neoclassical poetics, 83; theory, 82
Neoclassicism, English, 65, 79. *See also*
    Classicism; l'Honnêteté
Neo-Platonists: Desmarets and, 53
Newton, 180
Nicole, Pierre: et Desmarets, 51, 54, 55;
    Dissertation, 10–16, 22; *Epigrammatum
    delectus*, 9, 16; *Essais de morale*, 217–
    30; et Méré, 24, 25, 28; et Pascal, 15–
    17, 20, 21; "Querelle des *Imaginaires*,"
    49; et la raison, 40; et la rhétorique,
    22; *Traité de la vraie et de la fausse
    beauté . . .*, 36–37
Noël, P., 18
Notre-Dame, 51, 54

Optics, 197; Descartes and, 180–82
Ovid, 153, 158
Oxford Latin Dictionary, 152

Palais-Cardinal, le, 47
Paris Opéra, 54
Parish, Richard, 203
Parnasse, le: Boileau et, 39
Parody: by Desmarets, 53
Pascal, 9, 40, 126, 144, 221, 222. *De l'art
    de persuader*, 201–2; *Beauté poétique*,
    16, 18, 20; et le coeur, 35, 40; "La Ma-
    chine," 200, 201, 203; et Méré, 23, 24,
    27, 28; Nicole et, 15–17; *Les Pensées*,
    15–22, 143, 196–205; et la raison, 35–
    36, 42; système pascalien, 16–22. *See
    also* Davidson-Dubè Concordance
Passions: Nicole and, 228–29
Pelous, Jean-Michel, 110
Periphrasis: in La Fontaine, 144, 146, 149,
    150, 152, 156
Perrault, 51
Persuader: Pascal et, 20, 22, 201–2
Pfohl, Russell, 93
Phaedrus, 157
Picard, Raymond, 43
Plaire: et Descartes, 14, et Méré, 23–26; et
    Nicole, 10, 11, 13, 14; et Pascal, 22

Plaisir, le: et Descartes, 14; et Ferrand, 131, 133; et Nicole, 10, 11, 12; et Pascal, 17
Plato, 14, 29; Desmarets and, 53; la théorie du beau, 22
Plaute: *Auluraria*, 111, 115
Pléiade, la: and Aristotle, 171, 172; Desmarets and, 52, 53
Poésie, la, 7–8; et Méré, 25; et Nicole, 11, 12, 13; et Pascal, 18, 19, 21
Poétique, la, 3, 6; et Corneille, 82, 85; et Desmarets, 47; et Méré, 27, 28
Poisson, P., 14
Pope: as comic poet, 77–79; Epistle IV, 78; *An Essay on Criticism*, 79
Port-Royal, 9, 14, 21, 29, 219
Poulet, Georges, 212
Psalms, 47

Quarrel of the Ancients and Moderns, 29; Desmarets and, 50, 51, 55, 56; Méré and, 27; Nicole and, 10, 14, 15

Rabelais, 12
Racan: and Desmarets, 45, 51
Racine: *Andromaque*, 92, 131, 143, 144; *Britannicus*, 96; et Corneille, 93, 94–97; et la raison, 42–43; et Sophocle, 94; *La Thébaïde*, 82, 91, 92–96, 97
Raison, la, 5, 6; et Boileau, 34, 35, 39–40; et La Bruyère, 34, 40; et Corneille, 42; et Descartes, 36; et le goût, 40; et Méré, 27, 28; et Nicole, 10, 14, 229; et Pascal, 35–36, 42; et Racine, 42–43
Rambouillet, Mme de, 47
Recognition, 82–94, 97; *anagnorisis*, 82, 83
Règles, les: de l'art, 3; et Méré, 27; et Nicole, 11, 13; et Pascal, 19, 21
Régnier: *Epître au roi*, 51; and La Fontaine, 146–47, 148, 153, 154
Renaissance, the, 76
Representation: Descartes and, 183, 185
Reversal, dramatic: in *Cinna*, 102–6
Rhétorique, la, 6, 54, 104; et Méré, 25, 27, 28; et Nicole, 14; et Pascal, 20, 211
Richelieu: Desmarets and, 4, 45, 46, 47, 48, 51, 52, 55, 56
Riffaterre, 151

Robert, Paul: dictionnaire, 34, 36
Romain, Jules, 132
Romanowski, Sylvie, 183
Ronsard, 53
Rosicrucianism, 197
Rotrou: and Oedipus, 92, 93, 94, 97; *Venceslas*, 83

Saint-Amant: "Le Contemplateur," 171; "L'Hiver des alpes," 162; "La Solitude," 169
Saint Augustine: Nicole and, 217–19, 221, 223–27, 229; *De vera religione*, 22
Saint Bernard, 221
Saint-Evremond, 29
Saint François de Sales, 5–6, 9; *Introduction à la vie dévote*, 5
Saint Paul, 202, 204, 205; Nicole and, 221–22
Saint Vincent de Paul, 111
Satire: in Boileau, 72–73; in Ferrand, 133–34
Savreux, Charles, 9
Scepticisme, le: et Nicole, 10, 21; et Pascal, 19, 20, 21
Senecan model: in *Epistulae Morales*, 162–63, 166; and Nicole, 227
Sensibilité, la, 35
Shakespeare, 114, 118
Snell, 180
Socrates, 153
Soissons, la comtesse de, 127
Solitude, the, 169–71
Sophocles: and poetics, 82; *Oedipus*, 84, 93–98 passim
Spitzer, Leo, 144
Structuralists, Russian, 161–62

Taste. See Goût, le
Térence, 115
Thesaurus linguae latinae, 151, 152
Thomism: Nicole and, 218
Thou, de, 46
Tiefenbrun, Susan, 101
Todorov, Tzvetan, 208
Tragedy, 96
Tristan l'Hermite, 172; "Consolation à Idalie," 166–69; "Consolation à Ma-

dame la Princesse Marie," 165–66; "Consolation à son cher amy xxxx," 164–65, 166; "La Mer," 169–70; "Le Promenoir des deux amants," 170

Truth. *See* Vérité

Tyard, Pontus de: *Dialogues philosophiques,* 53

Uzès, la comtesse de, 126

Vallière, Mlle de la, 127

Vaugelas, 13

Vavasseur, P.: *De Epigrammate liber,* 9

Vérité, la: et Corneille, 47; et Descartes, 180, 184–85, 189–90; et Desmarets, 46–47, 54; et La Bruyère, 40; et Nicole, 10–12, 13, 14, 222; et Pascal, 19, 20, 22

Versailles, 117

Viau, Théophile de, 54, 172; "A Monsieur de L.," 169; "La Solitude," 170–71

Virgil: and the consolation, 165; Desmarets and, 50, 56

Voiture: Méré et, 24

Voltaire: and Corneille, 86, 89; Desmarets and, 56

Walker, Hallam, 111

Wilden, Anthony, 211

Wordsworth, 79

Zeno of Elea, 211